TRADE UNION RESPONSES TO GLOBALIZATION

A review by the Global Union Research Network

TRADE UNION RESPONSES TO GLOBALIZATION

A review by the Global Union Research Network

Edited by Verena Schmidt

INTERNATIONAL LABOUR OFFICE • GENEVA
GLOBAL UNION RESEARCH NETWORK

Copyright © International Labour Organization 2007
First published 2007

Publications of the International Labour Office enjoy copyright under Protocol 2 of the Universal Copyright Convention. Nevertheless, short excerpts from them may be reproduced without authorization, on condition that the source is indicated. For rights of reproduction or translation, application should be made to the Publications Bureau (Rights and Permissions), International Labour Office, CH-1211 Geneva 22, Switzerland, or by email: pubdroit@ilo.org. The International Labour Office welcomes such applications.

Libraries, institutions and other users registered in the United Kingdom with the Copyright Licensing Agency, 90 Tottenham Court Road, London W1T 4LP [Fax: (+44) (0)20 7631 5500; email: cla@cla.co.uk], in the United States with the Copyright Clearance Center, 222 Rosewood Drive, Danvers, MA 01923 [Fax: (+1) (978) 750 4470; email: info@copyright.com] or in other countries with associated Reproduction Rights Organizations, may make photocopies in accordance with the licences issued to them for this purpose.

V. Schmidt (ed.)
Trade union responses to globalization: A review by the Global Union Research Network
Geneva, International Labour Office, 2007

Globalization, multinational enterprise, workers rights, trade union rights, trade union role, international trade union, developed countries, developing countries

03.02.3

ISBN 978-92-2-119860-4

ILO Cataloguing in Publication Data

The designations employed in ILO publications, which are in conformity with United Nations practice, and the presentation of material therein do not imply the expression of any opinion whatsoever on the part of the International Labour Office concerning the legal status of any country, area or territory or of its authorities, or concerning the delimitation of its frontiers.

The responsibility for opinions expressed in signed articles, studies and other contributions rests solely with their authors, and publication does not constitute an endorsement by the International Labour Office of the opinions expressed in them.

Reference to names of firms and commercial products and processes does not imply their endorsement by the International Labour Office, and any failure to mention a particular firm, commercial product or process is not a sign of disapproval.

ILO publications can be obtained through major booksellers or ILO local offices in many countries, or direct from ILO Publications, International Labour Office, CH-1211 Geneva 22, Switzerland. Catalogues or lists of new publications are available free of charge from the above address or by email: pubvente@ilo.org

Visit our website: www.ilo.org/publns

Typeset by Magheross Graphics, France & Ireland *www.magheross.com*
Printed in Switzerland ATA

CONTENTS

Acronyms vii
About the authors/editors ix
Preface xvii
Acknowledgements xxi

Editorial overview (*Verena Schmidt*) 1

1   Sustainability and unions: International trade union action to implement sustainability norms at corporate level
(*Eberhard Schmidt*) 11

2   Social partnership at the global level: Building and Wood Workers' International experiences with International Framework Agreements
(*Marion F. Hellmann*) 23

3   Integrating labour issues in global value chain analysis: Exploring implications for labour research and unions
(*Lee Pegler and Peter Knorringa*) 35

4   Paving the path toward the unionization of high-tech sweatshops
(*Anibel Ferus-Comelo*) 51

5   Corporate governance reforms as a means of protecting and promoting worker interests: Shaping the corporation of tomorrow
(*Richard Tudway*) 63

6   Multinational companies in Bulgaria: Impact on labour and social development *(Nadejda Daskalova and Lyuben Tomev)* 73

7   Freedom of association and collective bargaining: The practice of multinational companies in Brazil *(Clóvis Scherer)* 85

8   Trade and development in South Africa *(Neva Seidman Makgetla and Tanya van Meelis)* 97

9   Migration in the global economy: Challenges and opportunities for Caribbean trade unions *(Ann-Marie Lorde)* 113

10 European Union enlargement, workers and migration: Implications for trade unions in the United Kingdom and Poland *(Jane Hardy and Nick Clark)* 125

11 More than bananas: Social responsibility networks and labour relations in the banana industry in the Urabá region of Colombia *(Maria-Alejandra Gonzalez-Perez and Terrence McDonough)* 139

12 The Labour Platform: An alliance of trade unions in Turkey *(Seyhan Erdoğdu)* 153

13 Transnational union networks, feminism and labour advocacy *(Mary Margaret Fonow and Suzanne Franzway)* 165

14 Action research in the garment sector in Southern and Eastern Africa *(Esther de Haan and Michael Koen)* 177

Conclusion 191

ACRONYMS

ACP	Africa, Caribbean, Pacific
AGOA	African Growth and Opportunity Act (US)
BWI	Building and Wood Workers' International
CIS	Commonwealth of Independent States
CPSU	Caribbean Public Sector Unions
CSR	corporate social responsibility
EFTA	European Free Trade Association
EU	European Union
GATT	General Agreement on Tariffs and Trade
GRI	Global Reporting Initiative
GUN	global union networks
GUF	Global Union Federation
GURN	Global Union Research Network
GVC	global value chain
FDI	foreign direct investment
ICEM	International Federation of Chemical, Energy, Mine and General Workers' Unions
ICFTU	International Confederation of Free Trade Unions
ICT	information and communication technologies
IFA	International Framework Agreement
IFBWW	International Federation of Building and Wood Workers
IFI	International Financial Institution
IMF	International Metalworkers' Federation
IMF	International Monetary Fund
ITGLWF	International Textile, Garment and Leather Workers' Federation

ITUC	International Trade Union Confederation
IUF	International Union of Food, Agricultural, Hotel, Restaurant, Catering, Tobacco and Allied Workers' Association
LDC	least developed countries
MFA	Multifibre Agreement
MNE	multinational enterprise
ODM	original design manufacturer
OEM	original equipment manufacturer
OFR	operating and financial review
PSI	Public Services International
SADC	Southern African Development Community
SME	small and medium-sized enterprises
SRN	social responsibility network
TNC	transnational corporation
TUC	Trades Union Congress
TUAC	Trade Union Advisory Committee to the OECD
UNI	Union Network International
WCL	World Confederation of Labour
WFBW	World Federation of Building and Wood Workers
WSF	World Social Forum
WTO	World Trade Organization

ABOUT THE AUTHORS AND EDITORS

Esther Busser has been trade policy officer in the Geneva office of the International Trade Union Confederation (ITUC) since August 2003, responsible for trade issues as well as for activities on bilateral and regional trade agreements of the Global Union Research Network. She holds a Masters in Economic Policy from the University of Nijmegen, the Netherlands, and worked previously as a consultant for the Social Finance Programme in the ILO and the Competition and Consumer Policies Branch in UNCTAD. Contact details: ITUC Geneva Office, Avenue Blanc 46, 1202 Geneva; e-mail: esther.busser@ituc-csi.org

Nick Clark is a policy officer in the Public and Commercial Services Union General Secretary's office in the United Kingdom. He worked in manufacturing before joining the independent Labour Research Department in 1983 and the research department of the print union SOGAT in 1987. Nick held lay union posts ranging from shop steward to national negotiator. From 1993 to 2005 he worked for the British Trades Union Congress (TUC), first leading a project setting up European Works Councils and ultimately covering migrant workers' issues. He sat on the Ethical Trade Initiative (ETI) Temporary Labour Working Group, led the TUC's Portuguese Workers Project and is TUC nominee on the Gangmasters Licensing Authority board. In 2003, he conducted a study programme on Migrant Workers and Trade Unions at Corpus Christi College, Oxford, and has published several papers on the subject.

Nadejda Daskalova is deputy director of the Institute for Social and Trade Union Research in Sofia, Bulgaria. The main research areas include trade union development, industrial relations and social dialogue, the labour market – in

particular policies for social inclusion, gender issues, social impact of privatization in the public services, European integration and social dimensions of globalization.
Contact details: Institute for Social and Trade Union Research, 1 Macedonia Square, Sofia-1000, Bulgaria; e-mail: nadyadas@yahoo.com

Luc Demaret is the focal point on migrant workers in the ILO Bureau for Workers' Activities. He previously worked at the ICFTU, first in charge of migration in the ICFTU Europe and Americas Department and later as Director of Information writing extensively on workers' rights and migration issues. He represented the ICFTU in the European Trade Union Confederation working group on migration in the 1970s and 1980s and in the ILO Committee on the Application of Conventions and Recommendations from 1983 to 1989. In 1999 he chaired the Jury for the International Federation of Journalists Prize for Tolerance in Journalism. This award is supported by the Council of Europe, the European Commission and the City of Strasbourg and was organized by the International Media Working Group Against Racism and Xenophobia (IMRAX).

Lawrence Egulu has been the macroeconomist for the ILO Regional Office for Africa since March 2006, where he is in charge of guiding and conducting policy-oriented research and socio-economic analysis, and reviewing their implications for decent work in Africa. He is also responsible for strengthening ILO relationships with other regional and international organizations. He coordinates the GURN web pages on PRSPs/IFIs. In 2005, Mr Egulu served as Research Officer for the ILO Bureau for Workers' Activities in Geneva on a short-term basis. Prior to joining the ILO, Mr Egulu was the Director of Economic and Social Policy at the ICFTU African Regional Organization (AFRO) from 1996. In 2003 he was seconded by the ICFTU to the World Bank headquarters in Washington, DC. He also worked with the National Organization of Trade Unions and the Ministry of Finance and Economic Planning in Uganda.
Contact details: ILO Regional Office for Africa, 6th Floor, Africa Hall, Menelik II Avenue, P.O. Box 2788, Addis Ababa, Ethiopia; mobile: +251-911-813251; fax: +251-11-5445573; e-mail: egulu@ilo.org

Seyhan Erdoğdu is teaching in the Department of Labour Economics and Industrial Relations at the Faculty of Political Sciences, Ankara University, Turkey. She is co-author of *Sendikacı Kadın Kimliği* (a book on trade union women in Turkey published by Imge Publication, Ankara, 1998) and author of *Küreselleşme Sürecinde Uluslararası Sendikacılık* (a book on the international trade union movement in the era of globalization, published by Imge

About the authors and editors

Publication, Ankara, 2006). She has written various articles on economic restructuring and labour issues in Turkey. She is active in the Turkish trade union movement as an advisor and educator.
Contact details: e-mail: serdogdu@politics.ankara.edu.tr

Anibel Ferus-Comelo has been engaged in labour research, education and training for the past ten years. She has worked extensively with unions and community-based workers' centres supporting the rights of low-wage workers, who are mainly migrants, in the United States and the United Kingdom. Her doctoral research explored globalization and labour strategies in the global electronics industry with a comparative focus on Silicon Valley in the United States and Bangalore in India. She is currently developing an education programme for the New Trade Union Initiative, a national independent union federation in India.
Contact details: anibelfc@hotmail.com

Mary Margaret Fonow is Director and Professor of Women and Gender Studies at Arizona State University. She is a sociologist by training, with research interests in gender and social movements, including feminist transnational labour activism. Her book, *Union women: Forging feminism in the United Steelworkers of America* (University of Minnesota Press, 2003) examines how a feminist agenda took hold in a male-dominated union. Fonow's scholarship is both multi-disciplinary and international. She is the co-author with Suzanne Franzway of *New feminist politics: Transnational alliances between women and labor* (University of Illinois Press).

Suzanne Franzway is Associate Professor in Gender Studies and Sociology and is a Key Researcher in the Hawke Research Institute for Sustainable Societies at the University of South Australia. Her research focuses on gender, work and labour movements, with current projects on engineers and workplace culture; care workers in elderly care and childcare; and the impact of domestic violence on women's work. Her books include *Sexual politics and greedy institutions: Union women, commitment and conflict in public and in private* (Pluto Australia, 2001) and *Staking a Claim: Feminism, Bureaucracy and the State* with R.W. Connell and Diane Court (Allen & Unwin, 1989). She is co-author with Mary Margaret Fonow of *New feminist politics: Transnational alliances between women and labor* (University of Illinois Press).
Contact details: School of International Studies, St Bernards Road, Magill, South Australia, 5072; e-mail: Suzanne.franzway@unisa.edu.au

Maria-Alejandra Gonzalez-Perez is a researcher at the Centre for Innovation and Structural Change (CISC) at the National University of Ireland,

Galway (NUIG). Her research interest is on corporate social responsibility, global production networks and international labour migration.
Contact details: CISC, NUIG, Galway, Ireland; e-mail: magonzalez@nuigalway.ie

Esther de Haan has extensive experience in researching and documenting labour practices in the garment industry in Southern and Eastern Africa. Since 1997 she has worked with organizations and trade unions in the region on action research and campaigning initiatives. She works in the Netherlands for the Centre for Research on Multinational Corporations (SOMO) and is also a campaign coordinator for the Clean Clothes Campaign, an international network campaigning on improving labour conditions in the garment industry. For SOMO she is also involved in research and campaigning on labour conditions in the electronics industry, and recently is working with organizations in Southern Africa on researching the extractives industry.

Pierre Habbard is a senior policy advisor to the Paris-based Trade Union Advisory Committee to the OECD (TUAC). His portfolio includes corporate governance, trade and investment, pension regulation and public governance. He is a member of the Global Reporting Initiative's Stakeholder Council. Born in 1972, he graduated from the Université Paris IX Dauphine and the London School of Economics and Political Science.

Jane Hardy is a Reader in Institutional Economics in Business School at the University of Hertfordshire, United Kingdom. Since 1990 Jane's research has been concerned with the transformation of the Polish economy. Specifically Jane has focused on the impacts of foreign investment, and the gender and labour market aspects of transformation. In 2006 Jane was awarded a grant from the British Economic and Social Research Council for a research project to look at cooperation between Polish and UK trade unions in organizing Polish migrant workers. She authored a book *Restructuring Krakow: Desperately seeking capitalism* (1996) and is currently writing another book entitled *Poland's new capitalism and its discontents* (2007). Jane is also an active trade unionist and on the national committee of the newly formed University and College Union.

Marion F. Hellmann is Assistant General Secretary of Building and Wood Workers' International (BWI) and responsible for relations to the industry, international financial institutions and development banks, Europe and Middle East. He has worked since 1991 for the BWI in Geneva. He started his professional career as typesetter in the printing industry and then studied and received a Masters degree in Sociology from the Free University of Berlin in

Germany. He also worked as staff member in the European Parliament on legal and economic issues. In the German Wood and Plastic Workers' Union (GHK), which merged with the German Metal Workers' Union (IG Metall), he was first secretary of the board dealing with European Union matters, economic and environmental issues.
Contact: Building and Wood Workers' International (BWI), 54 route des Acacias, Carouge, Geneva, CH-1227; e-mail: marion.hellmann@bwint.org

Michael Koen is part of the Civil Society Research and Support Collective (CSRSC) based in Durban, South Africa. He works extensively with organized labour in Southern and East Africa in research and facilitation. He has spent several years supporting garment sector initiatives of ITGLWF in Southern and East Africa including facilitating educational and strategic planning sessions with affiliates, developing educational materials, producing the ITGLWF Africa quarterly newsletter and conducting research in the sector at both regional and country level. He has also provided support for the South African labour movement, several Global Union Federations individually and collectively through the Africa GUF Forum and various international organizations that have labour-based initiatives in Africa.

Peter Knorringa is Associate Professor in Local and Regional Development at the Institute of Social Studies, The Hague, the Netherlands. He has worked on value chain analysis and the role of global buyers; small enterprise development, clustering and local economic development; the role of trust, social capital, and networks in industrialization. In recent years, Peter Knorringa has increasingly worked on income and employment generation as part of poverty alleviation programmes, and on fair and ethical trade. Most of his research and project work has been in India and Viet Nam, and some shorter research or advisory work in Indonesia, Ethiopia, South Africa and Siberia.

Ann-Marie Lorde was employed as a research officer of the National Union of Public Workers (Barbados) for more than nine years, and is presently employed by the Arawak Cement Company Limited as their Employee Relations Officer. Ann-Marie served as chairperson of the Caribbean Public Services Association Education and Research Committee for a number of years, and, until recently, was the National Coordinator for the International Migration of Women in the Healthcare Sector Project of Public Services International. Her research interests are trade union renewal, cross-border alliances and migration. She has presented a number of research papers in these areas to international forums and she is presently examining the possible link between cross-border alliances and migration to Caribbean public sector trade union renewal.

Terrence McDonough is the director of the CentreSTAGE project at the Centre for Innovation and Structural Change (CISC) and Senior Lecturer in Economics at the National University of Ireland, Galway. His research interests include globalization, American and Irish economic history, political economy, the history of economic thought and economics education for labour and community groups. He is co-author of *Minding your own business: Business education for labour activists* (Oak Tree Press, Dublin, 2001), co-editor of *Social structures of accumulation: The political economy of growth and crisis* (Cambridge University Press, 1994) and editor of *Was Ireland a colony? Economics, politics, ideology and culture in nineteenth-century Ireland* (Irish Academic Press, Dublin, 2005).
Contact details: Department of Economics, NUI, Galway, Ireland; e-mail: terrence.mcdonough@nuigalway.ie

Lene Olsen works in the International Labour Organization's (ILO) Bureau for Workers' Activities (ACTRAV) in Geneva. She is in charge of environmentally sustainable development issues in addition to being involved in the Global Union Research Network and the Global Labour University (GLU). She also covers issues in relation to information technology. From 1999 to 2001 Lene worked on the ILO/ACTRAV environment project "Trade Unions and Environmentally Sustainable Development" and two child labour projects aiming at developing national and international trade union strategies to combat child labour as well as actions against child labour through education and training. Before joining the ILO in 1999 she worked for the Norwegian Confederation of Trade Unions' Brussels Office for six years.

Lee Pegler spent a large proportion of his early career working as an economist/advisor to the Australian labour movement and various labour governments in that country. Further work has been carried out on labour relations in developed countries such as Japan, Sweden and the United Kingdom. Following an intense interest in developing countries, more recent times have seen him researching and publishing on the labour/industrial relations implications of "new" management strategies of TNCs in Brazil and Latin America in general. This has spread to a more focused interest in the implications of value chain insertion on labour/industrial relations, both for formal and informal workers, in countries such as Brazil, Colombia and Viet Nam. He currently works as a lecturer, project consultant and as convenor of the Human Resources and Employment Programme at the Institute of Social Studies, The Hague, the Netherlands.

Clóvis Scherer was a researcher at the Instituto Observatório Social, Brazil, from 2000 to 2004 and a research coordinator from 2004 to 2005. The institute carries

out research on corporate performance related to social, labour and environment aspects. He is now responsible for the Inter-union Department of Statistics and Socio-economic Studies' (DIEESE) office in Brasília, Brazil. DIEESE is the most important trade union research centre in Brazil covering the areas of public policy, labour market, collective bargaining, industrial relations, and so on.
Contact details: DIEESE, SQS 314-315 AE Proj 1, 1º andar, 70.383-400, Brasília, Brazil; e-mail: clovis@dieese.org.br

Eberhard Schmidt is an emeritus professor of political science at the Carl von Ossietzky University of Oldenburg, Germany. He is the coordinator of a network of academics and trade unionists dealing with problems of organizational learning in unions (www.hattinger-kreis.de) and works together with the Hans Boeckler Foundation.
Contact details: Eberhard Schmidt, Huchtinger Heerstr. 40, D- 28259 Bremen, Germany, e-mail: eberhard.schmidt@nord-com.net

Verena Schmidt is working in the ILO's Bureau for Workers' Activities in Geneva. She is coordinating the Global Union Research Network and teaching a course in the Global Labour University (www.global-labour-university.org). Her research interest is the social dimension of globalization, in particular with regard to trade unions, gender, migration and global production systems. Verena completed her BA at the London School of Economics and King's College, her MSc at the University of Edinburgh and her PhD at the Ruhr University Bochum. Her recent publications include *Gender mainstreaming – an innovation in Europe? The institutionalisation of gender mainstreaming in the European Commission* (Barbara Budrich Publishers, Opladen, 2005) and "Temporary migrant workers: Organizing and protection strategies by trade unions", in *Merchants of labour*, (International Institute for Labour Studies/ILO, Geneva, 2005).
Contact details: ILO/ACTRAV, 4, route des Morillons, CH-1211 Geneva 22; e-mail: schmidtv@ilo.org

Neva Seidman Makgetla completed her degree at Harvard University, and her PhD in Economics in Berlin, with a dissertation on international financial flows and development. Thereafter she lectured in economics at universities in Africa and the United States, including as senior lecturer at the University of the Witwatersrand in Johannesburg from early 1991 to late 1994. In this period, she was a member of the Department of Economic Planning of the African National Congress of South Africa, and in 1993/4 was economics coordinator of the Reconstruction and Development Programme. In 1994, Neva Makgetla joined the National Labour and Economic Development Institute (NALEDI), which is associated with the Congress of South African Trade Unions (COSATU). From mid-1995, she worked for the South African Government. In 2000, Neva Makgetla joined COSATU as coordinator for fiscal, monetary and public sector policy and, from early 2001, as head of the policy unit. Since October 2006, Neva Makgetla has worked for the South African Presidency as Sector Strategies Coordinator.

Lyuben Tomev is director of the Institute for Social and Trade Union Research in Sofia, Bulgaria. The main research areas include social policy, incomes and living standards, social impact of privatization in the public services, labour market, industrial relations, European integration and social dimensions of globalization. Contact details: Institute for Social and Trade Union Research, 1 Macedonia Square, Sofia-1000, Bulgaria; e-mail: ltomev@abv.bg

Richard Tudway is an economist by training. His career includes experience in the secretariat of the OECD, multinational companies and investment banking. He is currently a director of the Centre for International Economics and a Fellow of Huron University in London where he teaches on the university's MBA programme. He has written widely on issues of corporate governance, and is an adviser to the Trade Union Advisory Committee (TUAC) to the OECD. He is also a non-executive director of the Centre for Corporate Accountability, a London-based NGO committed to improving standards of worker safety, and making directors responsible for corporate manslaughter. He is an expert in corporate governance.
Contact details: www.tudway.com

Tanya van Meelis completed her Masters in Industrial Sociology at the University of Witwatersrand, South Africa. Her Masters thesis was on Social Movement Unionism in South Africa. After completing her Masters she worked as a researcher at the Sociology of Work Unit, at the University of the Witwatersrand. Her research focused on company and workers' responses to increased competition in an era of increased globalization. After two years of working closely with and researching the glass manufacturing sector, she left the university to work as the restructuring coordinator for the Chemical Workers Industrial Union (CWIU). This involved doing research, developing positions, training and education and negotiating restructuring. While at CWIU, Tanya also represented COSATU in the National Economic Development and Labour Council (NEDLAC) – the structure set up by law to negotiate social and economic policy. After working for CWIU for a number of years she joined COSATU, where she worked from 2001 until 2006 as Trade and Industry Policy Coordinator. Since May 2006 Tanya has worked for Standard Bank as Head of Strategic Issues Management.

PREFACE

This book is about trade union responses to globalization from different parts of the world. Globalization is a complex and multi-faceted process for workers worldwide as are the strategies they must develop to face its challenges.

Successful policies for development and poverty alleviation require the involvement of workers' representatives through trade unions in policy development and implementation. Trade unions are a crucial agent in implementing the ILO Decent Work Agenda and fighting for a fair globalization. This involves the struggle for transparent governance for a fairer globalization, the implementation of labour standards, employment creation, social protection, and poverty alleviation including meeting the UN's Millennium Development Goals and gender equality. But to engage effectively, trade unions – like all civil society organizations – need access to thorough research on globalization and development to inform their arguments.

Trade unions throughout the world are facing the challenges of rapid economic and social changes through a globalization process that is undermining existing regulations and arrangements without providing an adequate new regulatory framework. On national and global levels, trade unions need to strengthen their analytical capacity, their organizational efficiency and their political ability to represent working people effectively in social and economic policy debates in general, and to achieve economic and social justice. The issues of good governance, civil society development and people's involvement in development programmes within the Poverty Reduction Strategy Paper (PRSP) process or similar restructuring initiatives require a prominent role for workers' organizations. The PRSP approach was initiated by the IMF and the World Bank in 1999. A PRSP describes the macroeconomic, structural and social policies and programmes that a country will pursue over several years to promote broad-based growth and reduce poverty. These issues are also reflected in the follow up activities on the World Commission Report on the Social Dimension of Globalization which was established by the ILO in 2002.

In response to this the Global Union Research Network (GURN) organized a workshop on "Trade Unions, Globalization and Development" which took place in January 2005 before the World Social Forum in Porto Alegre, Brazil. This book is an outcome of this workshop. All contributions in the book were selected by means of a call for papers and were edited by coordinators and network partners of the Global Union Research Network: Pierre Habbard and Clóvis Scherer on multinational enterprises and corporate governance; Esther Busser on bilateral and multilateral trade agreements; Lawrence Egulu on international financial institutions; Luc Demaret and Lene Olsen on migration and Verena Schmidt on trade union development.

The GURN (see: www.gurn.info) is a platform for trade unionists and researchers dealing with the challenges of globalization from a labour perspective. It is a cooperation project of the International Trade Union Confederation (ITUC), the Trade Union Advisory Committee to the OECD (TUAC), the Global Union Federations (GUFs), the ILO's International Institute for Labour Studies (IILS) and the ILO's Bureau for Workers' Activities (ACTRAV). Currently, the ITUC, TUAC and ILO/ACTRAV form the steering committee of the GURN.

The objectives of the GURN are to:

- facilitate access to research carried out within the global trade union movement and allied research institutes;

- promote cooperation of trade unions and research institutes on common research issues;

- encourage knowledge and resource sharing, especially between the global North and South; and

- support efforts to enhance the capacity of trade unionists to develop analyses and to increase participation in debates and policy formulations.

The GURN initiates research, provides research information on issues relevant to the labour movement via the Internet, publishes regular newsletters, organizes workshops and online conferences on selected topics and facilitates the development of union-related networks. In cooperation with the Friedrich Ebert Foundation (FES), the GURN provides a database with the option to download labour-oriented research articles.

The GURN is currently focusing on the following topics:

- Bilateral and regional trade agreements
- Corporate governance
- OECD Guidelines for Multinational Enterprises
- Wages and collective bargaining
- Social security
- Economic alternatives and poverty eradication
- Poverty Reduction Strategy Papers (PRSPs) and International Financial Institutions (IFIs)
- Migration
- Global trade union strategies (union renewal)
- Sustainable development

The aim of the GURN and this book is to stimulate debate and discussion in trade unions about possible approaches to deal with globalization.

Guy Ryder
General Secretary, International Trade Union Confederation

John Evans
General Secretary, Trade Union Advisory Committee to the OECD

Dan Cunniah
Director a. i., ILO Bureau for Workers' Activities

ACKNOWLEDGEMENTS

The Global Union Research Network acknowledges financial support from the development branch of the Dutch trade union confederation FNV (FNV Mondiaal) as well as the Federal Ministry for Economic Cooperation and Development (BMZ).

Chapter 11

Financial support from the Irish Research Council for the Humanities and Social Sciences (IRCHSS), the Social Sciences Research Centre (SSRC) and the Centre for Innovation and Structural Change (CISC) at the National University of Ireland in Galway, and comments and suggestions by anonymous reviewers from GURN, are acknowledged by the authors.

Having promised anonymity, the authors are unable to mention the names of all banana workers, union leaders, political activists, government officials, engineers, academics, businessmen and other community members in Urabá who shared their experiences, energy, time and interest during our field work. Field research support by Vanessa González and Juan Carlos Henao Mejia is gratefully acknowledged.

EDITORIAL OVERVIEW

Verena Schmidt
Bureau for Workers' Activities, ILO, Geneva

There are deep-seated and persistent imbalances in the current workings of the global economy, which are ethically unacceptable and politically unsustainable. They arise from a fundamental imbalance between the economy, society and the polity. The economy is becoming increasingly global, while social and political institutions remain largely local, national or regional. None of the existing global institutions provide adequate democratic oversight of global markets, or redress basic inequalities between countries. These imbalances point to the need for better institutional frameworks and policies if the promise of globalization is to be realized. The imbalance between the economy and society is subverting social justice […].

(World Commission on the Social Dimension of Globalization, 2004, p. 25.)

Globalization can promote development, but only if it goes hand in hand with social justice. When we think of the impact of globalization on labour, we tend to think of its negative aspects: export processing zones (EPZs), child prostitution or forced labour. However, globalization has also enabled workers to organize transnationally, to negotiate with companies on a global level and to address global issues such as gender discrimination and sustainable development with actors from around the globe.

Some research and experience is now available on the impact of globalization on workers and the strategies adopted by workers and their organizations to deal with these challenges. Here, we present some important contributions to that pool of knowledge. The authors of the contributions have very diverse backgrounds. Some are trade union leaders, some are trade union researchers and others are university professors working closely with labour. Their detailed conclusions on which strategies should be adopted to deal with globalization vary, but they do have some important underlying themes in common. The authors of this book have no doubts about the reality of globalization. It is here to stay, and it is shaping our lives. But to what extent is it a good or a bad thing for workers? And which strategies do trade unions pursue in dealing with the challenges of globalization? The following section will give an overview about the different trade union responses to globalization addressed in the book at a national, regional and global level.

The empirical framework: Country, regional and global experiences

The trade union interest for integrating sustainable development principles within their policies is growing. Threats such as global climate change have caught the attention of trade unionists. The concern with sustainable development is no longer seen as a luxury topic of the global North but rather as an essential forward-looking strategy for all trade unions. The United Nations (UN) recognizes that unions are vital actors in achieving broader goals of sustainable development. In *Sustainability and unions: International trade union action to implement sustainability norms at corporate level*, Eberhard Schmidt argues that the new framework of global governance enables the unions to intensify those efforts, both by lobbying international institutions and by building alliances with non-governmental organizations (NGOs). But at the same time, the unions are confronted with the growing influence of the private sector. Many unions are concerned that voluntary corporate codes of conduct are not accompanied sufficiently strongly by measures of "accountability". If a multinational enterprise (MNE) violates social and environmental norms, the Global Union Federations (GUFs) can either react by initiating demonstrative action or they can take pro-active steps by making an offer to negotiate with the corporation on relevant agreements.

Those agreements are a formal recognition of social partnership at the global level, points out Marion F. Hellmann, Assistant General Secretary of one GUF, the Building and Wood Workers' International. International Framework Agreements (IFAs) are therefore qualitatively different to companies' own internal codes of conduct. His contribution (*Social partnership at the global level: Building and Wood Workers' International experiences with International Framework Agreements*) analyses the strengths and weaknesses of the IFA approach. International Framework Agreements reflect a commitment to observe core international labour standards. In principle, the employers who sign up are demonstrating that they favour good industrial relations at the workplace, feel responsible for the whole supply chain and are open-minded about trade union activities. However, social partnership is not a substitute for union organizing.

International Framework Agreements currently cover only a small portion of the world labour force, but they might hint towards the emergence of new forms of industrial relations in addition to collective bargaining at national level.

Lee Pegler and Peter Knorringa show in their paper *Integrating labour issues in global value chain analysis: Exploring implications for labour research and unions* that the enhanced coordination of productive activity between countries by multinationals highlights how the level of corporate governance appears to have increased in recent years despite the greater dispersion of production. In contrast, the labour impacts of these value chain strategies, combined with the reduced relevance of national labour legislation in many countries, has left a gap in terms of labour rights. The increasing integration of national economies in a single global market and the appearance of new world production systems are demanding a convergence of national and international trade union agendas (ICFTU, 2004, p. 7). This is a big challenge for trade unions which traditionally organize within a national context but which are facing increasingly international challenges resulting from globalization. The paper highlights some of the implications of these value chain developments for labour research and policy.

Using the case of the information and communication technologies (ICT) industry, Anibel Ferus-Comelo (*Paving the path toward the unionization of high-tech sweatshops*) examines the challenges and prospects for labour campaigns and trade union development in an era of globalization. Many countries in which ICT production takes place have laws that protect workers' rights generally. However, the low level of unionization and collective representation of ICT workers worldwide means that there is little oversight of the enforcement of these laws. Amidst the overwhelmingly pessimistic prognosis of workers' rights as transnational corporations (TNCs) seek the most cost-effective, "flexible'" workforce, the author argues that, while globalization poses tremendous obstacles to organizing, there are many opportunities for action to defend workers' interests. It is based on primary research in two different places – Silicon Valley (United States) and Bangalore (India) – which are key nodes in the global high-technology industry.

Governance and accountability of corporations are increasingly taken up by trade unions, especially since the recent corporate scandals and collapses of Enron and Worldcom in 2001, followed by Parmalat in 2003. Trade unions are campaigning for the implementation of an effective national and international framework of rules and standards to ensure good corporate governance and wider market integrity, along with regulatory systems to ensure effective implementation and enforcement (GURN, 2006a). Richard Tudway assesses what needs to be done if corporate governance arrangements are to better protect and promote worker and wider community interests (*Corporate governance reforms as a means of protecting and promoting worker interests: Shaping the corporation of tomorrow*). The mechanisms of governance in Anglo-American jurisdictions are seriously flawed and cannot be remedied by superficial "fixes". Unitary boards cannot provide adequate independent supervision. Shareholders continue to fail to meet their obligations as owners: acting more like absentee landlords than committed shareholders they are unable to control the behaviour of those companies in which they invest. Entrenchment of management power is the result. The challenge is to make tomorrow's company a better governed institution capable of generating sustainable wealth in a responsible and accountable fashion. In meeting this challenge directors of companies have to engage with shareholders and other stakeholders in determining commercial objectives. Directors also need to ensure that they are empowered to provide adequate supervision of the executives who run the business. Only in this way can directors ensure that companies aspire to attain the very highest standards of corporate responsibility. Institutional shareholders need, for their part, to ensure also that they play an effective and fully engaged role in this process along with the other "gatekeepers" on whose dedication and diligence the integrity of corporate governance ultimately depends.

In Bulgaria, as in many parts of Central and Eastern Europe, the arrival of the multinational companies was often seen as a positive development. Nadejda Daskalova and Lyuben Tomev found much to support that view (*Multinational companies in Bulgaria: Impact on labour and social development*). A survey of 29 subsidiaries of 18 unionized multinationals in Bulgaria showed that most of them have serious investment programmes aimed at technological renewal and the modernization of production. They are also making considerable investments in environmental protection and the social development of the local communities. The priority for multinational managements is to modernize work organization. Teamwork, with job rotation, has been introduced, leading to flexibility and the development of personnel skills, and increased labour productivity. Union density in the multinationals surveyed is 67.4 per cent, as compared with an average of 20–25 per cent for Bulgaria as a whole. But some trade union structures have been lost in the process of outsourcing and subcontracting. Pay and conditions in the local subsidiaries of multinationals are significantly better than those legally required and those existing in most Bulgarian enterprises. However, managements often try to exclude unions from wage-setting, and pay in the Bulgarian branches of multinationals remains lower than in other countries.

A study of freedom of association and collective bargaining in 16 subsidiaries of multinational companies operating in Brazil found that they follow the labour relations standards pertaining to Brazil, with little importation of standards from their countries of origin. But as Clóvis Scherer notes (*Freedom of association and collective bargaining: The practice of multinational companies in Brazil*), unionization rates in the companies studied were higher than the national average. This reflects a greater union presence, indicated by the number of union leaders employed in the companies. However, the workers surveyed did feel that their ability to collectively intervene in the internal labour conditions of the companies was limited by poor development of the right to organize at the workplace. Other indicators of union freedom (access to the workplace, recognition of union decisions and compliance with agreements reached) were, with some exceptions, found to be positive.

In *Trade and development in South Africa* Neva Seidman Makgetla and Tanya van Meelis argue that the opening of the South African economy had very mixed implications for unemployment and poverty. The focus on higher exports without adequate, targeted support for more labour-intensive sectors contributed to slower employment growth. Meanwhile, labour-intensive imports displaced employment, without lowering the cost of living for the poor. Also, the threat of capital outflows led to the adoption of a conservative fiscal policy up to 2000, with devastating effects on government services.

Cross-border migration can be seen as a result of failed development and the lack of decent work globally. More than 175 million migrants, including migrant workers, refugees, asylum seekers, permanent immigrants and others, live and work in a country other than that of their birth or citizenship. The ILO estimates that some 86 million of them have moved to find work (ILO, 2004a). These figures do not include those who have moved within their country. Neither the restrictive policies adopted by many governments or the newly adopted "security approach" have stemmed migration. Instead they have promoted irregular migration, forcing millions of people into illegality. New measures are needed to improve the situation of migrant workers and their families. The ILO emphasizes that all its standards apply to all workers, whatever their situation may be (GURN, 2006b). The following two papers look at migration from the point of view of trade unions from so-called "source countries", Barbados and Poland, and from the point of view of trade unions of the destination country, namely the United Kingdom.

The Caribbean is increasingly being affected by international migration. There is growing concern among trade unionists about the impact of international migration on the quality of social services, particularly health services, in developing countries. Ann-Marie Lorde focuses on the impact of migration on the health-care sector and seeks to examine the migration of health-care workers in the global economy, paying attention to caregivers (*Migration in the global economy: Challenges and opportunities for Caribbean trade unions*).

Nick Clark and Jane Hardy examine cross-border collaboration between the Polish Solidarity and the British TUC in particular, and initiatives providing information, seconding organizers from Poland and hosting training courses for union organizers from Eastern Europe (*European Union enlargement, workers and migration: Implications for trade unions in the United Kingdom and Poland*). The article illustrates the challenges facing Polish unions such as the impact of the "drain" of members and potential members and improving the rights of Polish workers in the European Union. The response of Polish unions, which have been hostile to the labour market restrictions being placed on Polish nationals, is explored and the contrasting views about how they should intervene in the issue of migrant workers are discussed. The chapter looks at the problems that British unions have faced regarding migrant Polish workers such as organizing in private firms, the role of temporary labour agencies and integrating Polish activists into union structures. The response of British trade unions is discussed, looking at grassroots projects and community cooperation, initiatives to recruit Polish workers, and the special focus this issue has been given by the TUC.

All in all, trade union action will improve, or at least mitigate, the effects of globalization. The "race to the bottom" in the global banana industry could put great pressure on the already low pay and conditions in Latin American banana production, Maria-Alejandra Gonzalez-Perez and Terrence McDonough point out in *More than bananas: Social responsibility networks and labour relations in the banana industry in the Urabá region of Colombia*. And yet there are encouraging developments in the Colombian banana-growing region of Urabá. With strong union participation, it is currently pursuing an alternative "high road" strategy, emphasizing the quality of the product itself, as well as its socially and environmentally "ethical" nature. Current trends towards ethical marketing have made it possible to pursue a higher-price strategy for such "socially responsible" products.

In Turkey, agreements with the International Monetary Fund have meant that government policy has been dominated by neo-liberalism since the 1980s. The consequences for workers and their trade unions have been severe. But, as Seyhan Erdoğdu reports, a union-led alliance has been opposing that line ever since 1999. Her contribution (*The Labour Platform: An alliance of trade unions in Turkey*) is the first study of its kind on Turkey's Labour Platform, and it aims to fill some of the gaps in research on labour resistance in Turkey to corporately driven globalization.

Union feminists are playing an important role in mobilizing women's participation in transnational campaigns for labour rights and economic justice. Mary Margaret Fonow and Suzanne Franzway's research (*Transnational union networks, feminism and labour advocacy*) suggests that union feminists, with their structural ties to both organized labour and the women's movement, are in a unique position to mobilize within both movements in response to the issues and concerns raised for workers by globalization. The authors examine several sites where union feminists are using transnational labour networks to build international solidarity, to create new discourses of advocacy, and to build alliances with activists from grassroots organizations, NGOs and other social movements. By building and mobilizing transnational networks and alliances, union feminists create political spaces for new workers and for a new understanding of workers' issues and concerns arising out of the impact of globalization on both workplaces and personal lives.

Moreover, what should be the role of research itself in promoting decent work and a socially just, sustainable globalization? Various contributors emphasize that more research is needed into the trade union role, and that future analyses should aim for greater quantitative precision and comparability. Above all, researchers need to focus on the information required by those most directly concerned, the trade unions. Esther de Haan and Michael Koen describe one approach to this issue (*Action research in the garment sector in Southern and Eastern Africa*). As garment production in Southern and Eastern Africa became more export-oriented, research revealed highly exploitative conditions in the export-focused factories. Yet unions' traditional organizing methods seemed to have little impact. So workers and their trade unions were forced to learn new ways of struggling for better working conditions and building international solidarity. "Action research" aims to support such efforts. It allows needs on the ground to control the research agenda to a large degree. By providing feedback of its findings at various stages to national and regional unions and international campaigners, action research is directly linked with taking action and making changes.

The global and different national responses of trade unions to globalization vary considerably. One issue that links all contributions is networking and alliance building. Another issue is the role of ILO standards for achieving a fair globalization. Each issue will be looked at separately.

Networking and building alliances

Many of our contributors agree that unions need to seek allies at various levels, in various ways. Unions are just one of the players within the global governance system. So they have to build alliances with each other and also with other civil society groups such as NGOs. However, unions and NGOs are different types of organization. Trade unions are membership based and they are accountable to their members. Their primary task is to defend the interests of their members. Non-governmental organizations can be membership based and are then sometimes referred to as grass-root organizations (Edwards and Hulme, 1996). Some NGOs are not membership based and are solely funded by one or several external donors (e.g. enterprises). Even though non-membership NGOs "serve" their constituents, they are usually not accountable to them (Baccaro, 2001, p. 11).

In addition to emphasizing the importance of alliance building, almost all authors stressed the relevance of the ILO and of labour standards in achieving a fair globalization.

The role of the ILO on globalization

Globalization is often defined from an economic perspective, i.e. that it is about new technology enabling better communication and transportation, which lead to greater interdependence with regard to trade, finance and global production systems. The ILO is concerned about the social dimension of globalization, i.e. the impact of globalization on men and women in different parts of the world.

The Constitution of the ILO (which was adopted in 1919) states that "universal and lasting peace can be established only if it is based upon social justice" (ILO, 2004b, p. 4). This is reinforced by the ILO Declaration of Philadelphia in 1944 which reaffirms the fundamental principles on which the organization is based and, in particular, that:

(a) labour is not a commodity;

(b) freedom of expression and of association are essential to sustained progress;

(c) poverty anywhere constitutes a danger to prosperity everywhere;

(d) the war against want requires to be carried on with unrelenting vigour within each nation, and by continuous and concerted international effort in which the representatives of workers and employers, enjoying equal status with those of governments, join with them in free discussion and democratic decision with a view to the promotion of the common welfare.

(ILO, 2004b, p. 23.)

Even though the term "globalization" did not yet exist, this extract of the Declaration of Philadelphia established the foundation for the ILO's work on fair globalization. This work was reinforced with the Report of the Director-General on the World Commission on the Social Dimension of Globalization which defines the ILO's role regarding globalization. The report states:

> The emphasis placed by the Commission on our Decent Work Agenda highlights the central role the ILO is called upon to play in contributing to a fair and inclusive process of globalization.

(ILO, 2004c, p. 3.)

The important role of the ILO and in particular the role of the constituents was further strengthened by the conclusions of the 2007 discussion of the 96th International Labour Conference on "Strengthening the ILO's capacity to assists its Members' efforts to reach its objectives in the context of globalization":

> Strong constituents lie at the heart of effective ILO action. The ILO should increase its support in building the capacity of its constituents to ensure their ongoing ability to engage in the ILO objectives and the Decent Work Agenda, realize these goals in the context of globalization and meet the needs of their constituents.
>
> (ILO, 2007, p. 23.)

This book is about how one constituent of the ILO, trade union organizations, responds to globalization. The varied and partly contradictory effects of globalization on labour in different countries require varied and sophisticated responses which are analysed in this book from national, regional and global perspectives. The contributions show that civil society and, in particular, trade unions as the most important organized part of civil society are key in influencing the rules of globalization to achieve a fair globalization. Trade unions also play a paramount role in implementing and enforcing these rules.

References

Baccaro, L. 2001. *Civil society, NGOs, and decent work policies: Sorting out the issues*, IILS Discussion Papers, DP 127/2001 (Geneva, IILS).

Edwards, M.; Hulme, D. (eds). 1996. *Beyond the magic bullet – NGO performance and accountability in the post-Cold War world* (Bloomfield, CT, Kumarian Press).

GURN (Global Union Research Network). 2006a. "Corporate governance". Available at: http://www.gurn.info/topic/corpgov/index.html [accessed 3 Jan. 2006].

—. 2006b. "Migration". Available at: http://www.gurn.info/topic/migrant/index.html [accessed 3 Jan. 2006].

ICFTU (International Confederation of Free Trade Unions). 2004. *A trade union guide to globalisation* (Brussels), second edition.

ILO (International Labour Organization). 2004a. *Facts on migrant labour* (Geneva).

—. 2004b. *Constitution of the International Labour Organization and Standing Orders of the International Labour Conference* (Geneva).

—. 2004c. *A fair globalization: The role of the ILO*, Report of the Director-General on the World Commission on the Social Dimension of Globalization, International Labour Conference, 92nd Session, Geneva, 2004 (Geneva).

—. 2007. *Report of the Committee on strengthening the ILO's capacity to assist its Members' efforts to reach its objectives in the context of globalization*, Provisional Record 23, fifth item on the agenda, International Labour Conference, 96th Session, Geneva, 2007 (Geneva).

World Commission on the Social Dimension of Globalization. 2004. *A fair globalization: Creating opportunities for all* (Geneva, ILO).

SUSTAINABILITY AND UNIONS: INTERNATIONAL TRADE UNION ACTION TO IMPLEMENT SUSTAINABILITY NORMS AT CORPORATE LEVEL

Eberhard Schmidt
Carl von Ossietzky University of Oldenburg, Germany

Trade unions and the challenge of sustainable development

The United Nations Conference on Environment and Development (UNCED), held in Rio de Janeiro in 1992, explicitly gave unions the task of contributing to the implementation of sustainable development because of their specific role and responsibility as representatives of workers worldwide. Chapter 29 of Agenda 21 of Rio stated:

> Trade unions are vital actors in facilitating the achievement of sustainable development in view of their experience in addressing industrial change, the extremely high priority they give to protection of the working environment and the related natural environment, and their promotion of socially responsible and economic development.
>
> (UNCED, 1992.)

In the meantime, the process of economic globalization has intensified and severe impacts on the social and environmental dimensions of work have become more and more visible. Transnational corporations, as the main actors of globalization, have come under pressure from NGOs and unions, who have called for standard setting to regulate global business activities. Responding to the growing pressure, the management of multinational corporations and their international associations, such as the World Business Council on Sustainable Development (WBCSD) and the International Chamber of Commerce (ICC), have promoted a new instrument – corporate social responsibility (CSR). Under the CSR banner, and with the help of the so-called codes of conduct, the business world has tried to provide a response that ensures they retain the initiative and keep agreements voluntary.

Trade unions are sceptical as to whether codes of conduct without independent monitoring can ultimately solve the problem of improving working conditions and the environment. Most of the union movement is of the opinion that voluntary industry initiatives should only supplement, and not substitute, government-based regulations or standards. Recently, the 18th World Congress of the International Confederation of Free Trade Unions (ICFTU) in Japan (2004) adopted a very detailed resolution and an action programme entitled the "Social Responsibilities of Business in a Global Economy". Among other important points, this programme states:

> 11. Congress finds that trade unions must not take an uncritical or a dismissive approach to CSR. CSR cannot be an objective or an end in itself, as the protection and advancement of workers cannot be based on a concept that centres on the role of management. On the other hand, CSR can provide trade unions with opportunities to engage companies about the social impact of their business activities. There is a proliferation of voluntary private initiatives, public–private partnerships and statements of ethical principles in the name of CSR, and a growing industry of enterprises offering services to business and investors. CSR is increasingly being incorporated into the policy and programmes of governments and intergovernmental organisations. CSR cannot be ignored because it can lead to changes in the environment in which workers and their trade unions relate to employers, business organisations, non governmental organisations, governments and international organisations.
>
> (ICFTU, 2004.)

The action programme lists, in detail, provisions for union activities concerning the international regulation of business.

In 1999, when UN Secretary-General Kofi Annan proposed the UN Global Compact – a global partnership initiative – the unions became part of it, together with other NGOs, the private sector, commercial enterprises and businesses and their associations. Its aim is to generate a "shared understanding" about how companies can help to promote UN principles within corporate domains. However, no accountability mechanisms were specified.

The World Summit on Sustainability and Development (WSSD) in Johannesburg (2002), resulting from many multi-stakeholder dialogues in the different regions of the world, demonstrated the intention of the UN to cooperate with all relevant partners in establishing global political implementation networks to boost the participation of NGOs and the private sector in international negotiations. However, to the unions, the outcome of the WSSD in Johannesburg concerning CSR, accountability and public-private partnerships appeared ambivalent and rather weak. "Corporate social responsibility is a fine enough idea in itself, but at times it suffers a fatal flaw in that it tries to make the private sector do what the public sector should do, i.e. regulate and implement for the greater good. There has to be more clarity on the boundary conditions on these different notions," noted John Evans, General Secretary of the Trade Union Advisory Committee (TUAC) to the Organisation for Economic Co-operation and Development (OECD). He added, "The protection and enforcement of civil, human and labour rights is a domain in which governments remain the primary and most legitimate actor" (Evans, 2002). But this obviously does not mean that the unions refuse to consider new partnerships. "Crucial to the issue of corporate accountability is the effective regulation and implementation of agreements" (Evans, 2002).

So the international trade union movement has had to develop a dual strategy: influencing the relevant international institutions through diplomatic action to improve the norms and standards of CSR (the main actor here being the ITUC), and negotiating at corporate level to conclude agreements which ensure that CSR includes adequate instruments of accountability (the global unions being the principal agents in this approach).

Trade union strategies addressing norms of sustainability

The level of union diplomacy

It is evident that the new framework of global governance enables the unions to intensify their efforts in lobbying international institutions and in building alliances with NGOs, especially those who are fighting for similar political goals. On the other hand, the emerging multi-stakeholder dialogues and the new global political networks are increasingly putting the unions face-to-face with the growing influence of the private sector.

This trend is clearly reflected by the most influential initiatives on this sector:

- *ILO Tripartite Declaration of Principles concerning Multinational Enterprises and Social Policy* (ILO, Geneva, November 1977, amended 2000);

- *OECD Guidelines for Multinational Enterprises* (OECD, Paris, revised version 2000);

- European Commission green paper, *Promoting a European framework for corporate social responsibility* (European Commission, Luxembourg, 2001);

- *UN norms on the responsibilities of transnational corporations and other business enterprises with regard to human rights* (UN High Commission on Human Rights, Geneva, 2003–2007);
- International Organization for Standardization (ISO) Working Group on Social Responsibility final draft and publication of International Standard ISO 26000 (planned for 2008).

The ILO Tripartite Declaration invites governments, employers' and workers' organizations and MNEs to observe basic human rights, including core labour standards, especially freedom of association and the right to collective bargaining.

The *OECD Guidelines for Multinational Enterprises* present recommendations addressed by governments to MNEs, providing voluntary principles and standards for responsible business conduct. They recommend that enterprises should communicate reliable information to the public, should practise within the framework of applicable law and labour regulations, should establish an appropriate environmental management system, combat bribery and act in accordance with fair business. But the document makes no mention of a system of monitoring. The observance of the guidelines is explicitly voluntary and not legally enforceable. As this is an instrument of external verification, there is only the possibility of cases being raised with the National Contact Points (NPC). National Contact Points are established by governments in the countries that adhere to the OECD guidelines. When issues arise concerning the implementation of the guidelines in relation to specific instances of business conduct, the NCP is only expected to help resolve them, no further action is provided.

Although the European Commission green paper points in the same direction of voluntary commitment by enterprises, it makes it quite clear that companies are embedded in a process of interaction with employees, shareholders, investors, consumers, public authorities and NGOs. Trade unions are explicitly named as being party to the monitoring process. Monitoring, which should "involve stakeholders such as public authorities, trade unions and NGOs, is important to secure the credibility of codes of conduct" (EC, 2001, p. 15). With regard to internationally agreed standards like the "Social Accountability 8000" system, the document emphasizes that "the involvement of stakeholders, including trade unions and NGOs, could improve the quality of verification" (EC, 2001, p. 19).

The *UN norms on the responsibilities of transnational corporations and other business enterprises with regard to human rights*, initially adopted by a UN panel of independent experts in August 2003, "bring together a range of obligations drawn from existing international human rights, labour and environmental conventions and are widely regarded as a first step towards binding regulation and monitoring of TNC activities by UN bodies, backed by national enforcement" (Koenig-Archibugi, 2004, p. 26). Unlike the OECD guidelines, the ILO Tripartite Declaration and the UN Global Compact, "the UN norms are not limited by clauses emphasizing their non-regulatory nature" (Oldenziel and Bohman, 2004).

In 2005 followed a report of the UN High Commissioner for Human Rights on the responsibilities of TNCs and related business enterprises with regard to human rights (E/CN.4/2005/91) and a Resolution which requests the Secretary-General "to appoint a special representative on the issue of human rights and transnational corporations and other business enterprises, for an initial period of two years, who shall submit an interim report to the Commission on Human Rights at its sixty-second session and a final report at its sixty-third session, with views and recommendations for the consideration of the Commission, with the following mandate:

(a) To identify and clarify standards of corporate responsibility and accountability for transnational corporations and other business enterprises with regard to human rights;

(b) To elaborate on the role of States in effectively regulating and adjudicating the role of transnational corporations and other business enterprises with regard to human rights, including through international cooperation;

(c) To research and clarify the implications for transnational corporations and other business enterprises of concepts such as "complicity" and "sphere of influence";

(d) To develop materials and methodologies for undertaking human rights impact assessments of the activities of transnational corporations and other business enterprises;

(e) To compile a compendium of best practices of States and transnational corporations and other business enterprises" (2005/69).

A statement by the International Federation of Human Rights (FIDH), a NGO with consultative status to the UN, nevertheless "does acknowledge the weaknesses and ambiguities of the norms adopted in August 2003 by the Sub-Commission on Human Rights, in particular the vagueness of notions [...]. It acknowledges that the norms leave open a crucial question: how the means of implementation, in particular regards to the State, ensure that no human rights violation committed by a transnational corporation is left unpunished and without remedy" (FIDH 2007). The FIDH insists that the responsibilities of States should be clarified and, if necessary, expanded, in order to meet the need to effectively protect the rights of the victims of the activities of transnational corporations.

Finally, the ISO, through an initiative by Brazil and Sweden, has started a process to develop a standard on social responsibility. An ISO Working Group on Social Responsibility (WG SR) has been given the task of drafting an International Standard for social responsibility. The Bangkok meeting of the WG SR (2005) communicated that the guidance standard will be published in 2008 as ISO 26000 and its use will be voluntary. It will not include requirements of monitoring and accounting and will thus not be a certification standard. The standard will reflect an international consensus among all the stakeholder categories impacted by social responsibility.

The pressure for mandatory mechanisms by the unions and involved NGOs is a reaction to the inadequacy of voluntary mechanisms for corporate accountability. The crucial point is whether the concept of CSR, favoured by the business sector and strictly based on self-regulation and voluntary participation, will achieve results in the sense of really improving the social and environmental conduct of multinationals and other corporations. Many unions are concerned that these voluntary codes of conduct are a public relations tool for the business world and are not sufficiently accompanied by measures of "accountability", i.e. reporting, monitoring, transparency and verification.

The level of negotiations and agreements

In the case of the violation of social and environmental norms by MNEs, the GUFs principally have two courses of action open to them. They can react by initiating demonstrative action or they can take proactive steps by making an offer to negotiate with the corporation on relevant agreements (Müller et al., 2003).

The first type of action, which can be described as "naming and shaming", is more aggressive and aims to publicize violations by the multinationals. This is done through publicity campaigns, by calling on potential clients to boycott products or by initiating such action as worldwide campaigns, for example the Clean Clothes campaign. This type of action is very close to the strategy of many NGOs and mostly done in alliance with them. Often, putting the company under pressure is the only way to force them to accept negotiations on social and environmental norms. The existence or the development of global union networks (GUNs), connecting the activities of European works councils or even world works councils and global unions, is very helpful in supporting this type of action (Müller and Rüb, 2005).

Today, the strategic priority of the unions lies more with the second type of action, i.e. negotiating with the central management of MNEs on the basis of dialogue structures, and trying to build up to producing agreements. Since 1995, examples of successful International Framework Agreements (IFAs), setting up social and environmental norms and formal ongoing relationships between MNEs and GUFs, have increased. By November 2005 43 agreements of this type had been concluded (for a complete list see Carley, 2005 or Pichot, 2006).

The International Union of Food, Agricultural, Hotel, Restaurant, Catering, Tobacco and Allied Workers' Associations (IUF) was the pioneering organization. In 1989, it concluded the first global agreement with the Danone Group on the issue of giving information about the economic development of the company to the workers' representatives and later, in 1994, regarding respect of trade union rights. Other global unions, such as the International Metalworkers' Federation (IMF), the International Federation of Chemical, Energy, Mine and General Workers' Unions (ICEM), the International Federation of Building and Woodworkers (IFBWW) and the Union Network International (UNI) followed by concluding global agreements with well-known multinationals such as Statoil (1998); Faber-Castell (see Köhnen, 2003), Freudenberg, Hochtief, Telefonica (2000); Chiquita (see Riisgaard, 2005), IKEA, Skanska, (2001); DaimlerChrysler, ENI, Volkswagen (2002); Rheinmetall, SKF (2003); Bosch, Carrefour, EDF, H&M, Lukoil, Renault (2004); and BMW, EADS (2005).

All these agreements contain the full catalogue of ILO core standards (trade union rights, workplace equality, protection of health, safety and the environment, information and training, ban on child labour and forced labour). In addition to the core ILO standards, in some IFAs protection of the environment and improvement of working and environmental conditions in accordance with international, European and national norms are explicitly stipulated.

These formal agreements, signed by the management of multinationals and the global unions, are different from the majority of codes of conduct which are unilaterally declared by some TNCs or are concluded bilaterally between TNCs and NGOs and only sometimes include workers' representatives at the company level.

An example of best practice is the agreement between the Faber-Castell Corporation and the IMF and the International Federation of Building and Wood Workers (IFBWW), concluded in 2000. Faber-Castell is a TNC based in Germany, producing all kinds of pencils and writing materials. It has 5,000 employees, 15 production units and 19 distribution units (the biggest company is in São Carlos in Brazil). The agreement fulfils all the criteria of the model code of conduct which the ICFTU published in 1997. Beyond the ILO core standards, the senior management committed itself to pay sufficient wages, not to require overtime, to guarantee acceptable working conditions and to abstain from intimidation, sexual harassment and ill-treatment of workers. These standards and recommendations are available at every single workplace in the relevant languages. Unions have access to all the information about working conditions at all company sites and the participation of the local unions and works representatives is guaranteed.

This code of conduct is implemented by making it an integral part of the management system, using special checklists. Verification takes place in close cooperation with the unions and workers' representatives at all levels. Every two years, a verification audit is carried out by a special monitoring committee with external observers and representatives from management, the unions and the elected workplace-level worker representatives. They analyse the reports and the checklists and may suggest solutions to problems. It is true that examples like Faber-Castell are still rare but they point in the right direction and provide principles to guide trade union policy (Köhnen, 2003).

Agreements between the unions and management are always the result of dialogue procedures established on the basis of international union networks. Without such structures in the background, a monitoring process for the agreements cannot be adequately put into effect. The European works councils and the few existing worldwide workers' councils (VW, DaimlerChrysler etc.) may be very helpful in initiating and supporting such dialogue procedures, because of their long experience in building up relations with the management of the TNCs. But if the workers' councils pursue a purely company-centred policy in order to extend their influence, this may be a cause of conflict with the global unions.

Preconditions and prospects for successful international union action

The experience of unions in their efforts to influence standard-setting on sustainability, both by lobbying international institutions and by negotiating agreements with MNEs on social and envionmental norms, have highlighted some basic problems.

Dealing with conflicts of interest

Conflicts of interest about the implementation of sustainability norms (whether voluntary or mandatory) exist not only between the unions and workers' representatives on the one hand and the TNCs on the other, but also within the union movement and between the workers of different nations and locations. Although globalization has put pressure on national policies, labour regulation is still to a large extent determined by national law and collective bargaining. So trade unions prioritize the national context for their action strategy and tend to defend the corporate interests of their clients. European works councils, which are often dominated by delegates from the parent corporation, are strongly linked to national or local interests, and this can make a fair reconciliation of interests at the global level difficult to achieve. Thus, sustainability norms have been viewed by some as instruments of a protectionist policy favouring the interests of workers in developed countries to the detriment of workers in developing countries.

Moreover, the winners and losers of globalization processes are not only separated by a North–South divide. Unions all over the world are faced with economic winners and losers among their own national or regional membership. So the task of convincing the membership of the need for active international solidarity, in the sense of "solidarity among the unequal", becomes even more of a challenge. The need to coordinate diversity has increased, but at the same time the preconditions for such an ambitious goal have not improved.

Capacity building and investment of resources

Not the least of the reasons for the weakness of international cooperation between the unions is a lack of resources. The lack of human and financial resources at global union level and the lack of trained personnel with international experience, are a consequence of the limited policy of the national unions. The global level suffers from a lack of powers because national unions are often afraid of losing influence and control on international issues by delegating decisions to an upper level or, even worse, give priority to an isolationist policy instead of promoting multilateral action. Unless national member unions enhance and re-evaluate the status of the global unions and the international confederations, no real progress in terms of strengthening the union influence on global standard-setting processes will take place. Instead of short-term action and short-sighted campaigns, there is a need for enduring action on the basis of ongoing capacity building. A major task in this context is to qualify union experts for work at international level. This includes willingness for intercultural learning and the capability to interact with people from different institutional backgrounds, such as NGOs.

Developing a policy of alliances

Trade unions are a single global player in the global governance system and not the strongest one. If they want to be successful in implementing strong norms of CSR, including mechanisms of accountability, they have to rely on the support of allies. Those allies can be both governmental agencies and NGOs. The NGOs have turned out to be the unions' natural allies on many issues, whether in conflicts with TNCs or at the level of UN commissions and multi-stakeholder dialogues. However, it has to be recognized that unions are the experts on the world of work and that NGOs often tend to ignore the importance of local unions. They have to learn that the participation of the local or regional labour movement is decisive for the efficient implementation and monitoring of codes of conduct.

The unions can profit, in these alliances, from the high credibility of the NGOs and they can learn from their flexible and innovative forms of action. As multi-stakeholder initiatives are often the best way to address the accountability gaps in TNCs, the unions are well-advised to secure the assistance and support of NGOs. These alliances should be based on their own transnational networks. But there are some preconditions to reconsider, and some barriers to overcome, if cooperation with NGOs is to bring benefits to the unions. Unions, in contrast to NGOs, are strongly embedded in national bargaining processes and have to take into consideration the impacts of their action on their bargaining partners. Unions are mainly linked to their company-based rank and file, and are less attuned to societal needs than are the NGOs. Also, many union members are exposed to global competition. This means accepting the consequences of standard-setting, which has impacts on their social welfare. Moreover, the different attitudes of unions and NGOs and their members are not without their potential for conflict.

Taking these differences into account, the unions have to prove the benefits of cooperation with NGOs in every individual case, and they have to convince their membership of the resulting advantages. There is also a need to broaden their policy approach. The moralizing and universal approach of NGOs may grate with a union movement which is still very much bound to protectionist and labour-centred values. So what is required from the unions is a cultural switch from a traditional work-centred policy to one which includes sustainability norms and the whole dimension of work–life relations. This does not mean that the unions should become like NGOs, but they have to adopt new values and a new sense of responsibility for civil and universal rights. In the meantime, the first steps in this direction have been taken by the unions.

All of this makes it necessary to invest in research about the implementation and the real impacts of IFAs. How do they really work? What problems are emerging with the implementation of sustainability norms? What about the relations between global unions and local unions affected by those agreements? Are sufficient instruments of accountability in place? Case studies are needed to improve the quality of these framework agreements and the further prospects for this instrument. Such an evaluation may end up showing that some of the IFAs are only pieces of paper and have little impact on the reality of industrial relations. But this research could also lead to more knowledge about the conditions for the implementation of IFAs, and help to improve this instrument and its handling by the global unions.

References

Carley, M. 2005. "Global agreements – state of play", in *European Industrial Relations Review*, Oct., pp. 14–18.

European Commission (EC). 2001. *Promoting a European framework for corporate social responsibility*, Green paper (Luxembourg).

Evans, J. 2002. *The WSSD Outcome: What it was and what it heralds*, presentation at UNEP consultative meeting with industry associations, 7 Oct., Paris, France.

FIDH (Féderation Internationale des ligues des Droits de l'Homme). 2007. Position Paper on the United Nations Human Rights Council, fourth session, 12–30 Mar. Available at: http:www.fidh.org/IMG/pdf/Position_Paper_HRC4-2.pdf

ICFTU (International Confederation of Free Trade Unions). 2000. *Employment, sustainable development and social justice – Programme for sustainable economic growth*, 17th ICFTU World Congress, 3–7 Apr., Durban, South Africa.

—. 2004. *Final Resolution – The social responsibilities of business in a global economy*, 18th ICFTU World Congress, 5–10 Dec., Miyazaki, Japan. Available at: http://congress.icftu.org/

ILO (International Labour Organization). 2000. *ILO Tripartite Declaration of Principles concerning Multinational Enterprises and Social Policy* (Geneva).

ISO (International Organization for Standardization). Forthcoming. Working Group on Social Responsibility, Final draft and publication of International Standard ISO 26000.

Koenig-Archibugi, M. 2004. "Transnational corporations and public accountability", in *Government and Opposition*, Vol. 39, No. 2, pp. 234–259.

Köhnen, H. 2003. *Die Durchsetzung von Arbeits- und Menschenrechten ist möglich. Das Beispiel Faber-Castell*, Working Paper No. 69 (Düsseldorf, Hans Böckler Stiftung).

Müller, T.; Rüb, S. 2005. *Towards internationalization of labour relations? Global Union Networks and International Framework Agreements – status quo and prospects* (Fulda, Germany, University of Applied Sciences, European and Global Industrial Relations Research Group), unpublished manuscript.

—; Platzer, H.-W.; Rüb, S. 2003. "Globalisierung und gewerkschaftliche Internationalisierung – zur Politik der Global Union Federations", in *WSI Mitteilungen*, Vol. 56, No. 11, pp. 666–672.

Oldenziel, J.; Bohman, A. 2004. *The added value of the UN norms: A comparative analysis of the UN norms for business with OECD Guidelines, the Global Compact, and the ILO Declaration of Fundamental Principles and Rights at Work* (Amsterdam, Centre for Research on Multinational Corporations).

OECD (Organisation for Economic Co-operation and Development). 2000. *OECD Guidelines for Multinational Enterprises* (Paris), revised version.

Pichot, E. 2006. *Transnational agreements and negotiated texts at company level*, European Commission study seminar on transnational agreements, 17 May, Brussels, Belgium (DG EMPL D/2).

Riisgard, L. 2005. *The IUF/COLSIBA – CHIQUITA framework agreement: A case study*, ILO Working Paper No. 94 (Geneva, ILO).

Schmidt, E. 2007. *International Trade Union Activities concerning Corporate Social Responsibility (Codes of Conduct, International Framework Agreements, ILO Core Labour Standards) – Bibliographical References (2000–2007)*. Available at: http://www.uni-oldenburg.de/politik/download/bibliography_CSR-Unions.rtf

UNCED (United Nations Conference on Environment and Development). 1992. *Report of the United Nations Conference on Environment and Development*, 3–14 Jun., Rio de Janeiro, Brazil (A/C.2/47/L.51).

UNHCHR (United Nations High Commission for Human Rights). 2005. *UN norms on the responsibilities of transnational corporations and other business enterprises with regard to human rights* (Geneva).

SOCIAL PARTNERSHIP AT THE GLOBAL LEVEL: BUILDING AND WOOD WORKERS' INTERNATIONAL EXPERIENCES WITH INTERNATIONAL FRAMEWORK AGREEMENTS

2

Marion F. Hellmann
Assistant General Secretary, Building and Wood Workers' International[1]

Sustainable, safe and secure jobs are the primary issue for workers. The Building and Wood Workers' International (BWI) industrial relations strategy is to promote long-term sustainable industrial development that includes social, economic and environmental dimensions. To strengthen national industrial relations, the BWI and its affiliates continue to promote social dialogue with multinational companies and employers' organizations. The strategy of BWI makes reference to a worldwide discussion on globalization and sustainable development, because the effects of globalization have heightened the awareness of society about the products they buy and use. Society has become more concerned about conditions of work, the use of child labour, moving manufacturing plants to sources of cheaper labour, exploitation, the environment and sustainable development. Multinational enterprises and governments are starting to heed public opinion and demands. Multinationals are developing internal codes of conduct and signing up to global CSR instruments such as the UN Global Compact and the guidelines of the Global Reporting Initiative (GRI).[2] Other global instruments for measuring the performance of MNEs are the *ILO Tripartite Declaration concerning Multinational Enterprises and Social Policy* and the *OECD Guidelines for Multinational Enterprises* as described in the previous chapter by Eberhard Schmidt.

---

[1] At its World Congress in Buenos Aires, on 9 December 2005, the International Federation of Building and Wood Workers (IFBWW) and the World Federation of Building and Wood Workers (WFBW) created a new global union federation, the BWI. It is the leading GUF for the protection of workers in the building, building materials, wood, forestry and allied industries. It brings together some 12 million members of 350 trade unions in 125 countries. The BWI's mission is to promote the development of trade unions in the building and wood industries throughout the world and to promote and enforce workers' rights in a context of sustainable development. Further information is available on its website (www.bwint.org).

[2] The GRI was established in 1997 to develop, at a worldwide level, a common set of reporting standards for use by companies in the preparation of their "social responsibility" and "sustainability" reports. International trade union organizations have become involved with the GRI in order to influence what is considered important.

As part of MNEs' business strategies, based in large part on outsourcing and subcontracting, they have adopted codes of conduct which apply to the labour practices of their suppliers and subcontractors. The GUFs, including the BWI, have abandoned the expression "code of conduct" in favour of "International Framework Agreement"(IFA). The reason is that the former expression is often used for unilateral initiatives by management, without any reference to ILO Conventions, and is therefore frequently of questionable value for labour. Many of these "codes" are instruments for PR or marketing purposes. These "supplier codes" were a response to negative publicity related to exploitation and abusive labour practices in the production of famous brand-name goods. Such codes became a means of "risk management" for brand reputations. Codes and management systems addressing other reputation risks, such as possible bribery and corruption scandals, were also developed. Risk management became one of the strongest motivations for MNEs to sign IFAs with GUFs, which have a worldwide network of member organizations. The value added for MNEs is that trade unions are able to discover serious workplace problems (not being solved locally) at an early stage and take action before they become an issue for the media and the company's brand is damaged. In this way, companies use workers and their trade unions as an early warning system, through which they receive "in house" information on bad management practices, corruption and bribery in subsidiaries or in the supply chain.

Multinational companies signing IFAs with GUFs commit themselves to respect workers' rights, on the basis of the core Conventions of the ILO. In addition, the company should also agree to provide decent wages and working conditions, as well as a safe and healthy working environment. In many cases, agreements include a grievance handling procedure and/or a monitoring system, and they also cover suppliers and subcontractors. International Framework Agreements are sometimes regarded as negotiated codes of conduct with built-in grievance handling. However, this is not a useful way of looking at these agreements, which are *qualitatively* different from codes of conduct. International Framework Agreements constitute a formal recognition of social partnership at the global level. They are intended to complement and not substitute agreements at the national or local level.

The BWI has signed a number of IFAs – with Ballast Nedam, Faber-Castell, Hochtief, IKEA, Impregilo, Lafarge, the Royal BAM Group, Schwan-Stabilo, Skanska, Staedtler and Veidekke. They provide for the active involvement of BWI affiliates in the MNEs' country of origin and countries of operation in the initiation, implementation and monitoring of the agreements. In principle, the employers who sign these agreements are demonstrating that they are serious and fair, and that they favour good industrial relations at the workplace, feel

Table 2.1 International Framework Agreements concluded between TNCs and BWI

Company	Employees	Country	Sector	GUF	Year
IKEA*		Sweden	Furniture	IFBWW	1998
Faber-Castell	6 000	Germany	Writing instruments	IFBWW	1999
Hochtief	37 000	Germany	Construction	IFBWW	2000
Skanska	79 000	Sweden	Construction	IFBWW	2001
Ballast Nedam	7 800	Netherlands	Construction	IFBWW	2002
Impregilo	13 000	Italy	Construction	IFBWW	2004
Veidekke	5 000	Norway	Construction	IFBWW	2005
Schwan-Stabilo	3 000	Germany	Writing instruments	IFBWW	2005
Lafarge	77 000	France	Building materials	IFBWW/ICEM/WFBW	2005
Royal BAM Group	27 000	Netherlands	Construction	BWI	2006
Staedtler	3 000	Germany	Writing instruments	BWI	2006
Royal Volker Wessels Stevin NV	16 700	Netherlands	Construction	BWI	2007

* The IFA with IKEA covers suppliers in the wood chain and the Swedwood group, with a total of several hundred thousand employees.

responsible for the whole supply chain in their company and are open-minded about trade union activities. However, it has to be realized that without vigilance from consumers, unions and other groups, companies are not likely to move forward very fast with a CSR process. It also has to be recognized that achieving real improvements in a company's CSR profile does take time and can be costly. Companies have to live up to their commitments, but so should governments and this is a serious problem in many countries.

With the development of an IFA, the BWI is becoming more relevant not only to developing countries but also to developed countries. International solidarity, for vast numbers of unions in developed countries, is seen primarily as political or moral support to unions in developing countries. Globalization has changed the landscape of industrial relations, with more and more workers being employed directly or indirectly by MNEs. The BWI is evolving not only as an organization for delivering solidarity but also as one that is directly involved in industrial relations at the global level.

Practical approaches to company agreements – the process

Initiation and negotiation

In general, discussions about possible agreements are initiated by BWI affiliates in an MNE's country of origin. Sometimes, initiatives are taken by European works councils (e.g. within Skanska) or through other forms of cooperation on, for example, sustainable development. This was the case with the French building materials company Lafarge, which invited the BWI to be represented on their Stakeholder Panel on Sustainable Development before signing the IFA. Together with the International Federation of Chemical, Energy, Mine and General Workers' Unions (ICEM) and the Christian World Federation of Building and Wood Workers (WFBW), the BWI negotiated and signed the IFA with Lafarge on 12 September 2005. This is a new approach, reflecting multi-unionism in certain countries, with unions affiliated to different GUFs, and new forms of cooperation such as that with the WFBW.

Figure 2.1   The process of setting up an IFA

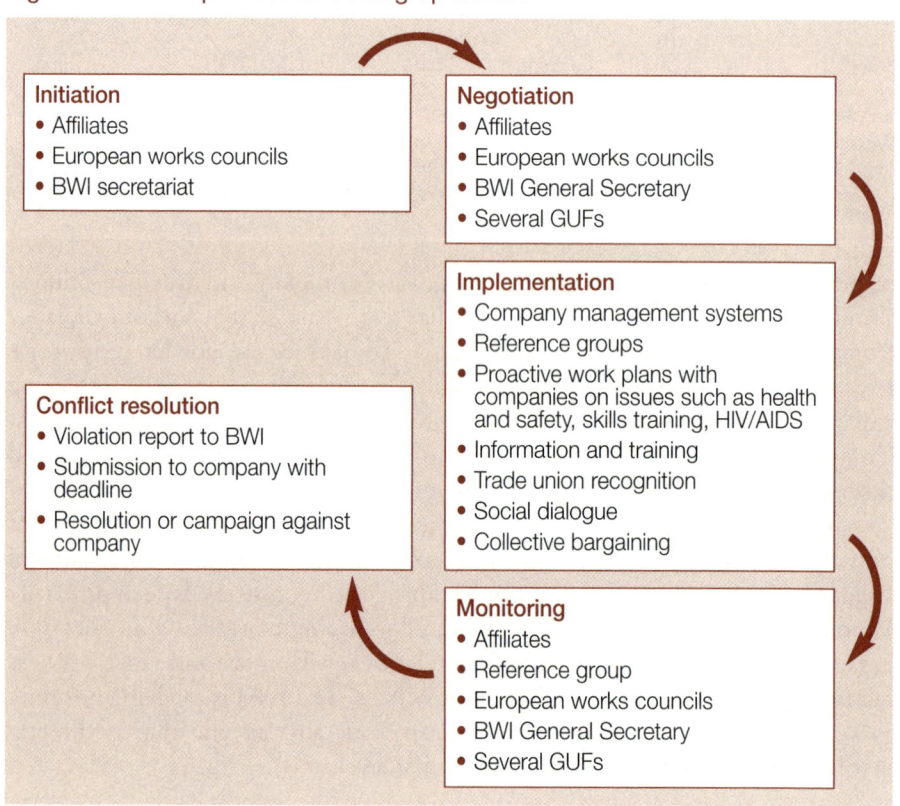

Initiation
- Affiliates
- European works councils
- BWI secretariat

Negotiation
- Affiliates
- European works councils
- BWI General Secretary
- Several GUFs

Implementation
- Company management systems
- Reference groups
- Proactive work plans with companies on issues such as health and safety, skills training, HIV/AIDS
- Information and training
- Trade union recognition
- Social dialogue
- Collective bargaining

Monitoring
- Affiliates
- Reference group
- European works councils
- BWI General Secretary
- Several GUFs

Conflict resolution
- Violation report to BWI
- Submission to company with deadline
- Resolution or campaign against company

The BWI has developed a model framework agreement as a minimum-level basis for negotiations. This commits the mother company, the supply chain and subcontractors to compliance with ILO core Conventions, but also to decent working conditions, health and safety, HIV/AIDS prevention, housing and employment relationships, with a process of monitoring and follow-up put in place.

Before reaching an agreement with a company, there are normally intensive contacts and discussions about the content of the ILO Conventions and the commitments into which the company would be entering. However, these meetings contribute to mutual understanding and trust and it sometimes takes up to two years before the agreement is signed. But this is an important investment for good implementation of the agreement. The agreement is signed by the BWI General Secretary, as the contractual partner on behalf of the BWI, and has to be endorsed by the BWI Management Committee.

Implementation and monitoring

Once an IFA has been signed, the company has to ensure that a management system is in place which guarantees implementation. However, the most important part of the implementation process is that the agreement should be given meaning and life through appropriate information and education campaigns. These must ensure that the workers affected by the agreement are aware of its existence and the meaning of its content. As part of the agreement, the BWI partner company has to inform its subsidiaries, suppliers or contractors about its content. The BWI, for its part, conducted a series of seminars and information campaigns for its members. However, the BWI discovered, through a survey carried out with its affiliates, that little information is available at workplaces and within trade unions around the world. This is one area of possible cooperation between the BWI and the MNEs. Both parties can develop a joint information and education programme, targeting a number of countries every year.

In practice, the implementation of IFAs is not as easy as companies would wish. In particular, they have serious difficulties in applying them to suppliers and subcontractors and there are many reasons for this. Often, the enforcement of certain standards will depend on the volume of a company's purchases from a supplier. Another difficulty is that, after a merger or takeover of a company in a country with a bad industrial relations record, management and sometimes also trade union attitudes and cultures take time to shift towards acceptance of a cooperative social dialogue. The BWI's experience is that companies are interested in safety, health and the environment, areas on which they are vulnerable and sensitive to any bad publicity. In the BWI Global Health and Safety Programme, a few initiatives with Skanska, IKEA and, most recently, Lafarge and the cement sector have been started on practical work for the prevention of injuries and ill health. In these areas, we can demonstrate the positive impact that organized workers with trade union safety representatives can have, in particular through joint management–union safety committees in the workplace.

The real challenge for strategies built around IFAs is largely one of monitoring and verification. The BWI sees the work of the reference or monitoring group, which is normally made up of BWI and management representatives, as that of exchanging and developing views on the management system and defined standards, and on their compliance or non-compliance with the agreement. In some cases, the BWI and its partner companies pay visits to suppliers' countries in order to have some reference points regarding the level of standards and implementation.

Responsibility for the monitoring of company performance lies primarily with auditing and accounting companies, providing certification on a commercial basis. There are many problems with this process, such as the auditors' ignorance about labour rights issues or the realities of working conditions; the extraordinary scale of subcontracting chains, which would require an army of auditors to verify compliance with the standard; and the marginalization of trade unions in the representation of workers' interests. Some IFAs which have been concluded between BWI and a TNC are verified by internal monitoring groups composed of union and company representatives, and by the unions nationally and locally. Currently, only a handful of unions are active in using the IFAs. Also, monitoring is expensive and time-consuming to organize for both trade unions and companies, depending on the complexity of the company concerned.

Trade unionists need to be careful about "monitoring", "independent monitoring" and "verification" of IFAs. The word "monitoring" implies a continuous presence of the kind that companies and their auditing companies cannot perform. For example, many of the ways in which workers can be intimidated, discouraged or prevented from joining or forming trade unions are difficult to detect. The only real test that workers' freedom of association or the right to collective bargaining are respected is the existence of a functioning trade union representation and a collective agreement. The BWI believes that the only real system of "independent monitoring" of workplaces is by the workers themselves through their trade unions. In this process the BWI secretariat is totally dependent on action by affiliates in countries of operation in reporting cases and by affiliates in the country of origin taking action and discussing with the head office of the MNE. Once the BWI secretariat receives information from the affiliate – in some cases by other groups such as the Dutch labour NGO SOMO (Centre for Research on Multinational Corporations) – the secretariat submits the case to the company and asks for corrective action. If there is no response

Social partnership at the global level

from the company or the company is not able to resolve the conflict, the BWI launches a global campaign to put pressure on the company.

How to use IFAs

The purpose of IFAs is to assist affiliates to gain recognition as unions and to start a social dialogue at the company and national level with companies, suppliers and subcontractors of BWI partner companies. This should lead to collective bargaining and finally to improved working conditions and better wages. However, the success of any IFA will depend on the strength of the unions at national level and at company level; full implementation of these agreements is only possible when workers are organized in free trade unions and are able to bargain collectively at national and enterprise level. Effective implementation of agreements should be seen as an ongoing and long-term process. Also important is the extent to which these opportunities are used to advance trade union work.

Currently, only a handful of unions are active in using IFAs and many are unaware of their purpose or even of their existence. The reasons for this may vary, but the most important is, of course, a lack of knowledge. Therefore, intensive training is required. There are also unions that are sceptical about the use of voluntary agreements as compared with legislative measures for companies. For negotiations about an IFA to be initiated there needs to be established social dialogue and good industrial relations in the country of origin of the MNE. In many countries, these conditions do not exist and therefore there is a certain scepticism about using the agreements.

Some affiliates have made breakthroughs in the use of these agreements. The Polish affiliates were able to organize 12 Swedwood companies, which are owned by IKEA. The Malaysian timber union also organized two IKEA suppliers. North American affiliates have been using these agreements with Skanska and Hochtief to establish unions at construction sites. Workers' representatives were elected in Faber-Castell factories in Malaysia and China. These are encouraging developments, but still far from what needs to be done. The BWI surveys among affiliates show that many of them do not know the companies covered by the agreements in their countries. Thus, organizing would be very difficult. Affiliates need to improve their organizing capacity.

Experiences with a partner company (IKEA)

The Swedish furniture company IKEA and BWI signed an agreement on the promotion of workers' rights at IKEA wood suppliers in May 1998. This process was initiated by the Nordic Federation of Building and Wood

Workers (NFBWW) and the Swedish Wood Workers' Union (now the Forestry and Wood Workers' Union). IKEA then developed its own code of conduct for its suppliers. A revision of the old IKEA/BWI agreement for wood suppliers was carried out in December 2001 to include references to this new company code of conduct, *The IKEA way on purchasing home furnishing products*, IWAY. IKEA established a compliance organization at IKEA International for the auditing of IKEA suppliers, reporting directly to Anders Dahlvig (CEO). The compliance group carried out workshops with the most important IKEA trading offices. IKEA is implementing an action plan for improving conditions at suppliers, according to the demands set out in the new code of conduct. IKEA states that its own staff at 43 trading offices around the world work closely with suppliers to implement the "IWAY" and to correct violations. Some 80 trained auditors carry out audits and establish action plans based on non-compliance. The auditors play an active part in the corrective measures taken by the suppliers. Numerous re-audits follow each action plan. According to IKEA, more than 20,000 corrective measures have taken place at IKEA's 1,600 suppliers in 55 countries and more than 50,000 corrective measures are in progress. IKEA also uses third-party auditing companies to carry out audits of suppliers and to verify working methods and results.

A year after the revised agreement was signed, IKEA prepared a new set of "IWAY" documents and requirements for their suppliers of home furnishing products, which came into force on 1 February 2003. The work of the monitoring or reference group – consisting of Kjell Dahlstrom, President of the Swedish Forestry and Wood Workers' Union, as representative of the NFBWW and Marion F. Hellmann from the BWI Secretariat, and of IKEA representatives – was not to monitor working conditions or measure the dust and noise level in different supplier companies and countries. It was rather to assist the development of IKEA standards and management systems for ensuring the implementation of internationally accepted labour standards and to develop good industrial relations between the suppliers and the BWI member unions. The monitoring group paid visits to suppliers in China, Hungary, the Lao People's Democratic Republic, Malaysia, Poland, Romania, Slovakia and Thailand.

Since 1998, the BWI has received complaints on violations of the "IWAY" from affiliates in Thailand, Malaysia, the United Kingdom, the United States, Canada and the Netherlands. Most of the complaints make reference to ILO Convention Nos 87 and 98, on the right to organize and collective bargaining, which are not respected by IKEA suppliers. The complaints have been followed up by the IKEA management.

The Dutch trade union confederation, FNV, undertook research on IKEA in order to obtain a general picture of the company. The FNV is of the opinion that IKEA provides very little public information and lacks transparency about the implementation of the "IWAY" standards, to what extent they are put into practice, and how compliance is monitored. The study concludes: "The case studies in India, Bulgaria and Vietnam, although showing a different situation, make it clear that there are still numerous violations of IKEA's code of conduct in all three countries in all factories researched." IKEA, the FNV, SOMO and the GUFs BWI and International Textile, Garment and Leather Workers' Federation (ITGLWF) met on 27 August 2003 to discuss the findings of the report. IKEA stated that the results of the research came as no surprise to them, as a result of IKEA's own audit system, and that these problems are not specific to IKEA suppliers or any particular industry. Some issues will take time to solve, because they require fundamental changes to society in certain countries. The unions expressed their appreciation for IKEA's efforts to improve working conditions at suppliers so far, but also pointed to the fact that IKEA's system is not transparent enough and that trade unions must be more involved in monitoring and verification at the workplaces.

The IKEA/BWI reference group meets regularly, at least twice a year, to exchange experiences on working conditions and social responsibility. The joint work programme covers the following issues:

- IKEA invited the BWI to assist in the improvement of working conditions for Chinese workers in their suppliers located throughout China (see box 2.1). This is within a current project on overtime reduction and increasing productivity carried out by the British consultancy Impact.

- IKEA invited BWI affiliates in Malaysia, Indonesia, Bulgaria and Romania to participate in a compliance audit in each country, so as to gain knowledge and understanding of the "IWAY" process and procedures. IKEA is continuing to develop its present auditing procedures in a dialogue with BWI.

- IKEA will become more transparent about auditing procedures and results. In 2004, IKEA published its first Social and Environmental Report, for 2003, and the reports for 2004, 2005 and 2006 have also been published. However, IKEA will not disclose general supplier information, e.g. supplier lists, for legal and competition reasons.

A good example of working together with IKEA within the framework of our agreement is the situation in Poland. Swedwood, IKEA-owned companies and the Polish and Swedish BWI member organizations started a social dialogue project in 2002 with the objective of establishing sound industrial relations and trade union representation at the company level in Poland. The unions report

Trade union responses to globalization

> **Box 2.1   Monitoring the IFA between BWI and IKEA in China**
>
> The IKEA Group and the BWI paid a visit to Beijing in late March 2003. This initiative was taken following the results from code of conduct audits of IKEA suppliers in China. The IKEA Group introduced its code of conduct, *The IKEA way of purchasing home furnishing products, IWAY*, on 1 September 2000 and since then extensive development and auditing of all IKEA suppliers have taken place, including in China.
>
> The audits performed by the five IKEA trading offices and the IKEA compliance team in cooperation with third parties identified specific difficult issues, such as a reduction in working time and an insurance plan for all employees, where special efforts were needed to make improvements in China. Specific areas, such as excessive working hours, lack of overtime compensation and poor handling of hazardous waste, were also among those addressed during the visit. Meetings were held with the Beijing Municipal Labour and Social Bureau, the China Enterprise Confederation, the Chinese Association of Environmental Protection Industry and the All-China Federation of Trade Unions to address the issues and discuss different views of the problems. The outcome of the meetings and visits was a better common understanding of the laws, practices and problems and some creative ideas on how to establish good practice involving all the important stakeholders. IKEA started a project at five suppliers in South China with the aim of reducing working hours and increasing productivity without reduction of wages. The BWI also attended an "IWAY" audit in China. The "IWAY" audits showed that the number of non-compliances decreased significantly during 2004. However, suppliers still need to deal with issues such as a further reduction of working time and an insurance plan for all employees.

that almost all Swedwood factories have been unionized in the meantime. The Polish unions very much welcomed this management/trade union approach because the unions are able to organize workers and start collective bargaining and are part of a sound industrial relations system.

Where do we go from here?

Before embarking on further new agreements, BWI affiliates are being invited to develop recommendations on how to effectively push forward and improve the implementation of these agreements. The following points summarize the outlook for future developments:

- Our *strength* is that we already have a global network of affiliates representing about 12 million members present in workplaces, including those where MNEs are operating.

- Our *weakness* is a lack of trade union strength in the building, wood and forestry sectors in many countries where many MNEs are operating. Informal work is common in these sectors, especially in developing countries, but illegal use of labour is also increasing in industrialized countries.

- There are *opportunities* to use the global agreements as a platform for a better social dialogue and for organizing efforts. This is our continuing strategy. However, BWI and its affiliates must continue to push the MNEs to implement these agreements and create more space for trade union involvement. In countries where labour legislation is weak, it is difficult for trade unions to work effectively and the informal economy dominates. So moving towards a stable labour market with representative social partners is a long process. Similarly, unions working in industries with substantial production in highly repressive countries, which do not respect workers' rights, have to recognize that the possibilities of strong and independent trade unions emerging in the short term are very slim. By establishing IFAs with companies investing in production in such circumstances, at least workers might be able to escape some of the more extreme denials of their rights, and some space might be created for trade union development.

- Among the *risks* involved is the possibility that companies may not make serious internal changes, but may use the agreement as a whitewashing tool, while the unions are accused of covering up for bad company practices.

- There is an urgent need for more and better involvement of affiliated trade unions, and they should take on more responsibility. This will require a training programme to assist unions to take up the challenge of recruiting and organizing in these companies. If activity is restricted to the work of the secretariat and staff alone, we will not be capable of handling the necessary organization for more than a handful of international company agreements.

- Substantially improved communication and global networking will also be needed.

- Another area that the BWI can explore with the MNEs is piloting implementation. The BWI and MNEs can identify countries where they can develop joint monitoring mechanisms, information and education programmes.

- Cooperation with the ILO is needed for training on the labour standards that workers and their unions are well-placed to monitor within workplaces.

In recent years BWI has served as a leading GUF in negotiating and implementing IFAs. While acknowledging that innovative IFAs have been developed by the BWI, delegates to the BWI World Congress in Buenos Aires in December 2005 commented that it was now time to reflect on past experiences with these endeavours. In November 2006 BWI started consultations for such a review. In autumn 2007 the BWI decision-making bodies will decide on the future direction of its policy on IFAs.

References

Justice, D.W. 2003. "The corporate social responsibility concept and phenomenon: Challenges and opportunities for trade unionists, in *Labour Education*, Vol. 1, No. 130 (Geneva, ILO-ACTRAV).

Müller, T.; Rüb, S. 2005. *Towards internationalization of labour relations? Global Union Networks and International Framework Agreements – status quo and prospects* (Fulda, Germany, University of Applied Sciences, European and Global Industrial Relations Research Group), unpublished manuscript.

Wick, I. 2003. *Workers' tool or PR ploy? A guide to codes of international labour practice* (Bonn, Friedrich-Ebert-Stiftung).

INTEGRATING LABOUR ISSUES IN GLOBAL VALUE CHAIN ANALYSIS: EXPLORING IMPLICATIONS FOR LABOUR RESEARCH AND UNIONS

3

Lee Pegler and Peter Knorringa
Institute of Social Studies, The Hague, the Netherlands

Introduction

Higher levels of international coordination of production within a value chain (rising corporate governance) appear to go hand-in-hand with low and even declining levels of labour protection (reduced labour governance). Nevertheless, some academics and policy-makers have implied that this situation can produce "high road" outcomes – that is, enterprise growth based on high quality production and with associated improvements in labour rights. However, whether and how this might occur is by no means certain or clear.

This debate is at the heart of the decent work initiative (ILO, 2002) and has particular importance for labour research and the future of unions in developing countries. This article[1] discusses the value chain approach, it investigates the assumed causality between company upgrading and improved labour conditions, and it explores implications for labour research and unions. To do this, the following section ("Global value chains and employment conditions") introduces the value chain approach and discusses the limited attention to labour issues in the first wave of the value chain literature. The subsequent section ("A leap of faith: High road causality in developing countries?") argues that more systematic attention needs to be given to labour issues, as improvements in labour and employment conditions do not automatically follow from upgrading strategies by firms in global value chains. Some key academic contributions in the field of labour studies and their relevance to the field of global value chain (GVC) studies are the focus of the

---

[1] This paper is based on a presentation at the 2nd GURN workshop, Nova Hamburgo, 23–25 January, 2005. It builds on an earlier paper presented at an European Association of Development Institute workshop, "Working in Small Enterprises – Job Quality and Labour Conditions in a Globalizing World", 17 January 2003, Free University, Amsterdam.

fourth section ("Relevance of labour studies to global value chain analysis"). The last section ("Value chains, labour research and unions – towards a "new" agenda") highlights a number of implications for labour research and unions.

Global value chains and employment conditions

In recent years the GVC approach has become very popular. A dominant feature in the GVC literature is the broad consensus on the "new competition" idea that, in order to cope with the pressures of globalization and to remain competitive, firms need to continuously upgrade (Best, 1990; Schmitz, 2004; UNIDO, 2002). Much less is known about how this drive towards upgrading impacts upon labour. Conceptually, broad brush views diverge from those who assume that economic globalization implies a cost-driven "race to the bottom" which inevitably leads to deteriorating labour conditions, while others expect that continuously upgraded processes and products also require higher skilled and motivated workers who can and will earn a premium in the labour market (ILO, 1999). Moreover, while the first wave of empirical GVC studies did not pay much attention to labour issues at all, more recent GVC studies have started to address specific labour issues in the value chain and country context of particular case studies (see for example Nadvi (2004) for a comparison of case studies, or Knorringa and Pegler (2006) for a set of working hypotheses on where and when firm upgrading and improved labour conditions are more likely to go together).

The value chain perspective draws attention to the sequence of activities stemming from product conception to the final consumer, stressing the importance of activities other than production itself, notably design, logistics and marketing (Gereffi and Kaplinsky, 2001, Kaplinsky and Morris, 2002). As formulated in the 1990s (Gereffi and Korzeniewicz (eds), 1994), the three key features of GVCs are: a) an input–output structure for the product; b) associated geographical aspects of production; and c) the governance structure by which production is coordinated. As a framework it thus moves from a firm-level approach, to inter-firm relations and then to networks, within and across regions. Various structures and formats have been suggested, the two main ones being producer- and buyer-driven value chains.

A general, but often implicit proposition from this literature is that more quality-driven or high road production entails higher levels of trust in inter-firm relationships in value chains (for a critical overview, see for example Humphrey and Schmitz, 1998). Lane (1998) argues that in the case of intensified quality-driven competition, trust has become more necessary but also more problematic. Her proposition is that trust is at present an even more important precondition for success than before, while at the same time intensified competition makes trust more difficult to develop and more risky to invest in.

Notwithstanding these difficulties, a quality-driven or high road environment may well offer more opportunities for organizational learning which, in turn, increases the likelihood of upgrading. Upgrading in the value chain literature is usually broken down into:

- process upgrading (doing things better);
- product upgrading (producing better goods);
- functional upgrading (engaging in additional and higher value-added activities) (Humphrey and Schmitz, 2002 and 2004).

The GVC debate has from the start looked at questions like how suppliers can be: "locked into dependent relationships across territories through considering issues of cooperation, competition, power" (Kaplinsky et al., 2002, p. 1160). The original formulation of the global commodity chain approach by Gereffi and Korzeniewicz (1994), draws its inspiration from Wallerstein's world system approach, with strong roots in dependency thinking. However, in the first wave of GVC studies the attention was almost exclusively focused on inter-firm relationships, basically neglecting impacts on labour. In more recent GVC studies labour is increasingly brought into the analysis, but we feel there is a need to further systematize attention for labour in GVC studies that aim to shed light on opportunities and threats from economic globalization on developing countries.

After all, positive impacts on the quantity and quality of employment as a result of inclusion and upgrading in GVC are often assumed by policy-makers, but such claims too often lack solid evidence (ILO, 1999). The findings from GVC studies are mixed (Kaplinsky et al., 2002; Nadvi, 2004). Moreover, the broad field of labour studies brings in some pertinent considerations that should alert us to be extremely cautious about sweeping generalizations when it comes to where and when firm upgrading may also lead to improvements in labour conditions.

Therefore, we argue that unless there is greater integration of labour studies issues into value chain analysis, policy suggestions for how GVCs can benefit developing countries will, at least, be incomplete and possibly misleading. The industrial upgrading related to inclusion in value chains may not automatically ensure "good" labour standards and conditions in firms.

In saying this we are not implying that most authors looking at the inter-firm level are ignorant of power relations. There are plenty of authors in the value chain literature who recognize the problematic, explicitly political and contestable nature of many of these behavioural linkages. Yet there is scant attention to the problematical impact of these measures on workers' attitudes (Nadvi and Barrientos, 2004). The acquisition, control and use of tacit knowledge by lead firms (vis-à-vis SMEs) is a theme which may have more serious implications than authors such as Palpacuer (2000) suggest. This applies equally for worker control and thus worker attitudes and their sense of security, and the quality of work in both large and small firms. Moreover, unequal power relations within the hierarchy of firms may have similarly negative effects on employment conditions, in particular in developing countries. This is due to the dependent and vulnerable position these firms often hold within value chains. Finally, where there is a combination of reduced union power, continuing antagonistic capital–labour relations and decreased national labour regulation, the promotion of "decentness" and "good" labour governance may not find an adequate substitute in new forms of international standards.

A leap of faith: High road causality in developing countries?

Nowadays it is relatively commonplace, among academics and policy-makers, to argue that firm upgrading is a key to sustained competitiveness (ILO, 1999 and 2002; UNIDO, 2002; Schmitz, 2004). Moreover, the promotion of job quality within this "new reality" of competitiveness is often expected to go hand-in-hand with four main elements – increased training and knowledge, integrating cost-conscious competitiveness with improved qualitative conditions, the promotion of self-help associations/collective solutions, and an appropriate facilitating regulatory environment (ILO, 1999, pp. 17–21). Upgrading, in this context, would then lead to improved employment conditions. However, we feel that the likelihood of this simultaneous upgrading of firm-based competencies and employment conditions should be tested empirically, instead of remaining an implicit assumption, and thus become an integral part of future studies (Knorringa and Pegler, 2006).

In the simultaneous upgrading scenario workers are too easily assumed to be highly-skilled and relatively scarce, and to possess significant tacit knowledge. In those situations, companies indeed are anxious to enlist and keep such "repositories of know-how". This conceptualization of workers and of owner–manager–worker relationships clearly has its merits in an increasingly knowledge-intensive globalizing economy characterized by the need to continuously adapt and learn. Moreover, while the initial conceptualization focused on R&D type of activities, at least parts of this logic can be extended to a broader variety of activities in the value chain such as design and marketing, and even as part of the actual production of goods (ILO, 1999; Palpacuer, 1997 and 2000). However, one should be careful not to over-generalize the extent to which this approach can serve as a model for all types of labour relations. In essence, it is a model primarily suited to the core workers who carry out core activities in core firms in the value chain. Therefore, this model does not fit well with the type of labour-intensive processing activities that constitute the bulk of production in developing-country suppliers in GVCs. In other words, adopting this model to conceptualize impacts on labour from economic globalization would amount to wishful thinking for the bulk of developing country low-cost suppliers to GVCs. Moreover, its already limited relevance may well diminish over time, due to possible further decline in core worker proportions.

In the still relatively few attempts to look empirically at these connections it has been found that among small firm clusters there are ample cases which seem "exceptional", in that poor employment conditions persisted despite firm upgrading (Nadvi and Schmitz, 1994 and 1999). In the first review of small firm clusters it was evident that the ideal high and low road trajectories do not seem to fit realities in the South (Nadvi and Schmitz, 1994, p. 43). The authors observed a less straightforward relationship between firm upgrading and employment conditions at cluster level. While it is debatable whether a straightforward high and low road trajectory ever existed in developed economies, it seems safe to assume that there is less likelihood of finding a high road strategy which also includes high road employment conditions in developing countries.

A recent and careful assessment of labour impacts in a set of GVC studies by Nadvi (2004) brings out two main points that also reverberate from other GVC studies that look at labour and employment issues (Bair and Gereffi, 2001; Kaplinsky et al., 2002). Firstly, lots of new jobs have been created in "greenfield" locations, poor areas that became attractive because of the supply chain logic of continuously searching for cheaper locations with sufficient skills for entry into GVCs. Jobs offered by final producers and some core supplier firms in such new locations often provide clearly better labour conditions compared with local alternative employment opportunities. From a development perspective this, at least initially, leads to an important pro-poor economic stimulus as it generates new and relatively better-paid employment in a specific locality (Nadvi, 2004).

Secondly, value chain inclusion is frequently associated with strongly segmented and differentiated employment conditions, increasing insecurity and longer hours, especially at the furthest end of the chain. In essence, this means that the general observation from labour studies about impacts of economic globalization – increased insecurity and precariousness (Standing, 1999) – is confirmed by those GVC studies that have paid attention to labour. Finally, while low wages may act as an initial inducement to value chain inclusion and growth via FDI, both FDI attraction and future export performance are strongly and positively correlated with the basic tenets of decent work – especially better labour rights and a more stable, equal representational environment (Kucera, 2001; Kucera and Sarna, 2004; see also Neumayer and de Soysa, 2006).

On the whole, we feel that the accumulated know-how around employment impacts in developing countries lags behind our know-how in other key areas of the research agenda on GVCs. In this light, based on a few pertinent examples, the following section looks at what labour studies can tell us in practice and theory about labour rights and conditions in both large firms and SMEs.

Relevance of labour studies to global value chain analysis

Within global value chain analysis and the new competition paradigm the potential contribution of labour studies to the issues of labour rights and conditions appears to revolve around two lines of questioning. First, how do we categorize those working in this type of firm or network and, second, what do we know about their employment conditions and labour relations, and the mediation of these by other actors? As discussed earlier, the combination of segmented labour market theory, labour process analysis and industrial relations studies provides some helpful clues on these issues.

For example, early authors on the topic, such as Thurow, pointed to a potential link between education, labour markets and firm level strategy. He suggested that it would be better to focus on the demand and supply of jobs rather than the demand and supply of labour (Thurow, 1970). This more explicitly opens up discussion of the methods used to produce a more flexible and homogeneous core labour force, for example selection and employer screening. The question then remains whether SMEs follow this lead or whether they are the "depositories" for many of those not able to be considered suitable for work in larger firms. Authors such as Mainwaring added to this in terms of a more variegated definition of secondary labour markets (first and second tier subcontractors, home workers, the self-employed, etc.) and others have added useful concepts concerning social stratification and conditioning influencing entry into the labour market (Thomas, 1990).

Using a number of developing country examples, the following paragraphs try to demonstrate how such labour process approaches continue to be central to understanding firm dynamics under new competition. First, there is growing evidence that "modernizing" large firms are implementing changes to work via such strategies as reduced hierarchies, the combination of tasks, teamworking and delegated responsibility (Humphrey, 1994; Pegler, 2000). There is a more striking finding in terms of the issue of labour conditions in SMEs. Industrial sociology has shown that many smaller firms, including first tier subcontractors and firms which have scaled down from being large firms, especially in more capital intensive industries, are now providing conditions similar to those of large firms, and this extends to some of the training, education and ancillary benefits (Bair and Gereffi, 2001; Gereffi and Kaplinsky, 2001; Fleury and Humphrey, 1993; Gitahy, 2000; Humphrey, 1995; Nadvi 2004).

In addition, the development of networks of firms has also been observed, along with many of the cluster synergies and linkages that many value chain researchers identify as important for industrial development. These have taken various forms. From the perspective of local economic development, there is the appearance of "virtuous" clusters of firms with business association linkages (Abreu et al., 1999; Ruas et al., 1994). At a firm level, many basic services and even accounting functions have often been externalized or quasi-externalized (Abreu et al., 1999; Pegler, 2000, chapter 4; Ruas et al., 1994). In other cases, such as the automobile industry, a new form has emerged of business-park or modularized production, with key selected suppliers on the same site as the TNC (Abreu et al., 2000).

However, this is about as close as the evidence gets to support a more optimistic vision of SME employment in value chains. As one moves from an analysis of objective factors to an analysis of subjective and attitudinal factors beyond the "core" firm, the evidence is more problematic and negative (Humphrey, 1999; Pegler, 2000, chapter 6). Moreover, examples of change in management methods and work must be seen within their specific economic, cultural and industrial relations context. In particular, to suggest that changes have or will occur in management attitudes towards cooperation and trust may imply that the organizational and behavioural traits of the "Japanese model" have been accepted at both large firm and subcontractor levels. As many studies have shown, such a model and its transferability are highly problematic issues, particularly in terms of what they suggest for labour rights and conditions in firms of all sizes in the recipient country.[2]

For example, a number of studies suggest that the acquisition of greater tacit knowledge within daily workplace routines has led firms to instigate stronger, but more subtle, forms of control to offset any dependence the employer may have on such skills (Fleury and Humphrey, 1993; Humphrey et al., 1998; Pegler, 2002b). There is also little evidence to suggest that many production workers have developed a commitment, allegiance or trust in their employer as a result of new production regimes (Leite, 1994; Pegler, 2002b). Teamwork, decentralized monitoring and similar strategies have added to work pressures, and the use of

---

[2] See Dedoussis, 1995; Delbridge, 1995; Elgar and Smith, 1994; and Humphrey, 1995, for various examples from developing and higher income countries.

more stringent selection and screening mechanisms are generally seen by workers as an additional control measure. These negative attitudes are only partially explained by the low wages paid to workers in such "privileged" modernized plants: workers also do not see themselves as more employable in the open labour market (Leite, 1994; Gitahy, 2000; Pegler, 2000, chapter 6). Yet employers of this type are generally seen as preferable to working for small-scale suppliers and parts producers. Therefore, managers in such "priviliged" modernized plants can use the implicit threat of dismissal as a significant source of bargaining power.

From a Brazilian, and also Latin American perspective, economic and labour market conditions probably heighten the uncertainty workers face during periods of change. A high degree of confusion, anguish and uncertainty comes through from discussions with Brazilian workers – from blue collar to white collar, from manager to production employee. For example, at a key white goods TNC in the state of São Paulo, one of the authors[3] found a major effect on the morale of both managers and production workers as its role as a product innovator and independent firm declined. Gitahy found that downsizing and reduced hierarchies were seen to have a similarly massive effect on managers' attitudes in other firms in the region (Gitahy, 2000). This same author also quotes a production worker as saying, "I am a spare part which cannot be milled anymore" (Gitahy, 2000, p. 14).

When one moves beyond the workplaces of these large and small firms, power and inequality are also very important issues, especially from an industrial relations perspective. For instance, those same firms which adopt flexibilization policies have made union representation all the more difficult through the use of more subtle anti-union policies (Ackers et al., 1996; Pegler, 2002a; Shaiken, 1994). Rather than transferring more consensual models of industrial relations into Brazil, many of these firms have simply imported new management models that emphasize flexibilization without also significantly investing in workers. Moreover, these same firms promote greater heterogeneity and flexibility in workplace conditions, even for firms in the same sector and region, which forces a vacuum of labour rights governance. This is particularly the case because national labour regulations have been peeled back to enable this flexibility.

The Indian context, as illustrated by the case of Crompton Greaves (an engineering company) highlights a different but equally problematic situation for organizational change and for labour rights and conditions (Humphrey et al., 1998, chapter 6). At this firm, the combination of more rigid and enforceable labour rights than in Brazil and most of Latin America, plus an apparently aggressive and representative union, has put clear limits on

---
[3] Company interviews, São Paulo, Brazil, December 2000–February 2001, by Lee Pegler.

the manner in which firms can change. Here fewer hierarchical changes have been introduced and agreements must be made when the firm wishes to introduce workplace change. Some change has come about, but worker acceptance of this has been contingent on the gaining of clear stability rights, improved pay, limited work intensification and some veto rights.

This situation is in stark contrast to the situation in Brazil and other developing countries where there is a low level of enforceability of labour rights and greater employment flexibility, even in large firms. Yet it should be noted that Indian employers (especially when linked to TNC capital) often choose to relocate to less aggressively unionized and lower wage "greenfield" sites (Humphrey et al., 1998, pp. 143–144). Experiences at these sites show how employers have much greater flexibility in respect to labour rights and conditions. The uncertain and potentially negative implications of these developments for labour rights and conditions apply to both large and small, core and non-core firms within a value chain network.

More generally, both the Indian and Brazilian cases highlight how the promotion of labour rights is contingent on a real, effective and appreciated role for union representation. Nevertheless, the mobility of capital means that union representation is not a sufficient condition. The discussion suggests that the building of trust and good employment conditions within the firms of any new "virtuous circle" of inter-firm relations will be based on a process of power and negotiation. Mutual gains to workers and their firm based on concepts such as trust and cooperation may require a unique combination of unions being both recognized and representative and workers showing allegiance to both company and union. In other words, advocates of new competition theory at the level of the firm and the value chain must re-adjust their views: the possible coexistence of increased control and worker trust needs to be based on clearer evidence than seems to exist at present.

Looking at power inequality from a national and international perspective suggests the need to take a cautionary view of value chain developments and their implications for labour rights and conditions. For example, since the mid-1990s there was a significant change in the differing standards of employment conditions within locally based firms and the quality of work across the Brazilian white goods value chain. At first it looked as if high-skilled input production of compressors in Brazil would provide a driving force for upgrading inter-firm linkages and employment. Even older white goods firms developed high-skilled R&D functions within the Brazilian market.

However, in recent years compressor production in Brazil has been downgraded, in the sense that Brazilian production is now just one hub amongst many for the main global suppliers. Moreover, R&D and product design functions have been transferred back to the United States and most other high-skilled work has been further standardized and outsourced, often to former employees and/or local SME branches of other well-known TNCs. Other authors have noted a similar agglomeration of TNC lead firms and their preferred overseas suppliers in the automobile industry in both Brazil and India (Humphrey, 1999). They have also argued, as highlighted by this less promising example of the Brazilian white goods industry, the difficulty that industry in developing countries will have in establishing and retaining sustainable, competitive niches within GVCs (Humphrey, 2003, pp. 20–21).

In summary, this section has suggested that there are some central behavioural dynamics within the field of labour studies that should become a more central part of GVC analysis. A number of theories, concepts and hypotheses within the field of labour studies suggest that trust building and knowledge development within firms cannot be taken for granted. This is due to the existence of uncertainty, control strategies, unequal power and differential labour market access. The next section of this paper provides a very brief sketch of what these observations imply for labour and union research. What the discussion suggests is that there may be great gains for unions through a more active role in value chain research, but there might also be some problems or ambiguities.

Value chains, labour research and unions – towards a "new" agenda

At the broadest level, the examination of the links between firm upgrading and labour rights highlights that the research agenda must focus more squarely on making GVCs more equal and inclusive. This means it must be focused not just on "nodes of value and their constraints" but also on the way labour is used and the labour conditions which exist at these nodes. This would suggest that unions should encourage industrial policy-makers to integrate the decent work agenda within national industrialization strategies. Finally, recognizing that firms are not the only mechanism for the promotion of improved security for workers, this approach must also consider, in the absence of a strong state role, how to promote better social protection within and around firms.

This might sound like a very tall order and outside unions' traditional agendas, however, one of the ways policy development of this type may be assisted could be through the use of research matrixes. Such matrixes could be used to systematize different hypotheses on where and when industrial upgrading and improvements in labour conditions go together, at various levels of analysis (see Knorringa and Pegler, 2006).

What then does this suggest for union involvement in the research process? First, at a general level, unions should be part of the process to methodically investigate labour rights both in main firms and in their supply (value) chain structure. Second, they should use this information to actively suggest ways in which better CSR might be promoted within these value chains. The objective would have three parts – to show that value chains could, in many circumstances, still be seen as one "firm"; to help bolster the argument that better labour rights are good business[4] and to put forth the argument that unions should be a more significant stakeholder in CSR.

More specifically, this labour/union research agenda would involve a series of stages, methodologies and decisions. For example, mapping supply chains is a complex process involving data from many different sources and from workers from both the informal and formal economies. Decisions will have to be made about which products and to which level (i.e. which tier or supplier) research is able and intended to reach. Second, as argued strongly by the preceding analysis, the research into employment relations and employment conditions within these lead firms and suppliers must be based on both objective and subjective indicators. Without such a focus, shop floor analysis, intra-firm relations and considerations such as trust and security will have little meaning.

Third, this may take many unions into uncharted waters, and they may have to get involved in investigating the relationships between firms – whether that be in terms of R&D, training, products and input trade, in terms of levels of trust or in terms of the possibilities for cluster synergy. Similarly, research into labour rights will often require union researchers to expand the focus of their analysis – beyond formal labour relations and on to consideration of informality, poverty and livelihoods outside of traditional workplaces.

Moreover, the joint promotion of industrial development and decent work may, especially in the case of buyer-driven chains, require that unions develop an understanding of why buyers choose suppliers in one location and not another. This too may take unions into less traditional areas – i.e. sourcing analysis and local development promotion. On the other hand, through involvement in the matrix construction referred to above, unions and labour researchers will have a potentially powerful research source at their disposal: a comparative perspective on labour rights and conditions within and across various value chains and countries.

Concluding remarks

Global value chain analysis has provided a most useful tool in the examination of globalization – its structures, levels and processes. Yet this paper suggests

---

[4] Essentially, the argument underpinning the concept of decent work and as pursued in the research of authors such as Kucera and Sarna (2004).

that the next generation of studies should integrate a more diverse and critical analysis of intra-firm labour conditions and labour market flows. When integrated more fully in this way, GVC studies may offer new insights on the sectoral variety of labour rights and conditions, as well as any regulatory changes which might be needed to promote decent work more widely amongst labour markets and countries. This appears to be most important in respect of employment in SMEs.

Most researchers in the GVC field appreciate the fact that power and inequality operate at many levels. However, the first wave of value chain studies insufficiently integrated labour issues, making these studies less useful to labour and unions. In this sense, unions now have an opportunity to expand and activate GVC analysis for their own use. This paper has indicated a number of possible ways in which this may be done.

In undertaking this research agenda unions may (once again) expose themselves to considering groups and themes that are outside their traditional priorities. In this regard, the vexed questions of a union role in local development promotion and possible links with other social actors and processes may require nuanced responses. However, the reality of the "world of work" in the 21st century seems to necessitate the more active engagement of unions with people affected by informality, poverty and gender inequality.

References

Abreu, A.; Beynon, H.; Ramalho, J. 2000. "'The dream factory': VW's modular production system in Resende, Brazil", in *Work, Employment and Society*, Vol. 14, No. 2, pp. 265–282.

—; Gitahy, L.; Ramalho, J.; Ruas, R. 1999. *Industrial restructuring and inter-firm relations in Brazil: A study of the auto-parts industry in the 1990s*, Occasional Paper No. 21 (University of London, Institute of Latin American Studies).

Ackers, P.; Smith, C.; Smith P. (eds). 1996. *The new workplace and trade unionism* (London and New York, Routledge).

Bair, J.; Gereffi, G. 2001. "Local clusters in global chains: The causes and consequences of export dynamism in Torreon's blue jeans industry", in *World Development*, Vol. 29, No. 11, pp. 1885–1903.

Best, M.H. 1990. *The new competition: Institutions of industrial restructuring* (Cambridge, MA, Polity Press).

Dedoussis, V. 1995. "Simply a question of cultural barriers? The search for new perspectives in the transfer of Japanese management practices", in *Journal of Management Studies*, Special issue, Vol. 32, No. 6, pp. 731–45.

Delbridge, R. 1995. "Surviving JIT: Control and resistance in a Japanese transplant", in *Journal of Management Studies*, Special issue, Vol. 32, No. 6, pp. 803–17.

Elgar, T.; Smith, C. (eds). 1994. *Global Japanization? The transnational transformation of the labour process* (London and New York, Routledge).

Fleury, A.; Humphrey, J. 1993. *Human resources and the diffusion and adaptation of new quality methods in Brazilian manufacturing*, IDS Research Report No. 24 (Brighton, IDS).

Gereffi, G.; Kaplinsky, R. (eds). 2001. *The value of value chains: Spreading the gains from globalisation – IDS Bulletin*, Special issue, Vol. 32, No. 3.

—; Korzeniewicz, M. (eds). 1994. *Commodity chains and global capitalism* (Westport, CT, Praeger Publishers).

Gitahy, L. 2000. *A new paradigm of industrial organisation: The diffusion of technological and managerial innovation in Brazilian industry*, PhD thesis (Uppsala University, Sweden).

Humphrey, J. 1994. "Japanese production methods and the changing position of direct production workers: Evidence from Brazil", in T. Elgar and C. Smith (eds): *Global Japanization – The transnational transformation of the labour process* (London, Routledge).

—. 1995. "The adoption of Japanese management techniques in Brazilian industry", in *Journal of Management Studies*, Special issue, Vol. 32, No. 6, pp. 767–787.

—. 1999. "Globalization and Supply Chain Networks: The auto industry in Brazil and India", in G. Gereffi, F. Palpacuer and A. Parisoto (eds): *Global production and local jobs*, (Geneva, IILS).

—. 2003. *Opportunities for SMEs in developing countries to upgrade in a global economy*, SEED Working Paper Series, No. 43, Geneva, ILO.

—; Schmitz, H., 1998. "Trust and inter-firm relations in developing and transition economies", in *Journal of Development Studies*, Vol. 34, No. 4, pp. 32–61.

—; —. 2002. "How does insertion in global value chains affect upgrading in industrial clusters?" in *Regional Studies*, Vol. 36, No. 9, pp. 1017–1027.

—; —. 2004. "Governance in global value chains", in H. Schmitz (ed.): *Local enterprises in the global economy* (Cheltenham, Edward Elgar), pp. 95–109.

—; Kaplinsky, R.; Saraph, P. 1998. *Corporate restructuring – Crompton Greaves and the challenge of globalisation* (New Delhi, Response Books).

ILO (International Labour Organization). 1999. *Job quality and small enterprise development*, SEED Working Paper Series, No. 4 (Geneva).

—. 2002. *Small enterprises, big challenges – A literature review on the impact of the policy environment on the creation and improvement of jobs within small enterprises*, SEED Working Paper Series, No. 23 (Geneva).

Kaplinsky, R.; Morris, M. 2002. *A handbook for value chain research*, report for International Development Research Centre (Ottawa, IDRC).

—; Readman, J. 2001. *How can SME producers serve global markets and sustain income growth?* (Brighton, IDS), mimeo. Available at: www.ids.ac.uk/ids/global/valchn.html [accessed 20 Nov. 2002].

—; Morris, M.; Readman, J. 2002. "The globalization of product markets and immiserizing growth: Lessons from the South African furniture industry", in *World Development*, Vol. 30, No. 7, pp. 1159–1172.

Knorringa, P.; Pegler, L. 2006. "Globalisation, firm upgrading and impacts on labour", in *TESG Journal for Social and Economic Geography*, Vol. 97, No. 5, pp. 468–477.

Kucera, D. 2001. *The effects of core worker rights on labour costs and foreign direct investment: Evaluating the "conventional wisdom"*, Decent Work Research Programme Discussion Paper No. 130 (ILO-IILS).

—; Sarna, R. 2004. *How do trade union rights affect trade competitiveness?*, Working Paper No. 39 (ILO, Geneva, Policy Integration Department).

Lane, C. 1998. "Introduction: Theories and issues in the study of trust", in C. Lane and R. Bachman (eds): *Trust within and between organizations: Conceptual issues and empirical applications* (Oxford, Oxford University Press), pp. 1–30.

Leite, M. 1994. *O futuro do trabalho: Novas tecnologias e subjectividade operária* (São Paulo, Pagina Aberta).

McCormick, D.; Schmitz, H. 2002. *Manual for value chain research on homeworkers in the garment industry* (Brighton, IDS).

Nadvi, K. 2004. "Globalisation and poverty: How can global value chain research inform the policy debate?", in *IDS Bulletin*, Vol. 35, No. 1, pp. 20–30.

—; Barrientos, S. 2004. *Industrial clusters and poverty reduction – Towards a methodology of poverty and social impact assessment of cluster development initiatives* (Vienna, UNIDO).

—; Schmitz, H. 1994. *Industrial clusters in less developed countries: Review of experiences and research agenda*, IDS Discussion Paper No. 339 (Brighton, IDS).

—; — (eds). 1999. *Industrial clusters in developing countries – World Development*, Special issue, Vol. 27, No. 9.

Neumayer, E.; de Soysa I. 2006. "Globalization and the right to free association and collective bargaining: An empirical analysis", in *World Development*, Vol. 34, No. 1, pp. 31–49.

Palpacuer, F. 1997. *Competitive strategies, competencies management and inter-firm networks: A discussion of current changes and implications for employment*, paper for International Workshop – Global Production Systems and Labour Markets, IILS (Geneva, ILO).

—. 2000. "Competence-based strategies and global production networks: A discussion of current changes and their implications for employment", in *Competition and Change*, Vol. 4, No. 4, pp. 353–400.

Pegler, L. 2000. *Workers, unions and the "politics of modernisation": Labour process change in the Brazilian white goods industry*, PhD thesis (University of London, LSE).

—. 2002a. *Factory modernisation and union identity: New challenges for unions in developing and transitional economies*, paper for ISA World Congress, Brisbane, Australia, July.

—. 2002b. "Dependência do empregador e 'lealdade' do trabalhador na fábrica do futuro: evidência com base no Brasil", in *Revista Brasileira de Ciências Sociais*, Vol. 17, No. 48, pp. 133–157. (Available in English in Working Paper Series, paper No. 17, School of Social Sciences, Cardiff, UK, Oct. 2001).

Ruas, R.; Gitahy, L.; Rabelo, F.; Antunes, E. 1994. *Inter-firm relations, collective efficiency and employment in two Brazilian clusters*, World Employment Programme Research, WEP 2-22/WP.242 (Geneva, ILO).

Schmitz, H. (ed.). 2004. *Local enterprises in the global economy* (Cheltenham, Edward Elgar).

—; Knorringa, P. 2000. "Learning from global buyers", in *Journal of Development Studies*, Vol. 37, No. 2, pp. 177–205.

Shaiken, H. 1994. "The new international division of labour and its impact on unions: A case study of high-tech Mexican export production", in J. Belanger, P. Edwards and L. Haiven (eds): *Workplace industrial relations and the global challenge* (Ithaca, NY, ILR Press).

Standing, G. 1999. "Global feminization through flexible labour: A theme revisited", in *World Development*, Vol. 27, No. 3, pp. 583–602.

Thomas, H. 1990. *Labour and work in small scale enterprises*, ISS Working Paper No. 79 (The Hague, Institute of Social Studies).

Thurow, L. 1970. *Investment in human capital* (Belmont, CA, Wadsworth).

UNIDO (United Nations Industrial Development Organization). 2002. *Industrial Development Report 2002–2003: Competing through innovation and learning* (Vienna).

PAVING THE PATH TOWARD THE UNIONIZATION OF HIGH-TECH SWEATSHOPS

4

Anibel Ferus-Comelo
New Trade Union Initiative, India

Introduction

Globalization has led to a significant spatial restructuring of industrial production as TNCs seek the most cost-effective, "flexible" workforce (Dicken, 1998). A majority of commodities in the international market are produced through a series of complex subcontracting chains that cross national borders of industrialized and developing countries (Gereffi and Korzeniewicz, 1994). Some scholars have characterized this type of economy as "networked capitalism" which increasingly relies on information and communication technologies (ICT) (Castells, 1996). As ICT companies are becoming powerful players in such a globalizing economy, it is critical to understand their restructuring practices and employment patterns as they have significant implications for unionization.

Driven by the rapid pace of technological advancements amidst plummeting prices of computers, mobile phones and other electronics products, ICT firms are cutting their costs by outsourcing production to contract manufacturers and several tiers of suppliers, and relying increasingly on temporary employment agencies to supply their labour needs. While this has been a successful corporate strategy, it has detrimental consequences for workers further down the supply chain in different parts of the world (CAFOD, 2004; Ferus-Comelo, 2005). Working in the IT industry frequently means having precarious employment in a highly stratified occupational structure with casual or short-term contracts, in a factory or as part of home-based work, with all the attendant health and safety risks. Women and migrants are an integral part of the global electronics production workforce (Ferus-Comelo, 2006).

Using the case of electronics manufacturing, this paper argues that, while globalization poses tremendous obstacles to unionization, there are many opportunities for labour action that need to be seriously considered. It presents three inter-related points for consideration: first, the perception of "footloose" capital, which breeds fatalism among unions, needs to be tempered by a sober analysis of the extent of and conditions under which industrial mobility occurs with the aim of identifying potential ways of "pinning down" capital; second, the challenge of globalization lies in identifying and exploiting existing vulnerabilities in the structure of capital using the strengths of the international labour movement; lastly, the concept of the "labour movement" needs to be expanded beyond unions to include alternative organizations whose remit and activities may make them powerful allies in the struggle for social and economic justice. This analysis is based on research in two different places, Silicon Valley (United States) and Bangalore (India), that are key nodes in the North and the South of the global high technology industry (Ferus-Comelo, 2005).

Global capital, local labour?

A major inhibitor of labour organizing in the face of capital's transnational operations is its fickle nature in relation to place, i.e. its proven record of settling temporarily in a location and jet-setting off to a different site. The power of capital in this regard cannot be underestimated; however research on the electronics industry in Bangalore and Silicon Valley questions the notion of "footloose" capital.

The extent of industrial (im)mobility

Interviews with corporate managers suggest that the electronics industry is less mobile than generally assumed as it relies on the supply chain system as well as local geographical characteristics. For instance, India currently represents an untapped, large and lucrative consumer market for the electronics industry. Thus, finding a production site within the country and a reliable subcontractor locally is important to both foreign multinationals as well as domestic corporations in order to secure a substantial percentage of this emerging market. Bangalore is a key location in India for both foreign and domestic electronics firms due to two major factors. First, managers in Bangalore highly value the skills of the large pool of workers drawn to Bangalore from other parts of southern India. More than a hundred technical institutions provide state- and company-certified training to meet the specific labour needs of the industry. Although low labour costs in India is a significant criterion, it is not the primary reason for companies to continue operation there since other countries in Asia, especially China, offer comparable labour cost savings for higher productivity. Second, the current IT policy of the state government of Karnataka (of which Bangalore is the capital) sets out a variety of generous fiscal incentives, including land subsidy and tax holidays with minimal conditions attached to promote the establishment of hardware manufacturing units. Labour regulation in the state is also being downgraded to be on par with the practice in Taiwan (China), Singapore, the Republic of Korea and the Philippines, India's primary competitors in the high technology sector. In the Philippines, for example, employers use temporary factory closures as an opportunity to delay contract negotiations and weaken or eliminate unions (ICFTU, 2006). In India, the 1982 amendment to the Industrial Disputes Act requires that firms employing more than 100 workers obtain state government permission before they lay off workers. According to some union activists in Bangalore, government-sponsored voluntary retirement schemes (VRS), conceived as a "safety net" in the form of funds for retraining and other support for retrenched workers, are used by many employers to circumvent the law and close down their enterprises without notice, especially when they want to get rid of the existing union.

While the availability of a large pool of skilled labour, necessary even for assembly jobs, and the business-friendly policies of the state makes Bangalore a key node in the global electronics industry, Silicon Valley retains its significance to the high technology industry due to its transformation as a launch pad of highly specialized, niche products. The quality infrastructure of Silicon Valley permits manufacturing of technologically complex products during the initial stages of their development before they are transferred to low-cost regions around the world for high-volume production. Contract manufacturers and subcontractors in Silicon Valley can rely on supplier firms in the vicinity. Being close to R&D centres in the region also gives them a competitive edge in the bidding war for contracts from original equipment manufacturers (OEMs) or original design manufacturers (ODMs). Production managers in Silicon Valley favourably rated a flexible local regulatory framework in terms of electricity use, labour laws, chemical use and occupational health and safety regulations. In sum, the availability of qualified labour, proximity to markets and governmental subsidies are specific place-based factors that draw and retain electronics manufacturers in both regions.

Moreover, manufacturing is a significant part of the two regional economies in this study but is either concealed among small units subcontracted by larger companies in Silicon Valley or overshadowed by the fame and fortune of the software industry in Bangalore. Governmental statistics and industrial projections in both places suggest that low-end assembly jobs are expected to grow. Industry groups such as the Manufacturers' Association for Information Technology

(MAIT) in Bangalore and the Silicon Valley Manufacturing Group (SVMG) lobby their respective governments to enact and implement policies, which promote production locally. The number of jobs in the semiconductor and electronic component manufacturing industry, including processors, operators and assemblers, in Silicon Valley are projected to increase, not decline between 2004 and 2014, according to the Santa Clara County Employment Development Department. This trend toward the retention and expansion of jobs in local electronics production reinforces the need to organize a growing workforce, while turning on its head the image of the manufacturing sector as constantly on the move.

Subsidy-linked labour standards

Besides taking note of the place-fixed nature of capital, the labour movement would benefit from exploring the associated liabilities that may be exploited on the behalf of workers. By receiving corporate welfare in the form of public subsidies, the industry opens itself to greater scrutiny and demands for corporate accountability. There is a great deal of public investment in the high-tech industry, specifically for job creation and economic development. Dell recently received a lavish US$242 million package of incentives to build a computer assembly plant in the American state of North Carolina after triggering a bidding war among the local governments offering additional subsidies (Seccombe and Cherrie, 2004). These incentive packages are generally presented with minimal qualification criteria and virtually no oversight.

One way that the labour movement can advocate on behalf of workers is to create public support for the attachment of decent standards of employment as conditions for state subsidies, and challenge the social burdens (e.g. poor job quality, low return for investment, pollution, etc.) imposed by corporations on local communities. The Living Wage campaigns in the United States, which have linked public subsidies to labour rights, particularly the right to organize in a neutral environment, demonstrate that the participation and intervention of workers' representatives in debates about the use and impact of public funds can complement union organizing campaigns.

Shifting the scale of campaigns

Organizing workers employed within complex supply chains in factories, small production units or their own homes around the world poses tremendous challenges. Three important questions that arise in the process are: whom to target for improvements in employment conditions? Where are the weaknesses in the corporate armour that can be used on behalf of workers?

And who are potential allies to put pressure on the (direct and indirect) employers? Mapping the politics of supply chains geographically based on a combination of workers' knowledge and corporate intelligence can be a powerful tool to explore these issues.

Redefining the employer and the collective bargaining unit

Certainly, corporate accountability for labour conditions is elusive when production for OEMs or ODMs is carried out in units that do not belong to them, by workers who are not their direct employees. However, the garments and automobile industries provide valuable lessons for the electronics industry in this regard. In a careful study of industrial dynamics and power relationships in the garments sector, labour activists concluded that justice campaigns needed to target fashion retailers and name-brand "manufacturers". These "sweat" the subcontractors and, indirectly, the seamstresses through several tiers of the production network in a cut-throat industrial environment (Louie 2001; Nutter 1997). Hence, the garment workers' union sought to inform and mobilize fashion consumers, most notably middle-class women and university students, to develop a broad-based anti-sweatshop movement. A parallel approach based on the politics of consumption in the high-tech industry may imply targeting large institutional buyers such as schools, universities, hospitals and government offices.

There have also been successful attempts to extend union protection to workers at suppliers of firms where unions are already recognized in the automobile and garments industries. Jobbers' agreements or joint liability which hold the manufacturer responsible for conditions in its contracting shops, originated in the experiences of the garment workers' union in New York (Bonacich, 2001). In a similar style, the Canadian Auto Workers (CAW) developed new collective bargaining concepts of "work ownership" and "satellite bargaining" to challenge the artificial organizational boundaries that restrict the terms and conditions outlined in union contracts to the corporation's direct employees (Holmes, 2004). At the international scale, IFAs are a form of corporate codes of conduct that GUFs, such as the International Federation of Chemical, Energy, Mining and Factory Workers (ICEM) and the International Union of Food, Agricultural, Hotel, Restaurant, Catering, Tobacco and Allied Workers' Associations (IUF), are negotiating with large corporations to cover direct and in some cases indirect employees. Although this approach is not easy to achieve or problem-free to implement, as Bonacich (2001) and Wills (2002) suggest, it points to directions in which labour organization needs to move to re-define the traditional collective bargaining unit in accordance with predominant contracting systems.

The weakest link

Highly decentralized networks of production deployed by interdependent corporations, while consolidating corporate power, also allow labour to assert its demands. As Moody (1997, p. 280) notes, TNCs "have deep pockets to resist strikes or other forms of action, but they are also vulnerable at many points of their cross-border production chains". This vulnerability to local activism is apparent in the transnational production arrangements in the electronics industry.

Managers in both Silicon Valley and Bangalore agreed that shortening the time absorbed in transporting goods from one point to another and eliminating storage is vital in this industry due to the high obsolescence rate of electronic products. The time it takes for a fully assembled product to get to the shop shelf or customer from the production line has a huge impact on its market value. Just-in-time systems, described by a company manager in Bangalore as "the right materials at the right place and at the right time" in this climate are indispensable. Rather than being stored for long periods of time in warehouses, materials and components are pulled directly into production lines and into the final products within just hours of their delivery. Several tiers of suppliers are linked to each other under similar high pressure settings on the basis of a strict forecasting schedule from OEMs or CMs, making punctuality and right quantity of delivery essential.

As Herod (2000) has argued using the case of the United Auto Workers (UAW) 1998 strike at two General Motors plants in Flint, Michigan, a well-calculated work stoppage or slowdown at key points in the arteries of global production networks could raise the financial stakes of union resistance. A supply chain analysis can also help identify other important players who could provide leverage for workers. Beukema and Coenen (1999) suggest that companies which provide logistics services, or "the planning, execution, and control of the flow of goods from purchase up to and including distribution to end-users" can also be important sites of resistance (Beukema and Coenen, 1999, p. 142). Using the case of a Dutch distribution company, they demonstrate that, due to their contact with and knowledge about important clients of their employer firm, logistics workers (e.g. transport workers) can play a significant role in providing leverage to workers at the weaker links in global production networks. High union density in the transport industry and active networks of organized labour that exist in this sector internationally open up some space for worker action and solidarity across industries.

International worker exchanges

The potential for the geographical relocation of electronics jobs makes it evident that a purely localized organizing strategy is no longer adequate in today's capitalism. As workers are divided by the geographies of production, unifying workers across national boundaries must be a central component of organizing in the electronics industry. Reports about worker exchanges and international meetings among workers from specific multinationals, such as those organized by the Maquila Solidarity Network (MSN), affirm the benefits of personal contact and information exchange among workers. Protectionist measures adopted by unions to prevent jobs moving from one place to another can be replaced by pressuring corporations to create better jobs *wherever* they operate.

One approach is to bring together assemblers who are involved in the supply chains of a single company like International Business Machines (IBM) regardless of their direct employer or location of employment. It would be essential to include workers from places that have strategic significance to the company. During the summer of 2002, a delegation of workers formerly employed by the multinational electronics firm the Radio Corporation of America (RCA – now Thomson Multimedia) in the northern county of Taoyuan, Taiwan (China), toured the United States to seek solidarity from American labour and environmental organizations in their struggle for just compensation. The tour was organized by the self-help association of former RCA employees which was founded in 1998 to support hundreds of RCA workers who are suffering (or the families of those who have died) from cancer developed from exposure to toxic substances in their workplace. Workers' representatives visited five major cities, including Silicon Valley, to present their story to American electronics workers and allies. Their aim was to build support for a public hearing and lawsuit to hold their former employer accountable for serious environmental pollution and a huge cancer cluster. In the process, they were able to share information and develop personal ties directly with workers in other places. In Silicon Valley, the RCA workers were struck by the ethnic diversity of workers and their stories of unfair treatment in the industry. Thus, a cross-border worker exchange can result not only in practical campaign support but also create a realistic image of working conditions in places around the world through personal contact.

Global Union Federations, such as the IMF, which recognizes that labour organizing in the ICT sector "requires special trade union effort" can play a vital role in internationalizing labour campaigns in the industry (IMF, 2002, p. 8). Such international union structures can lend institutional pressure in labour disputes, conduct corporate research, lobby governments, raise public awareness in several countries, and mobilize union members for coordinated days of action through their national affiliates. As several well-known cases have shown (e.g. the 1997 UPS-Teamsters strike), international solidarity mobilized through these organizations can make a huge difference in contract negotiations and struggles for union recognition. Other examples were provided in chapters 1 and 2 of how GUFs have used IFAs to create international solidarity.

Linking with the "other" labour movement

Despite the need for labour organization and potential opportunities that exist for it, research in the two regions exposes a fundamental dilemma. Not only is the electronics industry globally marked by a very low degree of unionization but trade unions in Bangalore and Silicon Valley have not yet been successful in establishing an institutional presence in the industry. In Bangalore, unionization is limited to the traditional public sector electronics companies set up just after India's independence, leaving the relatively newer private sector unorganized. In Silicon Valley, the industry remains a union-free zone despite a couple of notable attempts to organize workers in the 1980s and mid-1990s (cf. Early and Wilson, 1986). However, here, as in many other hot-spots of the electronics industry, many non-profit, community-based organizations and issue-based social movements are filling the gap in the organization and representation of workers. It is therefore critical to develop and strengthen local collaboration between unions and these diverse social actors if workers' rights are to be protected.

Organizing through services

One arena of productive ties between social organizations and unions is meeting workers' needs beyond the workplace. In Bangalore, the Bharat Electronics Employees Union, a public sector union, launched a monthly women's legal clinic with the pro bono services of a sympathetic public interest law firm in 2001. By facilitating the provision of a service to female (and male) workers on matters that are not necessarily workplace related, the union increases the value and relevance of collective organization in workers' lives. Union leaders aim to make this monthly legal clinic available to members of the residential community around the production facility, thereby promoting unionism beyond the workplace. Women members of the Malaysian Trade Union Congress (MTUC) run two hostels for women who work in the EPZs in the suburbs of Kuala Lumpur (David, 1996). Besides providing workers with safe, decent and affordable housing, these hostels are places where women can discuss their problems and raise their awareness of the benefits of unions. Not only has this initiative been replicated elsewhere but a small group of women who lived in these hostels have also participated in the creation of a new union in the electronics industry. Health and safety education for electronics workers in Silicon Valley was the focus of a NGO – the Santa Clara Center for Occupational Safety and Health (SCCOSH). Its Working Women's Leadership Development Project (WE LeaP) was a popular education initiative conceived in the 1990s to lay the foundation for organizing the predominately female and immigrant workforce around the issue of health and safety in the workplace.

Besides legal aid, housing and safety training, there is a myriad of services that would benefit workers, e.g. medical care, vocational skills, literacy or English proficiency. Meeting these needs through a structured programme in the neutral space of a community-based organization would draw workers, allowing unions to build relationships of trust with them. But there are many other reasons for such a long-term, circumspect strategy. First, it takes into account the fact that many workers value their jobs no matter how bad they seem as their opportunities to secure suitable, decent paying jobs are severely limited. This does not, however, preclude their awareness of the need to fight for equality and dignity as workers. Secondly, the process of connecting with other workers outside the workplace setting can contribute to the formation of a political identity as workers, particularly important for women who are often defined only by their roles in the family. In general, getting involved in an organization gives workers an experience of how collective action can change people's lives.

Cross-movement alliances

Given the environmental degradation and health risks that the electronics industry poses to workers and communities, environmental activists in many high-tech clusters around the world such as Taiwan (China), Thailand, Silicon Valley and Scotland have proven to be workers' allies for CSR. A number of high-profile, landmark lawsuits have been filed against TNCs such as IBM, RCA (now Thomson Multimedia) and Seagate Corporation by environmental justice organizations on behalf of workers and their descendants, whose health has been permanently damaged due to their exposure to a "witch's brew" of chemicals and hazardous materials in the workplace.

The Silicon Valley Toxics Coalition (SVTC) is one such organization which grew out of inter-related concerns about environmental degradation, public health and workers' issues. For around 20 years SVTC has been conducting research, public education and advocacy centred on the environmental impact of the electronics industry, starting with groundwater contamination in the 1970s resulting in ground-breaking environmental policies in the United States. The coalition's demands for environmental accountability of the industry has had significant implications not only within the region or the country but beyond through the formation of the International Campaign for Responsible Technology (ICRT), a network of public health specialists, labour activists and environmental advocates in the 1980s. The Rio Tinto campaign, which brought together a similar cross-border coalition of indigenous people's organizations, unions and environmental groups, is an example of how the ICRT could serve as a platform upon which local labour campaigns can be linked to global issues of business practice, corporate governance, shareholder value and social responsibility (Sadler, 2004).

Conclusion

Working conditions in the IT manufacturing sector, particularly for workers at the bottom end of subcontracting chains, can frequently be summarized by the term high-tech sweatshops. Research in Bangalore and Silicon Valley has shown that the unionization of this industry, although virtually non-existent at present, may not be impossible. However, in order to begin envisioning the possibility, it is important to find ways out of the pessimistic cul-de-sac that the rhetoric of globalization conjures up about contemporary capitalism and the labour movement. The image of fluid capital scouring the globe for the cheapest labour and the most lax legislative regimes does not always fit the electronics industry everywhere it operates. The state has a definite role to play in the regulation of private industry and this is remarkably evident in high-tech manufacturing which benefits enormously from generous subsidies. Rather than accepting defeat before the battle has even begun, unions can draw upon lessons learnt in similar industries in order to plan out a strategy.

Although the numerous challenges associated with the global structure of electronics manufacturing cannot be underestimated, there are also inspiring examples of workers' struggles that can be supported and amplified. This calls for a bold, creative and collaborative effort from various parts of the labour movement. The study in two key sites of the IT industry suggests that the organization of global production in a time-sensitive industry such as high-tech manufacturing is not immune to well-coordinated labour action. By analysing and taking strategic advantage of the openings for collective resistance, mobilizing political allies from other social movements, and re-drawing the contours of campaigns to include workers across borders and in households, unions and community-based organizations together can begin the arduous process of establishing dignity and respect for electronics workers.

References

Beukema, L.; Coenen, H. 1999. "Global Logistic Chains: the increasing importance of local labour relations", in P. Leisink (ed.): *Globalization and labour relations* (Cheltenham, Edward Elgar), pp. 138–157.

Bonacich, E. 2001. "The challenge of organizing in a globalized/flexible industry: The case of the apparel industry in Los Angeles", in R. Baldoz, C. Koeber and P. Kraft (eds): *The critical study of work: Labor, technology and global production* (Philadelphia, PA, Temple University Press), pp. 155–178.

CAFOD (Catholic Agency for Overseas Development). 2004. *Clean up your computer: Working conditions in the electronics sector* (London).

Castells, M. 1996. *The information age: Economy, society and culture. Vol. I: The rise of the network society* (Oxford, Blackwell).

David, N. 1996. *Worlds apart: Women and the global economy* (Geneva, ICFTU).

Dicken, P. 1998. *Global shift* (London, Chapman), third edition.

Early, S.; Wilson, R. 1986. "Do unions have a future in high technology?", in *Technology Review*, Vol. 89, pp. 56f–65f.

Ferus-Comelo, A. 2005. *Globalisation of production and labour organisation in the electronics industry*, PhD thesis submitted to the University of London, unpublished.

—. 2006. "Double jeopardy: Gender and migration in electronics manufacturing", in T. Smith, D. Sonnenfeld and D. Pellow (eds): *Challenging the chip: Labor rights and environmental justice in the global electronics industry* (Philadelphia, PA, Temple University Press), pp. 43–54.

Gereffi, G.; Korzeniewicz, M. (eds). 1994. *Commodity chains and global capitalism* (Westport, CT, Praeger Publishers).

Herod, A. 2000. "Implications of just-in-time production for union strategy: Lessons from the 1998 General Motors-United Auto Workers dispute", in *Annals of the Association of American Geographers*, Vol. 90, No. 3, pp. 521–547.

Holmes, J. 2004. "Re-scaling collective bargaining: Union responses to restructuring in the North American auto industry", in *Geoforum*, Vol. 35, No. 1, pp. 9–21.

ICFTU (International Confederation of Free Trade Unions). 2006. *Philippines: Annual survey of violations of trade union rights* (Geneva).

IMF (International Metalworkers' Federation). 2002. *IMF Action Programme, 2002-2005: Dealing with global challenges*, adopted at the 30th IMF Congress, 11–15 Nov. 2001, Sydney, Australia (Geneva).

Louie, M.C. 2001. *Sweatshop warriors: Immigrant women workers take on the global factory* (Cambridge, MA, South End Press).

Moody, K. 1997. *Workers in a lean world: Unions in the international economy* (London and New York, Verso).

Nutter, S. 1997. "The structure and growth of the Los Angeles garment industry", in A. Ross (ed.): *No sweat: Fashion, free trade, and the rights of garment workers* (London and New York, Verso), pp. 199–213.

Sadler, D. 2004. "Trade unions, coalitions and communities: Australia's Construction, Forestry, Mining and Energy Union and the international stakeholder campaign against Rio Tinto", in *Geoforum*, Vol. 35, No. 1, pp. 35–46.

Seccombe, J.; Cherrie, V. 2004. "Winston-Salem wins", in *Winston-Salem Journal*, 23 Dec.

Wills, J. 2002. "Bargaining for the space to organise in the global economy: A review of the Accor-IUF trade union rights agreement", in *Review of International Political Economy*, Vol. 9, No. 4, pp. 675–700.

CORPORATE GOVERNANCE REFORMS AS A MEANS OF PROTECTING AND PROMOTING WORKER INTERESTS: SHAPING THE CORPORATION OF TOMORROW

Richard Tudway
Adviser on corporate governance to TUAC, Paris
Fellow of Huron University USA in London
Director of the Centre for International Economics, London

Introduction

There is a continuing crisis which centres on the corporation, its ownership and governance, and its wider economic and social responsibilities. This is not a new problem. It is, however, one that has been brought into sharp relief as a result of the major corporate scandals in the United States, Europe and elsewhere. Enron and WorldCom in the United States, Parmalat in Italy, Ahold in the Netherlands and Marconi in the United Kingdom are some of the best known examples, in a much longer list, where the abuse of corporate power has had devastating consequences for working people. Many of these problems in turn flow from the arrangements in place in respect of corporate governance.

There is a pressing and important need for trade unions to influence, in a practical and commercially realistic manner, the case for change. This can best be sustained by a programme of coordinated research aimed at promoting a clear understanding about what needs to be done to address these problems and how best to proceed. This paper explores more fully the nature of the problem and identifies the high ground of a response.

The nature of the problem

The process of corporate governance is controlled and directed at the highest reaches within the corporation – by the board of directors. In British and American jurisdictions there is no distinction in law between the corporation as an entity and the board which is there to protect shareholder interests and the interests of other stakeholders. This is a constitutional anomaly. This issue is addressed in German law through the existence of the supervisory board.[1] The supervisory board represents the interests of the company, employees and other stakeholders. Other detailed aspects of governance arrangements in Anglo-American jurisdictions are also inadequately defined in law. Those concerning directors' fiduciary duties[2] are neither clearly nor objectively[3] defined. Some important requirements are currently left to the discretion of directors to interpret under comply or explain arrangements.[4]

Overall this is an unsatisfactory state of affairs. It undermines the credibility of corporate governance. There are no easy or obvious remedies. Reform has to be driven by strong, empirically sound, commercially realistic arguments. Global trade unions need to support practical research aimed at shaping these reforms.

The framework of governance in Anglo-American jurisdictions and elsewhere points to serious systemic weakness. The self-regulating disciplinary functions of the market have broken down. The passing of the Sarbanes Oxley Act by the United States Congress in 2002, in the wake of the Enron scandal, is a welcome step aimed at improving the framework of control and tightening the enforcement of relevant laws. Parallel moves have been taken in the United Kingdom and other European countries. They all aim to strengthen corporate governance and accountability. But this make-do-and-mend approach is only a start. More fundamental and forward-looking reforms are needed in shaping tomorrow's corporation.

The linchpin of corporate accountability is the publication of audited accounts. Accounts focus, however, on past activities. Whilst accurate company accounts and other financial disclosures are crucial ingredients of effective governance, shareholders and stakeholders need to have a full understanding of the direction and content of business development intentions. The report of the British Company Law Reform Steering Group (CLSRG) has, to its credit, recommended that larger publicly quoted corporations should in future prepare and present an OFR (Operating and

---

[1] See the German Co-determination Act 1976. See also the German Corporate Governance Code 2005 http://www.corporate.governance-code.de/index-e.html

[2] Directors' fiduciary duties in Anglo-American jurisdictions and their interpretation by the courts have evolved from ancient trust law and the law of equity, alongside common law. A common complaint is that directors in the contemporary setting are "protected." by equity in those jurisdictions and that the full force of common law does not therefore apply. See Penner, J.E., 2002, *The law of trusts*, Butterworths for a treatment of these issues. See also Parkinson, J., 1995, *Corporate power and responsibility*, Clarendon Press, (Chapter 4), for a discussion of managerial efficiency.

[3] Although the extension of statute law in the United Kingdom and the United States has resulted in greater objectivity of standards. Examples of this would include section 214(4) of the British Insolvency Act 1986 and its application in Norman v. Theodore Goddard (1991). In this landmark judgment, objective standards by which negligent behaviour by directors can be measured in terms of what might be expected from a reasonably diligent person were set out. The passing of the Sarbanes Oxley Act by the United States Congress in 2002 has had a similar impact. But in a number of other aspects directors' duties remain exempt from these higher standards.

[4] See the [British] Companies Act 2006, Chapter 2: General Duties of Directors, section 170 onwards.

Financial Review).⁵ This will require the directors of the board to declare any material changes it sees in the prospective business activities of the corporation and any environmental or other liabilities that it foresees impacting upon the business. Being informed after the event can no longer be accepted as normal in effective and progressive corporate governance. Corporations need to engage before the event, with shareholders and other stakeholders – especially trade unions – in the articulation of commercial strategy.

Resistance to change

Existing habits and practices in Anglo-American jurisdictions discourage this sort of thinking. Corporations operating in Germany (and Austria, Belgium, France, Luxembourg and the Netherlands) often behave differently. The supervisory board oversees the executive board. Its role is to debate and agree matters of strategy and commercial policy with the executive board. In Anglo-American unitary board jurisdictions there is little appetite for this sort of dialogue. There is a widespread abhorrence in Anglo-American jurisdictions of supervisory boards, which are regarded as a distraction from reaching sound and effective business decisions. There is also little effective leadership from shareholders, as beneficial owners of the corporation, to promote fundamental change. There are complex reasons which explain shareholder inertia on the key issue of board involvement. Inertia arises from the fact that in reality shareholders in Anglo-American jurisdictions are largely institutional investors managing very large portfolios in a large number of different publicly quoted corporations.⁶ As risk arbitrageurs they would be conflicted if required to nominate board directors from within their own ranks. The stark reality is that these risk arbitrageurs are not shareholders in the normal sense of the term and have no appetite for any day-to-day involvement in the affairs of the corporation. They arc happy to sell if they are not satisfied rather than press for improvement where management is seen to be failing. There are no straightforward answers. But solutions can be found if there is a will to do so. The role of trade unions and workers' capital will continue to play an important strategic role in this area. Workers' pension funds are a major source of investment in industry. Trade unions must ensure that pension fund trustees play an effective role in forcing through progressive changes in corporate governance.

---

⁵ This provision, approved by Parliament in March 2005, was repealed on 12 January 2006 because of an existing obligation on companies to provide a Business Review, a requirement of the European Accounts Modernization Directive 2003/51/EC of the European Parliament and the Council of 18 June 2003 amending Directives 78/660/EEC, 83/349/EEC and 91/647/EEC.

⁶ This pattern of behaviour is, however, being fundamentally transformed by the activities of hedge funds and private equity whose strategy is to secure a small but significant shareholding and then insist upon and secure strategic changes from the incumbent management. The route often preferred is to de-list the target company, thus weakening further governance and accountability.

Resolving the paradox of shareholder ownership in Anglo-American jurisdictions is central to arriving at sensible, commercially viable reforms. How best to bring this about needs to be carefully explored and evaluated. It must result in shareholders and other stakeholders, including trade unions, being fully consulted. The constitutionality of corporate governance and the law that underpins this must uphold this commitment at every level in the corporation. Anything less will not do.

Promoting effective corporate governance

The global challenge facing citizens in general and trade unions in particular centres on fostering the development of a credible, transparent and participative system of corporate governance. The reason for this is that under existing arrangements corporations are not adequately accountable to shareholders or other stakeholders, including trade unions. The existing framework of governance allows these defects to remain unchecked. This needs, urgently, to be understood and addressed on the basis of practical and commercially realistic remedies.

In moving the debate forward the language of governance has first of all to be opened up and demystified. If, as it is argued, shareholders are the beneficial owners of the corporation then two questions at least have to be asked and answered. First, how do shareholders exercise their ownership rights and responsibilities? If they are the owners of the corporation then what is expected of them as owners in ensuring the full and proper accountability of the managers and directors who run the corporation on their behalf? A closely allied second question inevitably centres on the role directors play in ensuring the full and proper accountability of the corporation to shareholders and other stakeholders.

Seeking proper answers to these key questions reveals a raft of queries which cannot be adequately or credibly explained. On close inspection the language of governance is rhetorical, tautological and self-serving. A few examples will illustrate the difficulty that questioners have. The notion of shareholder ownership is inherently ambiguous. The term "ownership" on which great store is often placed is, in practice, defined as meaning just about anything other than what ownership is normally understood to mean. An honest reading of the language leaves the questioner sensing that there is something odd if not specious about the way in which the term ownership is used and understood. Ownership by shareholders must also entail duties and responsibilities if shareholders are to avoid being classified as absentee landlords caring little about governance issues and only interested in dividends and capital growth.

Demystifying the corporation

There is a concealed reason for this ambiguity. The ambiguity and ambivalence is a linguistic device to prevent the viewer from distinguishing between rhetoric and reality in respect of the underlying issue of ownership. A fair conclusion is that in reality publicly quoted corporations in Anglo-American jurisdictions are not owned, in any meaningful sense, by the shareholders. Lawyers in their search for a means to circumvent this difficulty have successfully argued that the corporation is not owned by anyone but is in reality a nexus of contracts with shareholders who enjoy rights to participate in dividends in proportion to their ownership of equity. Whilst this is an ingenious solution it is also one which is intuitively unsound. It is a device which masks the reality that directors control the corporation as if they were owners, which in law they are not. This appears to give them the best of both worlds: effective, if concealed ownership, without responsibility. Because shareholder ownership cannot be defined as having any operational meaning the ownership of the corporation is itself tainted with ambiguity. This inevitably undermines legitimacy and public confidence.

Corporations, as we are all aware, are fictional personifications in law. In law they may be sued, as legal persons, for acting unlawfully even though their existence is fictional. Yet corporations are not capable of actions or thoughts. The directors are the parties who speak for and act for the corporation. In practice the directors, or certain directors to be precise, are the controlling mind of the corporation. This confers massive undisclosed power on those directors whose actions are in turn governed, in law, by their fiduciary duties to shareholders and stakeholders. A close inspection of their fiduciary duties reveals, however, a pervasive vagueness of definition. The repeated theme throughout is that the director's first duty to is to act in the best interest of the company and the members. This, in turn, is defined as seeking to maximize shareholder value. At no stage, however, is this objective specifically or meaningfully defined.[7]

Though there are other important, complementary questions, the issues that have been identified call for proper, detailed scrutiny. Trade unions must, with patience and determination, resist arguments advanced by parties who have an interest in discouraging wider discussion and debate of these issues. Sadly, the OECD in its current review of the Principles of Corporate

---

[7] There is, for example, no reference to the forward time frame. This invites the criticism that directors of companies in Anglo-American jurisdictions systematically pursue short-term profit-maximizing strategies which may compromise longer-term sustainability.

Governance[8] has not grasped the unique opportunity the review presents to examine honestly and openly these issues. This arises because of resistance from certain governments and the business enterprise sector to any debate which might lead to change. There are powerful interests that want permanent closure of debate in this area.

Moving our understanding forward

Corporations are vitally important social and economic institutions. On their prosperity rests the prosperity of society at large. What trade unions and other citizen interest groups need to ensure is that the corporation operates within a clear ownership structure where elected directors have a constitutional independence from the corporation and can be seen to act in the best interests of the corporation, the shareholders in ownership and other stakeholders, in maximizing long-term shareholder value. In doing so it is important that any recommendations for change address the practical reality that corporations have to prosper if they are to survive. They can only survive if they can operate effectively in competitive markets. It is only if corporations are effective and profitable that investment can be sustained and employment protected and enlarged. Any changes must therefore recognize the importance of ensuring that the fairytale goose that lays the golden egg is not unreasonably hampered by the framework of corporate governance. The old-style negative response to capitalism does not offer a viable way forward. There is a soundly based consensus that private corporations of all shapes and sizes, offering the widest possible range of goods and services in competitive markets, are the best safeguard against tyranny. But there has to be a proper and credible response to the huge accretion of corporate power that has occurred, especially in the largest publicly quoted corporations, if fully competitive yet fair and responsible markets are to be created and maintained.

There are some important principles that should guide us in this process, each of which needs to be fully researched.

Principle 1

We need to know and understand how some European corporations fare that share, explain and react constructively to debate and discussion with share-

---

[8] This review is being managed by the OECD Secretariat. Debate of the important issues raised by TUAC in a number of written submissions has been prevented by the actions of certain OECD member governments and the Business and Investment Advisory Committee (BIAC) to the OECD. OECD civil servants for their part failed to ensure that the debate was full, frank and inclusive. The progress of these discussions can be followed on TUAC's website <www.tuac.org> Attention is drawn, in particular, to the "TUAC Evaluation of the 2004 Review of the OECD Principles of corporate governance".

holders and stakeholders about future commercial aims and objectives, when compared with Anglo-American corporations that don't.

Principle 2
Corporations and their boards need to consult with their shareholders and stakeholders if valuable business opportunities are to be spotted and acted upon. Corporate Social Responsibility is seen by the best and most effective corporations as a serious strategic business development commitment, not some PR-motivated bolt-on.

Principle 3
The maximization of shareholder value, as a prime objective of corporate endeavour, has to be "unpacked" in terms of what it means and how it should be interpreted and implemented. The underlying objective must be the long-term growth and prosperity of the corporation, its shareholders and stakeholders.

Principle 4
There is a need to clarify the fiduciary duties of board directors in ways that will encourage them and empower them to look widely and think deeply about their responsibilities in maximizing shareholder value as foreseen by Principle 3.

Principle 5
It is important that institutional investors play their part in improving both the quality and relevance of governance and the underlying constitutionality of the corporation and the board of directors. The socially responsible investment initiative is a good and worthwhile example of how institutional investors can reward progressive management and penalize those which are not prepared to embrace change.

Principle 6
The gatekeepers – the auditors, legal advisers, investment banks and commercial banks – have a key role to play in promoting better, higher and more relevant standards of governance. This is because of their close link to capital markets and the critical influence they have on those markets.

The importance of trade-union-driven research

The corporation has been subjected for the best part of half a century to the most detailed scrutiny by scholars, researchers and instructors in business schools and other academic institutions, mostly in OECD countries and most particularly in the United States. One cannot but marvel at the sheer scale of research output. This needs to be qualified. Most of this research has been focused on the activities of American corporations operating within American-style capital markets. The scale of Nobel Prize-winning contributions from American researchers bears testimony to the domination of American research in this area and the vast knowledge and understanding of American markets and American practices and predilections to which this bears witness. In contrast, much less is known about the operation of capital markets and the performance of the corporation within those markets in other jurisdictions, notably in Germany and Japan.

It is important that the global trade union movement takes proper and effective ownership of its own programme of research in this field. The research needs to be focused, policy-oriented and above all commercially realistic. It also needs to achieve some level of critical mass and for its results to be widely disseminated and debated in the media. There can be no doubting that the time is right for an honest, open debate between the social and economic partners whose collaborative efforts have the potential and the capacity to build effective and prosperous businesses. We need to act now.

References

Allen, F.; Gale, D. 2000. *Comparing financial systems* (Cambridge, MA, MIT Press).

Brudney, V. 1985. "Corporate governance, agency costs, and the rhetoric of contract", in *Columbia Law Review*, Vol. 85, pp. 1403–1444.

Easterbrook, F.H.; Fischel, D.R. 1991. *The economic structure of corporate law* (Cambridge, MA, Harvard University Press).

Eisenberg, M.A. 1989. "The structure of corporation law", in *Columbia Law Review*, Vol. 89, pp. 1461–1525.

Faccio, M.; Lasfer, A.M. 2001. *Institutional shareholders and corporate governance: The case of UK pension funds* (Turin, Center for Research on Pensions and Welfare Policies).

Government Commission on German Corporate Governance. 2003. *Framework of German Corporate Governance*.

Hoffmann, J. 2004. *Co-ordinated continental European market economies under pressure from globalisation* (Toronto, York University, Canadian Centre for German and European Studies).

Marens, R.; Wicks, A. 1999. "Getting real: Stakeholder theory, managerial practice, and the general irrelevance of fiduciary duties owed to shareholders", in *Business Ethics Quarterly*, Vol. 9, No. 2, pp. 273–294.

Mitchell, L.E., 1992. "The economic structure of corporate law", in *Texas Law Review*, Vol. 71, No. 1, pp. 217–242.

Norman, W.; MacDonald, C. 2004. "Getting to the bottom of 'Triple Bottom Line'", in *Business Ethics Quarterly*, Vol. 14, No. 2, pp. 243–262.

Parkinson, J. 1995. *Corporate power and responsibility* (Oxford, Clarendon Press).

Penner, J.E. 2002. *The law of trusts* (London, Butterworths).

Stapledon, G.P. 1996. *Institutional shareholders and corporate governance* (Oxford, Clarendon Press).

Tudway, R. 2002. "The juridical paradox of the corporation", in F. Macmillan (ed.): *International corporate law*, Vol. 2 (Oxford, Hart Publishing), pp. 79.

MULTINATIONAL COMPANIES IN BULGARIA: IMPACT ON LABOUR AND SOCIAL DEVELOPMENT

6

Nadejda Daskalova and Lyuben Tomev
Institute for Social and Trade Union Research, Bulgaria

Introduction

In 1999, the Institute for Social and Trade Union Research (ISTUR) carried out a survey of eight subsidiaries of MNEs located in Bulgaria (Daskalova and Tomev, 2000). A new 2004 survey covered 29 subsidiaries of 18 MNEs in Bulgaria.[1] In selecting the MNEs to be included in the sample three main criteria were considered: the presence of trade union organization; the size of the MNE (i.e. the largest MNEs in any given sector were chosen); and it must have been included in the original survey. The findings, therefore, cannot be applied to all multinationals operating in the country. For the purposes of the survey, fellows of the Institute interviewed the chairpersons of trade union organizations and human resource managers, using a semi-structured questionnaire. The research aimed to reveal the links between global and local development in the Bulgarian context, to outline the changes in industrial relations in multinational subsidiaries in Bulgaria in the previous five years and to identify good practices. The expectations concerning direct foreign investments, even at the start of the country's transition, had been that they would be an important means of achieving structural change within the economy, the technological renovation of enterprises and the transfer of a new organizational culture and industrial relations practices (Daskalova and Tomev, 2004). Today, 15 years after the start of change and the entry of foreign investors into the Bulgarian economy, the extent to which these expectations

---

[1] The subsidiaries studied operate in 16 sectors, and the headquarters of the parent companies are situated in 12 countries: Belgium, the Cayman Islands, Denmark, Germany, Greece, Iceland, Italy, Luxembourg, the Netherlands Switzerland, Turkey and the United States.

have been fulfilled can be realistically assessed. The results have proved to be quite varied, as the paper shows.

The study shows that MNEs have controversial effects on the labour market and industrial relations in Bulgaria. They create many new jobs and preserve many others. Nevertheless, in all companies privatized by MNEs there were significant job losses. Both favourable and adverse effects were registered on industrial relations practices as well. The study identified potential for the Europeanization of industrial relations, albeit with differences according to sector, country of origin and type of company. Alongside the best practices of many MNEs that transmit European social values and patterns of cooperative management and social partnership, in some MNEs attempts have been made to erode industrial relations and social dialogue and to marginalize trade unions.

The role of the multinationals

The MNEs play a major role in the process of establishing a global system of markets and production. Foreign direct investment (FDI) involves both capital flows and the means for the transfer of technologies, management skills and new methods of work organization from country to country. Inflows of foreign direct investment (FDI) were substantial in 2005. They rose by 29 per cent to reach US$916 billion, having already increased by 27 per cent in 2004. It was attributed to some 77,000 MNEs and their 770,000 affiliates abroad (UNCTAD, 2006).

The MNEs operate a kind of "transmission", transferring industrial relations practices from the country of origin to the host countries where their subsidiaries are based, while in some cases undermining or putting pressure on the specific national regulatory mechanisms – including trade union recognition and collective bargaining mechanisms.

The possibility of moving production and investments from country to country makes job protection and terms of employment rather difficult. The export of capital and technologies is often directed to countries where labour is cheap, trade unions are weak and governments are corrupt. Such practices can be viewed as "social dumping" – a problem that deserves special attention.

Social dumping and erosion of labour standards

Social dumping can be observed in many countries, mostly in developing and transition countries. In general terms, it is an expression of the urge of an enterprise to benefit from any differences in the economic situation and labour legislation and to extract economic profit or competitive advantage.

What are the key factors and differences on which social dumping practices are based?

- **The difference in the price of labour.** The gap here is very large indeed. The minimum monthly wage in 25 European Union (EU) Member States on 1 January 2007 ranged from 172 euros (Latvia) to 1,572 euros (Luxembourg) per month. In the two newest EU Member States – Bulgaria and Romania – it was 92 and 114 euros respectively (Regnard, 2007). Social dumping based on lower payment is the most widespread form in developing and transition countries.

- **The labour legislation.** The issue here is most often the practice of resorting to atypical contracts of employment: fixed-term, temporary, replacement, on probation, etc. Unregulated work hours and ease of evasion of regulations can serve as a basis for social dumping.

- **The role of social partners and their capacity for collective bargaining.** Social dumping can flourish in countries where the influence, collective bargaining power of trade unions and coverage of collective agreements are low.

- **The existence of economic sectors with a labour force surplus.** This is logically a prerequisite for the hiring of cheap skilled labour, especially in areas with a high unemployment level.

- **The significant role of the informal sector** in developing and transition countries creates room for social dumping both between countries and within the country itself.[2]

The most frequently used forms of social dumping involve contracts for outsourcing, with consequent export to third countries, contracts for subcontracting, sub-suppliers, and so on. Yet, as practice has shown in the past few years, a number of corporations resort to delocalization to other countries. In 2007 two large multinationals – American Bunge and Anglo-Dutch Unilever suddenly closed their production operations in Bulgaria and moved to Romania.

Social dumping has many faces but ultimately there is one common denominator – it is used as an instrument for the erosion of labour standards. Naturally, it should be noted that not every delocalization is related to the practice of social dumping, and clearly the distinctive line here is the level of investment and production expansion and the observation of national social and labour laws.

---

[2] According to some expert estimates, the size of the informal economy in Bulgaria is 30–35 per cent of GDP.

The use of cheap labour is particularly widespread in light industry. Bulgarian garment manufacture operates almost entirely as a subcontractor of western partners, but the net wage can be as low as US$173 per month. All this is happening against the background of the growing share of garments in the export of industrial goods – up to 20 per cent of the country's total exports, meaning a balance of payments surplus in that subsector. Yet the hourly pay rate there is about 98 cents.[3] As the campaign for the defence of fundamental labour rights in the workplace of the Confederation of Independent Trade Unions in Bulgaria shows in a number of garment companies owned by foreign investors relocated to Bulgaria from neighbouring countries, the widespread practice is to work 14–16 hours a day for minimum pay – in drastic violation of the social and labour laws.[4]

Multinational companies in Bulgaria: Changes in the labour market and industrial relations

Over the last decade, Bulgaria has been slowly but irreversibly entering the global economy, following the processes of European integration and the penetration of foreign capital, especially from MNEs. Globalization is creating challenges for the Bulgarian trade unions, but also new opportunities for the development of labour relations based on the promotion of fundamental human and labour rights and effective social dialogue with business.

At the beginning of the transition period, FDI was expected to be one of the core instruments for structural change in the economy and the technological renovation of enterprises. It was supposed to usher in a new organizational culture and new industrial relations practices in Bulgaria. It was expected that FDI would catalyze change and impact on employment and the quality of jobs as well as living standards. Today, 15 years after the changes began, assessments of social and economic development and industrial relations are contradictory. Bulgaria is not at the centre of strong foreign investment attention, unlike Hungary, the Czech Republic and Poland. Bulgaria attracts only 3.3 per cent of FDI in the EU accession countries. In 2002, Bulgaria attracted only US$60 per capita, which is 20 times less than the amount for the Czech Republic, and 13 times less than for Estonia (CANSTAT, 2003). In the following years, the situation changed and the FDI flows to the countries of south-east Europe and the Commonwealth of Independent States (CIS) increased, reaching, in 2005, a relatively high level (US$40 billion). Inflows were fairly concentrated: three countries – Ukraine,

---

[3] National Statistical Institute, data for the first quarter of 2007.
[4] Since 1998 the largest trade union organization in the country, the Confederation of Independent Trade Unions in Bulgaria, began a permanent campaign in support of the ILO Declaration on Fundamental Principles and Rights at work.

Romania and the Russian Federation – accounted for close to three-quarters of the total. Bulgaria received US$2.2 billion, three times less than Romania (UNCTAD, 2006).

The impact of MNEs on the Bulgarian labour market is contradictory. The location of MNEs in the country creates employment, but in most cases restructuring after privatization by MNEs is accompanied by mass lay-offs, tension and conflict. At the same time, activities are being outsourced – mainly catering, transport, maintenance, and so on. This sometimes leads to the liquidation of these activities, and in other cases to the establishment of new companies, but with poorer employment conditions. While creating new jobs, the big trade chains (Metro, Billa, Ramstore, etc.) exercise competitive pressure on SMEs, leading to liquidations or job losses. Some of the enterprises bought by foreign investors have already been liquidated. Others are narrowing their investments. Taken together, all this has had a negative effect on the labour market, living standards and the economy in the regions concerned. Of course, there are also many MNEs that demonstrate strong economic interest in the country and continue to invest, some of them opening new subsidiaries and transferring good industrial relations practices.

In some cases, the labour legislation and core labour standards are neglected, undermining or putting under pressure the specific national regulating mechanisms, including trade union recognition and collective bargaining.

The survey reveals that on the whole MNEs have a positive impact on enterprise development in Bulgaria.[5] They bring new technologies and management skills, renovate labour organization and develop the culture of work. However, the point at issue is this: what is their role in the transformation of the organizational culture of enterprises and industrial relations? Should we assume that the European MNEs transfer European social values and models of corporate management, or rather that labour relations are threatened by erosion as a result of social dumping being applied?

The main survey findings show:

- Most of the MNEs surveyed have serious investment programmes aimed at technological renewal and the modernization of production.

- Corporate social responsibility is part of the MNEs' strategies in Bulgaria. Considerable investments are being made in environmental protection and the social development of local communities – mainly in health care, education, sport and infrastructure.

---

[5] It should be borne in mind that a simple extrapolation of the survey findings to the overall situation in the country is impossible – more than 150 MNE subsidiaries are operating in the country and we intentionally included in the survey only some of those with a trade union presence.

- Human resource management practices are being implemented and new programmes for staff training and development are being developed. Some of these programmes pay special attention to inculcating company aims and values in the staff, instilling a new work culture and motivation with the aim of increasing labour productivity and quality.

- During employment restructuring, new practices previously unknown in the Bulgarian system are being used, such as early retirement and voluntary redundancies accompanied by major compensation (severance payment equal to 3 to 17 times the gross monthly wages). A comparatively small number of companies has offered retraining courses prior to the workers being laid off.

- The priority for MNE managements is to modernize work organization. Nearly 70 per cent of the subsidiaries surveyed have made changes to their work organization, with the aim of increasing work efficiency and improving production quality and labour productivity. Teamwork, with job rotation, has been introduced, leading to flexibility and the development of personnel skills. Quite a number of MNEs have implemented schemes to collect employee suggestions for innovating on quality and productivity, work organization, management, and so on.

- In the MNEs surveyed, the trade union presence is significant. The trade union density is 67.4 per cent as compared with an average of 20–25 per cent for the country as a whole. In some MNEs, union membership is as much as 90–98 per cent (the subsidiaries of the Solvay Group, Belgium; American Standard, USA; Carlsberg Breweries A/S, Denmark). Trade union membership is stable, with new members being recruited in some MNEs. But some trade union structures, mainly in catering, transport and the maintenance departments of companies, have been lost in the process of outsourcing and subcontracting.

As shown by practical experience and existing traditions, industrial relations and social dialogue in Bulgaria are better developed in existing enterprises privatized by foreign investors than in enterprises built through "greenfield" investments – the more so as trade unions are not allowed into many such enterprises due to anti-union attitudes by employers. Privatized enterprises usually undertake significant reorganizations, more often than not causing redundancies. The new employers are interested in negotiating these changes with the trade unions, thus providing a balance of interests between the workers and the company.

Analysis of past phases in the development of the Bulgarian subsidiaries of MNEs points to the gradual establishment of a pragmatic and realistic pattern of collective bargaining. In most instances of dialogue and cooperation, the parties participating in the negotiating process seek a working formula through the application of modern practices typical of successful companies in pursuit of a common goal: higher productivity, stability and enterprise prosperity. As a rule, the labour and social terms agreed are better than those stipulated by law and significantly better than the average for the country.

The atmosphere during the process of bargaining and conclusion of collective agreements in most of the subsidiaries of the MNEs surveyed in Bulgaria is conducive to a new type of industrial relations, more adjusted to changes in economic life and society at a time of transition.

The findings of the survey show that the agreements reached in the area of remuneration are characterized by high wage levels (differentiated by job and staff categories) and as a rule these levels are much higher than both the average wage for the country and than for the corresponding sector. Higher compensation than that prescribed in the Bulgarian Labour Code and additional payments, as compared with the minimum standards required by the law, are agreed, i.e. for night shifts, hazardous working conditions and work on rest days and holidays.

The general impression is that in most cases the management and the trade union leaders categorize the terms agreed in the field of social policy as "good" and even "ideal" for Bulgarian conditions. In a number of cases, social benefits are reported to be "preserved" and even "further developed" after privatization. Thus, the collective agreements involving employees of MNEs are recognized as a tool for alleviating some negative consequences of the transition.

Despite these achievements, however, the practice shows that the wage levels in the Bulgarian subsidiaries are considerably lower than those in the subsidiaries in the developed countries; moreover, the largest number of rejected trade union and worker proposals and most frequent cases of refusal to bargain are registered in the social sphere, for example, concerning support for rest homes, preventive medicine facilities, sports facilities, swimming pools, etc. (on the pretext that they do not fit the company's priorities). At the same time, however, they are seen to be among the priorities of the corporate policy of the same multinationals in other countries, Eastern European countries included.

The examples of the successfully developing corporations included in the survey show that, in the course of negotiations, the parties agree to paid annual leave that is two to ten days above the provisions stipulated by the law. The agreements reached in the area of introducing additional pension and health insurance funded by MNEs can also be regarded as a positive development (American Standard Inc., USA; Nestlé, Switzerland; and the Solvay Group, Belgium can be cited as good examples in this area).

Comparison of the major agreements reached with MNEs and those at the sectoral and subsectoral level shows the MNEs in a favourable light. The better investment and technological climate and the established relations of bipartite cooperation in the subsidiaries of MNEs shape their behaviour – for example, they use sectoral collective agreements as a frame of reference and a principle rather than for the fixing of numerical values. In that section of the survey, the majority of union activists quote higher levels of negotiated minimum and start-up wages, higher compensation in case of employment contract termination, additional payments, and so on.

A good example of a balance between investment policy and social development in Sevlievo

People started talking about the "Bulgarian Hong Kong" in the middle of the 1990s, as the first results of a successful privatization project in Sevlievo (a small town in central northern Bulgaria with a population of 30,000 people) started to become apparent. Of major importance for the development of the town and the municipality was the "aggressive investment policy" of an American company planning to invest there. In 1992, a joint venture was created between Vidima (a company specialized in the production of bath and kitchen products, and fixtures and fittings for industry) and the American company, which then owned 51 per cent of the capital. Later on, following privatization in 1996 when Vidima was transformed into a joint stock company, the American corporation's equity increased to 99.2 per cent.

What are the major characteristics of this "aggressive policy"?

- In 1998, the biggest enterprise within the American company was opened in Sevlievo – for bath and kitchen fixtures and fittings, with 1,300 employees. Three new enterprises were opened in 2001 and 2002. By the end of 2006 the total investment by the American company amounted to over US$100 million, and also included the building of a four-star hotel and the construction of a gas main to the city. Over 2,100 jobs have been created.

- An extensive brand programme is under way, tailored to the needs of the clients. From the establishment of the joint venture up to the present day, production capacity has increased more than threefold. In terms of technical equipment, the technological level and working conditions, the Bulgarian enterprise does not differ from the company's branches elsewhere.

- The investment programme envisages improvements in the management system, information services and the skills level of the staff. Investment in human capital is a major priority, which in turn guarantees the competitiveness of the company on the international market. Over 300 people receive on-the-job training each year.

The sponsorship and charity initiatives of the MNE have strongly boosted the social development of the city and the municipality. Not only activities receive funding. The social infrastructure is also being refurbished and new infrastructure is being built. There are many examples of good work carried out for the benefit of the citizens and the development of the city.

Although most indicative, the example of the American company. is not an exception. A number of other foreign investors have launched projects in Sevlievo and this has greatly boosted the economic and social development of the region.

According to the United Nations Development Programme *Bulgaria Human Development Index* (UNDP, 2002), the economic profile of the municipality is exceptionally high. The gross value added per employee is above the average for the country and the municipality falls into the group of the best-developed economic regions in the country. The highly competitive environment generates on-going interest in modernization of the production units and further diversification of products and, very positively, even greater attention is paid to the introduction of up-to-date strategies for HRM and the development of the skills level of the staff.

Multinational enterprises and the challenges for the trade unions

Despite all the positive practices described above and the scope of the collective agreements in the MNEs, the survey shows that in some cases, the behaviour of certain foreign investors (large ones included) with respect to the liberalization of labour and social legislation creates difficulties for collective bargaining and gives rise to conflict situations.

The analysis of the findings from the interviews reveals that the most recurrent conflict issue in the process of collective bargaining is remuneration. In the key sectors and the large enterprises, it is the management who decides when, in what manner and by how much the remuneration and benefits will grow, and they do not allow the trade unions into consultations and negotiations on this matter. A serious problem is the lower remuneration level of the employees of MNEs in Bulgaria as compared with the branches of these companies in other countries. This is basically due to the low cost of labour and the lower living standards in the country.

Some of the new owners postpone or slow down the negotiations. Sometimes this results from a policy, spoken or unspoken, of ignoring the trade union organization in the enterprise, while in other instances it is determined by the stagnation of the market and the financial problems of the enterprise. In both cases, however, there is an attempt to cultivate conciliatory behaviour in some trade union leaders.

In some, albeit isolated, cases the trade union organizations have problems in getting all the necessary timely and comprehensive information from the employers, as needed for the preparation and signing of collective agreements. Normally the excuse is that this is a "company secret".

The trade union organizations in the MNEs are still experiencing difficulties in coordinating the collective bargaining process with the appropriate European trade union organizations and international trade union structures. They do not fully avail themselves of the latter's experience, standards, models and practices already in place, nor of the existing potential for positive influence and integration.

There are numerous examples of "greenfield" MNE investments where the employers obstruct the establishment and functioning of trade union organizations, or ban them overtly. This is a serious challenge to the national trade union organizations and a possible field for cooperation both with the trade unions in the subsidiaries in developed countries and with the GUFs.

The survey reveals that the collective bargaining practices and the collective agreements signed in the MNE branches strengthen the positive image of the trade unions. These have become important tools for the maintenance of trade union organization and a significant motivating factor for trade union membership. Furthermore, they are increasingly recognized as an instrument of CSR. This counteracts the attempts at uncontrolled liberalization of industrial relations, while promoting the sustainable development of the companies.

To face the challenges of globalization, the trade unions must reconsider their organizational structures and areas of action and internationalize them towards the promotion of the Decent Work Agenda. The extent to which unions succeed in changing the previously "standard" and tested patterns of trade union behaviour will determine how far they succeed in overcoming the dangers posed by globalization, namely deregulation and the disintegration of social protection and labour rights.

The growing influence of globalization and MNEs on the daily life of workers in Bulgaria and in south-east Europe increases the need for trade unions to strengthen their analytical capacity and cooperation with research institutions. In the countries of the region there is a lack of research on the problems of globalization and its impact on social, economic and trade union development during the transition process. It is necessary to undertake impact studies and research on industrial relations, trade union activities in MNEs, CSR, globalization, flexibilization, deregulation and liberalization, taking labour standards and ILO Conventions into account. The outcomes of research in these areas could become an instrument for strengthening the organizational structure, policy and bargaining power of trade unions in negotiations with MNEs and governments.

References

CANSTAT (National Statistical Institute). 2/2003.

Daskalova, N.; Tomev, L. 2000. *Multinational companies in Bulgaria: Challenges to industrial relations and trade unions* (Sofia, ISTUR and Friedrich Ebert Foundation). In Bulgarian.

—; —. 2004. *Multinational companies in Bulgaria: Challenges to industrial relations and trade unions – five years later* (Sofia, ISTUR and Friedrich Ebert Foundation). In Bulgarian.

Hoffmann, J.; Hoffmann, R. 1997. *Globalization: Risks and opportunities for labour policy in Europe*, Discussion and Working Papers, DWP 97. 04.01 (Brussels, ETUI).

Regnard, P. 2007. "Minimum wages 2007. Variations from 92 to 1,570 euro gross per month", in *Statistics in focus: Population and social conditions*, No. 71/2007 (Luxembourg, EUROSTAT).

Sengenberger, W. 2002. *Globalization and social progress: The role and impact of international labour standards* (Bonn, Friedrich Ebert Foundation).

UNCTAD (United Nations Conference on Trade and Development). 2005. *World Investment Report 2005. Overview. Transnational corporations and the internationalization of R&D* (New York and Geneva).

—. 2006. *World Investment Report 2006. Overview. FDI from developing and transition economies: Implications for development* (New York and Geneva).

UNDP (United Nations Development Programme). 2002. *Bulgaria Human Development Index: Municipalities in the context of districts* (Sofia).

Vitols, S. 2003. *Management cultures in Europe: European works councils and human resource management in multinational enterprises* (Berlin, Social Science Research Center).

FREEDOM OF ASSOCIATION AND COLLECTIVE BARGAINING: THE PRACTICE OF MULTINATIONAL COMPANIES IN BRAZIL

7

Clóvis Scherer
Instituto Observatório Social, São Paulo, Brazil

Introduction

This contribution presents the results of studies on 18 subsidiaries of MNEs operating in Brazil, concerning their practices in relation to freedom of association and collective bargaining. Although generalizations cannot be made about the conduct of all of the multinationals in Brazil[1] in relation to trade unionism, this synthesis seeks to assist in the analysis of this issue.

Instituto Observatório Social (IOS – Social Observatory Institute) has been researching corporate conduct in Brazil as a form of social vigilance over large national and multinational companies. The institute works closely with Brazilian trade unions, foreign trade union confederations and global unions. It is hoped that the study will stimulate social dialogue between trade unions and the corporations in order to achieve solutions to the problems identified by the research.

The companies that were the subject of these studies are part of large corporate groups in Brazil. Focusing on the specific interests of the trade unions that requested the studies, the scope of the research generally was limited to one or more subsidiary companies or specific plants in the case of industrial companies, or one or more areas of operations for service sector companies. This limit was defined in cooperation with the trade unions and was often negotiated with the companies themselves.

These studies were conducted at different times between 1999 and 2003, when Brazil was undergoing a phase of low economic growth, high

---

[1] The census of foreign capital in Brazil conducted by the Central Bank found 9,712 companies with 50 per cent or more of their capital controlled by foreigners in Brazil in the year 2000.

Table 7.1 Company revenue and number of employees Brazil, 1999–2003

Companies	Revenue or sales (R$ million)	Employees of the corporation in Brazil	Employees in subsidiary companies studied
Akzo Nobel	849	2 426	1 052
Banco Real	784	22 247	22 247
Bayer S.A.	1 190	1 510	1 143
Bompreço S.A.	3 309	21 823	21 823
Embratel	7 270	7 206	7 206
Light Serviços de Eletricidade	8 577	5 200	5 200
Moto Honda da Amazônia	–	–	3 876
Nokia Brasil	773*	1 466	1 087
Parmalat	1 155	4 803	382
Philips da Amazônia	2 400	4 000	1 092
Robert Bosch Ltda	2 500	11 413	7 637
Santander Meridional	430	8 250	1 323
ThyssenKrupp Elevadores	2 880	–	571
ThyssenKrupp Fundições Ldta	–	–	1 341
Unilever Divisão Higiene e Beleza	7 300	15 000	1 203
Wal-Mart do Brazil Ltda	780	6 000	–

Source: Social Observatory Institute.
* million euros

unemployment and oscillating currency exchange rates. The period was also marked by initiatives for the flexibilization of labour relations, such as the use of subcontracting systems, flexible hours and variable pay. This environment contributed to tense labour relations.

The companies were chosen because they were among the leaders in their segments. Their annual sales or revenues exceeded R$700 million (US$227 million at the average exchange rate for 2003). Where data were available, the number of people employed by each group was at least 1,400 directly contracted workers (see table 7.1).

Most of the companies/plants (12) were located in the south-eastern part of the country, which is Brazil's most industrialized region and has the strongest tradition of union activity. Three of the companies were located in the north, in the Manaus Export Processing Zone. Two are in the southern region[2] and one in the north-east.

---

[2] One of the studies focused on business units located in Brazil's southern and south-eastern regions.

Table 7.2 Companies studied, sectors of activity, controlling group and country of origin

Subsidiary studied	Sector	Controlling company	Country
Wal-Mart do Brazil Ltda	Retail sales	Wal-Mart	USA
Light Serviços de Eletricidade	Electrical energy	Electricité de France	France
Parmalat	Food industry	Parmalat	Italy
Moto Honda da Amazônia	Metalworking	Honda Motor	Japan
Santander Meridional	Financial	Santander	Spain
Banco Real	Financial	ABN-Amro	Netherlands
Embratel	Telecommunications	MCI	USA
Nokia Brasil	Electronics	Nokia	Finland
Akzo Nobel	Chemical and pharmaceutical	Akzo Nobel	Netherlands
Unilever Divisão Higiene e Beleza	Chemical	Unilever	Netherlands
ThyssenKrupp Elevadores	Metalworking and services	ThyssenKrupp	Germany
ThyssenKrupp Fundições Ldta	Iron and steel	ThyssenKrupp	Germany
Philips da Amazônia	Electronics	Philips	Netherlands
Bompreço S.A.	Retail sales	Ahold	Netherlands
Bayer S.A.	Chemical and pharmaceutical	Bayer	Germany
Robert Bosch Ltda	Metallurgical	Bosch	Germany

Source: Social Observatory Institute.

The national origin of the capital in these companies was predominantly European, coming from six countries (see table 7.2). This, to a large degree, is a reflection of the partnerships that the Social Observatory Institute (IOS) has maintained with Dutch and German trade union centres. There is a low representation of American companies in the group (two), although more of the multinationals operating in Brazil are headquartered in the United States than in any other country.

The companies conduct industrial, service and retail operations. The industrial companies were dominated by those in metalworking, chemicals, electronics and food. The service companies were in the financial, telecommunications and electrical energy sectors. In commerce, the companies studied operate in the supermarket sector.

References for evaluation of the companies

The IOS adopted the ILO Declaration on Fundamental Principles and Rights at Work (Core Labour Rights – CLR) as its reference for the evaluation of working conditions and union relations at the companies. The themes of health and safety at work were added as well as environmental protection, given their importance for the workers.

Two steps were necessary so that these international standards could be used as references in the analysis of company practices. The first was to convert international and national standards into criteria for the evaluation of corporate conduct. The second was to compare international standards with the Brazilian reality, legislation and practice of labour relations.

To define the indicators related to the right to freedom of association, it was necessary to consider that the corporatist model of union organization in Brazil guarantees the right to unionization. The model allows the existence of only one union for each professional category that legally represents workers, even those who are not union members, in their territorial area of operation. There are legally representative unions for the large majority of waged workers in the country.[3] Most of these unions have a small territorial base (73 per cent of them cover just one municipality) and small memberships (93 per cent have fewer than 5,000 members). But the single union system does not prevent various unions from operating at a given company, because they are divided into different occupational categories. Subcontracting aggravates the negative effects of this division, because a large portion of the subcontracted workers are not part of the majority union membership, which is normally the most active in the company.

On the other hand, the representation of workers and the presence of union representatives within companies and at workplaces are quite rare in Brazil. Less than half of the unions of salaried urban workers have a union delegate at their workplace. There are only 168 works councils (factory commissions) in Brazil and only 1,000 of nearly 10,000 unions said they were aware of the existence of a works council.

In relation to the right to freedom of association, the indicators chosen focused on the possibilities for a worker to join the existing union, the existence of representative organizations of employees, the presence of union representatives at the workplaces and recognition and respect for union decisions, movements and agreements (table 7.3).

Concerning the right to collective bargaining, labour issues in Brazil are regulated by the Federal Constitution (1988) and principally by the Consolidated

---

[3] According to Instituto Brasileiro de Geografia e Estatística (IBGE), in 2001, unions of urban employees in Brazil represented 31.7 million workers (total union base) and there were 9.2 million union members (*Pesquisa Sindical 2001*, 2001). In that year, there were 36.7 million employees in non-agricultural activities in the country (Pesquisa Nacional por Amostra de Domicílios [PNAD] data).

Freedom of association and collective bargaining

Table 7.3   Freedom of association – indicators and description

Indicator	Description
Freedom of organization	Workers' freedom to unionize
	Respect for the right to organize at the workplace
	Freedom of union entities to draw up their own rules
Freedom of union action	Access of union leaders to the workplace and freedom of communication with workers
Union recognition	Recognition of the decisions of union organizations, as approved in assemblies
	Respect for the right to strike
	Compliance with decisions taken in agreement with the union

Source: Social Observatory Institute.

Labour Laws (1943). Standards issued by the federal Government define the implementation of the regulations and, above all, decisions of the Labour Court establish the interpretations of or may even, at times, create rules.

Since the 1990s, there has been debate in Brazil about making this legislation more flexible, partly through a series of "isolated" changes in labour regulations such as: permission for so-called "hour banks" (flexibilization of the work shift and overtime payments), the creation of temporary labour contracts, institutionalization of lay-offs, stimulation of flexible pay schemes, and so on.

Collective bargaining effectively returned to the country in the late 1970s and is thus relatively recent and quite limited. It is complementary to the law and principally defines the annual pay rise, basic pay, benefits and some union rights. Collective agreements and company agreements usually have a duration of one or two years and are no longer valid after they expire. This places workers at a disadvantage because they are faced with the possible automatic loss of their rights, creating pressure on them to sign a new agreement. The alternative is to request the intervention of the Labour Court. This can also be required by the Government, if there is a strike.

Thus, the existence of direct negotiations between the company and the union and the conditions needed so that workers' representatives, whether they are unionists or not, can undertake effective negotiations, are the central indicators related to the right to collective bargaining. The other indicators derive from these, since information about the companies or units is one of the necessary conditions for effective bargaining. In the case of MNEs, it is essential that the Brazilian subsidiaries have the authorization to negotiate, and that they do not threaten to transfer their activities as a negotiating ploy (table 7.4).

Table 7.4   Collective bargaining – indicators, description and sources

Indicator	Description
Right to collective bargaining effective	Direct negotiations between company and union
	Offer workers' representatives the conditions needed for negotiations
	Make possible direct negotiations in each country of operation
	Do not threaten to transfer activities to other countries in order to influence negotiations
Right to information for collective bargaining	Offer the information necessary for effective negotiations, with data about the units and the company as a whole

Source: Social Observatory Institute.

Results

Freedom of association

In all of the cases studied, there were unions legally recognized as representatives of the predominant category of qualified workers employed (such as metalworkers, chemical workers and so on). But there were also other unions representing specific smaller groups of qualified workers. So, most companies had more than one representative union and sometimes even dozens. For example, 12 unions were noted at Akzo, 20 at Bompreço and more than 30 at ThyssenKrupp Elevadores.

There were also union representatives of occupational categories other than the major ones, such as engineers, secretaries, mid-level technicians, and others, within each corporate unit.

The workers in subcontracting companies are not represented by the same union as represents the directly contracted personnel, but this union often intermediates for subcontracted workers and seeks a solution to problems with the contracting company.

The rate of unionization is quite varied. Based on the average rate of unionization among waged urban workers in the country, which is 29 per cent,[4] an arbitrary five-level scale can be constructed: very low = 0–10 per cent; low = 10–20 per cent; medium = 20–35 per cent; high = 35–70 per cent; very high = above 70 per cent. In these terms, of the 18 distinct situations, 13 can be considered medium to very high, while the other five are below medium (see table 7.5). This reflects a positive general situation.

---

[4] Calculated according to *Pesquisa Sindical 2001*, by IBGE.

Freedom of association and collective bargaining

Although the number of employees with a union mandate at these companies is quite variable, we can surmise that the information about the two banks is applicable to all of the banks in the country. Similar generalizations cannot be made on the basis of the studies in other sectors. However, only two companies did not have union leaders among their employees, which shows the importance that these companies have within the union membership (we do not have information for the other four companies).

The union leaders have access to the workplaces to undertake communication activities with the workers, but frequently depend on the authorization of company management. This can be considered a potential limiting factor, especially during disputes with the company. In addition, access by leaders of the workers' organizations who were not employees of the company was even more difficult. In some cases, their access to certain areas of the establishments was prohibited or restricted.

At only one company (Bayer S.A.) did the studies find the existence of an organization that represented personnel, such as a works council, as defined by

Table 7.5   Freedom of association – results

Company	Unionization rate	Union representatives	Discrimination against union participation (%) *
Akzo Nobel	Low/Medium	0	–
Banco Real	High	298	–
Bayer S.A.**	Low/High	2 and 17	2.4
Bompreço S.A.	Medium	–	–
Embratel	–	–	–
Light Serviços de Eletricidade	Very high	–	5
Moto Honda da Amazônia	Medium	5	40
Nokia Brasil	Very low	0	–
Parmalat	–	–	–
Philips da Amazônia	Medium	4	37
Robert Bosch Ltda **	High/Very high	5 and 7	8 and 16
Santander Meridional	High	100	–
ThyssenKrupp Elevadores	Medium	3	3
ThyssenKrupp Fundições	Medium	7	8
Unilever	Very low/High	–	30
Wal-Mart do Brazil Ltda	Very low	1	–

Source: Instituto Observatório Social.
* Percentage of responses stating that there was discrimination against union participation in the company.
** Two different plants were studied.

the collective agreement and exclusively composed of elected representatives. But, even so, the relationships between the factory commission and the union were negatively affected by standards that restrict the participation of unionists in the election to the commission. Another company had a mixed commission with representatives nominated by the company and elected by the workers. This served to channel demands to the company. On the other hand, all the companies studied were required to have operating internal accident prevention committees, and all do so.

In contrast, some companies also have some form of internal participation by the employees in activities linked to the improvement of production and the quality of the product and process.

In general, no open discrimination against unionization was found as a company policy. But the unionists interviewed frequently accused managers of exercising some type of pressure against unionization or participation in union activities or of inducing the workers to think that it would be harmful to their employment or professional careers. Despite the different formats of the surveys, at seven companies the percentage of responses indicating some type of discriminatory action against unionization or participation in union activity was 2–16 per cent of the total. Only in three cases did responses of this type reach significant percentages, of 30–40 per cent, but this was in companies where the rate of unionization was average or high.

The sample studies revealed that the workers did, as a rule, receive printed material from the unions (70–90 per cent of those interviewed), but that a much lower percentage maintained direct contact with trade unionists.

The studies identified two concrete cases of attitudes contrary to union organization, in the form of lay-offs of union leaders either in the past or during the studies. Other complaints concerned discrimination against union leaders regarding career advancement and salary increases. But the most critical points were certainly the lack of coordination among unions that represented workers within one company and the absence of employee representation bodies within each workplace.

Collective bargaining

The studies show that the companies were governed mainly by collective agreements negotiated between the local unions and the employers' organizations (13) (see table 7.6). Ten companies had direct negotiation processes with local unions. Only one of the companies was governed by an agreement signed directly with the majority union.

The central issue here is the limited scope of the collective bargaining. No company negotiated internal standards (for example, job and wage plans

Freedom of association and collective bargaining

Table 7.6 Collective bargaining – results

Company	CCT	ACT	Profit sharing bargaining participant
Akzo Nobel	X	–	–
Banco Real	X	X	–
Bayer S.A.	X	X	Trade union + commission
Bompreço S.A.	X		One of the many local trade unions
Embratel	–	–	–
Light Serviços de Eletricidade		X	Trade union
Moto Honda da Amazônia	X		–
Nokia Brasil	X	X	Trade union
Parmalat	X	X	Trade union
Philips da Amazônia	X	X	Commission
Robert Bosch Ltda	X	X	Trade union
Santander Meridional	X	X	Trade union
ThyssenKrupp Elevadores	X		Commission
ThyssenKrupp Fundições	X	X	Trade union + commission
Unilever	–	–	–
Wal-Mart do Brazil Ltda	X	X	None

Source: Instituto Observatório Social.

CCT: Convenção Coletiva de Trabalho (collective labour contract signed between trade union and employer organization)

ACT: Acordo Coletivo de Trabalho (collective labour agreement signed between trade union and a company)

or personnel management policies) with the unions. Many unionists interviewed did not know of and did not interfere in decisions concerning job and function descriptions, pay scales, job promotion mechanisms, criteria for performance evaluation and other aspects of personnel management.

The standard practice is for the union to be limited to negotiating the so-called basic wage (sectoral minimum wage) upon which companies build their pay structures. Since the agreements apply to a municipality or region, each of them has a different basic wage, resulting in different pay structures within a single company. This was quite clear at companies in the retail sector, which have quite broad areas of operation.

Another theme which completely escapes the realm of collective bargaining is that of training, which is considered a prerogative of the employer.

It should be noted that the implantation of flexible systems for work shifts and pay is, by law, conditional on negotiation with the union (or with a commission of employees). So the companies usually seek to negotiate with the unions in such a way as to obtain advantages from these systems (reduction of additional wages and of social security payments). Various unions have not agreed to negotiate some of these points, precisely because of the adverse circumstances and the threat of a reduction of labour rights.

Profit- and income-sharing is the most visible form of flexible remuneration in the country. A distinction can be made between companies that identify the union as the interlocutor in this negotiation, and those that opt to give priority to specific commissions for this discussion. The attempt to exclude the union is evaluated as a form of weakening the employees' negotiating capacity. Thus, at seven companies this negotiation took place with the active participation of the union and at two others, with a commission with little or no union participation. In one of the cases, the rules were simply not negotiated, while in the other, only one of the many unions had discussed them (i.e. the others were excluded). There was not enough information about five companies.

The lack of the information needed for effective negotiations appears to be a critical issue. In addition to the dearth of information about internal personnel management norms, in most cases unionists do not have access to indicators and data about company performance. Most of the companies studied do not have publicly traded shares and are thus not required by law to disclose their balance sheets, much less to publish a social report.

On the other hand, there is one way in which information is made available to workers' representatives, through developments where companies have sought to be more transparent to the internal and external public, either through management systems that seek the involvement of workers or through the diffusion of the concept of CSR (the issuing of social reports, for example).

It is important to mention the limited coordination of the negotiating processes, reflecting the type of union organization previously described. Only at the two banks studied, and in an initial stage at Unilever and Bosch, were there some types of union organization that could promote this coordination. The very studies and parallel activities undertaken by the labour confederation Central Única dos Trabalhadores (CUT – Single Workers' Confederation) and the IOS sought to support and stimulate the creation of union committees or networks that could conduct negotiations in a more joined-up way.

Conclusions

The results show that there is no uniform conduct among the companies studied. It is apparent that these MNEs follow the labour relations standards pertaining in Brazil, with little importation of standards from their countries of origin. This is the case, for example, for representation at the workplace.

The Brazilian union model guarantees the existence of unions and certain general conditions for freedom for unionization that company practices can limit, but not entirely suppress. The rates of unionization at the companies studied were higher than the national average and reflect a greater union presence, indicated by the number of union leaders employed at companies.

The major restriction noted by the workers employed at these companies, concerning their ability to collectively intervene in the internal labour conditions of the companies, was that the right to organization at the workplace is poorly developed.

The results related to the other indicators selected for the theme of freedom of association, considering the differences between companies and certain isolated restrictions, were positive (in terms of access to the workplaces, recognition of union decisions and compliance with agreements reached).

Concerning collective bargaining, it was also found that there are prevailing practices of both sectoral and direct negotiations. The deficiencies in this case are more closely linked to the lack of information about the companies and the absence of coordination for negotiations at the corporate or group level. This point is particularly critical when a company undergoes a restructuring process that has a strong impact on employment.

So what could and should trade unions do to make a difference? It should first be considered that a process is under way to transform labour relations in Brazil, with the Government proposing to address some of the issues cited, such as the demand for a real legitimacy for unions, financial contributions linked to negotiation and a new system for conflict resolution in collective bargaining and workplace-level organizing. This reform will have a strong impact on all of the points examined here, if in fact the current model of union organization is altered.

Putting this reform, which still has to pass through the legislative process, to one side, Brazilian unions that act within large companies can limit their deficiencies if they give priority to creating ways to coordinate their actions and, in particular, the collective bargaining processes. The experience of the Social Observatory Europe Project[5] is illustrative, because it resulted in the creation of forums for social dialogue among some of these companies and groups of unions, confederations and the CUT (Bayer, ThyssenKrupp, Akzo Nobel, Bompreço). The impacts reported in these experiences were the broadening of freedom of activity of union leaders among the workers at these companies and greater access to information about company strategies. It is hoped that concrete measures that can improve working conditions will be implemented in the medium term.

---

[5] This project was a partnership between the IOS, the German DGB [Deutsche Gewerkschaftsbund] and the Dutch FNV (Federatie Nederlandse Vakbeweging) and aimed at the promotion of dialogue among trade unions, works councils and companies of three German MNEs (Bayer, Bosch and ThyssenKrupp) and three Dutch multinationals (ABN-Amro, Ahold and Unilever).

Brazilian unions can also use their own networks as instruments for information exchange and mutual preparation for talks with the companies.

To improve worker representation, the study showed that it would be possible to build up a broad network of trade unionists and other types of worker representatives within these companies, including members of internal accident prevention committees, as a way of broadening union power to influence working conditions in companies. To do so, it is important to revive this objective, which was one of the main issues for trade unionism in the 1980s and which was ignored in the defensive phase of the 1990s.

Concerning the social indicators chosen and the methodology employed, one consideration is that, as the IOS became known within the companies, and principally to the unions, doors were opened to the realization of more complete studies, with the use of more refined research techniques. It is important to note that in the more recent studies, the companies agreed to open their doors so that researchers could survey workers' opinions by means of questionnaires on the basis of statistically representative samples. In this sense, it is already possible to argue that the evaluation indicators should be redefined, to allow greater quantitative precision and greater comparability among companies and to accompany changes over time with greater precision. These steps may be very useful in the near future, when an important reform may be implemented.

References

All research reports of the studies on which this paper is based are available at the IOS website (www.observatoriosocial.org.br).

Boito Junior, A. 2004. *O sindicalismo tem futuro*, mimeo.

Cacciamali, M.C.; Brito, A. 2002. "A flexibilização restrita e descentralizada das relações de trabalho no Brasil", in *Revista da Abet*, Vol. 2, No. 2, pp. 91–120.

Cardoso, A.M. 2000. *Brazilian central union federations at the crossroads*, paper prepared for delivery at the conference "National Labor Confederations in Brazil and South Korea", Berkeley, CA, 13–14 May.

IBGE (Instituto Brasileiro de Geografia e Estatística). 2001. *Pesquisa Sindical 2001*.

ICFTU (International Confederation of Free Trade Unions). 2001. *A trade union guide to globalisation* (Brussels).

Krein, J.D. 2003. "Balanço da reforma trabalhista do governo FHC", in M.W. Proni and W. Henrique (eds): *Trabalho, mercado e sociedade: o Brasil nos anos 90* (São Paulo, Editora Unesp; Campinas, Instituto de Economia da Unicamp), pp. 279–322.

Tuma, F. 1999. *Participação nos lucros ou resultados: incentivo à eficiênica ou substituição dos salários?* (São Paulo, Editora LTR).

TRADE AND DEVELOPMENT IN SOUTH AFRICA

8

Neva Seidman Makgetla and Tanya van Meelis
Congress of South African Trade Unions, Johannesburg

Introduction

Debates on trade have generally failed to question the assumption that free trade supports development. For its part, the international labour movement has essentially argued that core labour standards are necessary to prevent a race to the bottom. But if trade leads, not to development, but to worse poverty and unemployment, core labour standards will not do much to improve conditions for workers.

The South African experience demonstrates both that trade in itself is not necessarily developmental, and that labour rights alone do not ensure better pay. The opening of the economy following the ending of apartheid in the early 1990s was associated with both growing exports and imports and soaring unemployment – in 2007 close to 30 per cent.[1] In these circumstances, although the democratic state introduced strong labour rights, workers saw falling pay and continual pressure on their conditions.

The main reason for extraordinarily high unemployment lay in the structure of the economy developed under apartheid. Given this economic trajectory, the State's efforts to encourage increased access to foreign markets, especially with countries in the South, tended to undermine light industry. They increased opportunities principally for capital-intensive sectors, notably minerals, chemicals and car manufacture, which did not create much employment.

This experience points to the need for a strong structural policy to support sectors that can create employment, especially agriculture, light industries and

---

[1] This figure does not include those who would immediately take paid employment, but are too discouraged actively to seek work. Inclusion of these people as unemployed raises the unemployment rate to 40 per cent.

services. That, in turn, requires a trade policy that encourages and supports employment-creating activities. The challenge for labour becomes to engage both within South Africa in defining more specific policy measures and internationally to ensure that international and bilateral arrangements leave space for measures to support specific sectors.

This paper first reviews the central challenges facing the South African economy, above all, those of unemployment and growth. It then looks at the impact of trade on poverty and employment. The third section outlines the nature of labour rights and assesses the trends in workers' pay and conditions. Finally, we consider the implications for the labour movement's claims regarding trade.

Unemployment and economic growth in South Africa

From the first democratic elections in 1994, the unemployment rate rose steadily from 16 per cent to around 30 per cent in 2002. In the early 2000s, it declined to just over 25 per cent. In these circumstances, it is not surprising that inequalities related to class, race and gender persisted and possibly even deepened. The former homeland areas – the reserves where about half of Africans were legally confined under apartheid – lagged far behind the rest of the country. Despite the emergence of a small but vibrant black elite in the state and the private sector, most Africans continued as poorly paid workers, or scraped out an existence as hawkers or subsistence farmers in the former homeland areas (see UNDP, 2003; PCAS, 2003).

The combination of high unemployment and, in some sectors, very poor pay meant that South Africa remained amongst the most inequitable economies in the world. Soaring unemployment was associated with relatively slow growth, particularly in the late 1990s. South Africa's economic performance did not match up to other middle-income countries for most of the period after independence.

In the mid-2000s, the economy began to grow much more rapidly, at over 3 per cent a year. This upswing largely reflected a short-term speculative inflow of foreign capital combined with a relaxation in fiscal and monetary policy. It was associated with a substantial increase in the balance of trade deficit.

In this period, retail trade and construction accounted for well over half of all employment growth. This pattern reflected the roots of growth in cheap imports and government investment. The sustainability of the expansion and the resulting jobs thus remained rather dubious, since it depended largely on maintenance of high real interest rates by international standards combined with strong prices for mining products.

In short, while the South African State made considerable progress in overcoming the legacy of apartheid, results did not match up to the (admittedly very optimistic) expectations held by much of the population before 1994.

Shortcomings emerged primarily in the inability to overcome the interlinked challenges of high unemployment and massive inequalities in incomes and assets. The question here is how the opening of the economy from the early 1990s contributed to this outcome.

Trade, employment and poverty

To understand the impact of trade on poverty and employment, we can look at its effects on:

- employment;
- the structure of ownership;
- government's ability to provide services; and
- the prices of commodities needed by low-income consumers.

The impact on employment and household incomes depends largely on the structure of trade. If it is dominated by capital-intensive sectors, even a substantial improvement in exports may do little to alleviate poverty. Moreover, if imports are dominated by light industry, firms may respond by mergers and retrenchments in order to take advantage of economies of scale to compete with imports.

The effects on the public treasury are even more ambiguous. If trade stimulates overall growth, the government should have more resources available. But increased economic openness is usually associated with greater freedom for capital flows. Many governments respond by adopting conservative fiscal and monetary policies in an effort to attract and retain speculative inflows. That, in turn, can lead to substantial cuts in anti-poverty programmes and in public-sector employment. Moreover, it may have a contractionary impact on the economy as a whole.

Finally, the effects of trade on consumption depend largely on income distribution. The poor usually rely on imports for only a small share of their needs. If labour-intensive imports displace local producers, the net benefits for the poor may be limited indeed.

In the event, analysis of South Africa's trade indicated that it did little to create jobs or alleviate poverty. First, exports remained concentrated in highly capital-intensive sectors, while imports competed heavily with light industry. Second, the Government cut the budget through the late 1990s explicitly to retain foreign portfolio investment. This limited its ability to provide services for the poor. Finally, concentrated retail networks generally did not pass on the benefits of cheaper imports of food and clothing to consumers.

For trade to assist in alleviating South Africa's overwhelming unemployment problem, a much more differentiated approach was required. Simply growing trade on the existing trajectory might help maintain macroeconomic stability, but would not do much to create employment, increase equality or enhance economic diversification. That would require, in particular, much more coherent and substantial efforts to support relatively labour-intensive sectors.

To understand the impact of trade on economic structure requires a brief overview of the historic growth path of the South African economy. The subsequent section explores how trade affected poverty and employment.

The South African growth path

Historically, the South African economy was focused on extractive industries. This structure formed a central factor behind persistent high unemployment (see Makgetla, 2004a). The formal sector, historically centred on minerals and, more recently, heavy chemicals and automobile manufacture, are relatively capital intensive, and cannot create employment on a large scale even when expanding. Moreover, this kind of capital-intensive industry generally fosters highly concentrated ownership.

Largely to generate cheap labour for the mines and white-owned estates, the colonial and later apartheid State deprived the majority of the population of productive assets and opportunities. From the turn of the 20th century until 1994, Africans in particular – over three-quarters of the population – were largely denied access to land, education, training, and formal-sector facilities such as the banking sector and retail marketing. As a result, most people had little scope for earning a living outside of paid jobs in the formal sector.

Shifts in economic structure since 1994 did little to remedy these problems. The main changes were:

- In the minerals sector, a move from gold to platinum mining, plus growth in aluminium, ferro-chrome and steel refining.

- In manufacturing, faster growth in heavy chemicals and automobile manufacture, with relative stagnation in light industry.

- Rapid expansion of business services, in value terms in finance and in employment in security and retail, with a decline in the public sector.

- A decline in construction through the 1990s, followed by very rapid growth from the early 2000s, initially for a high-income housing boom and, from the mid-2000s, for public investment projects.

- Rising capital intensity and substantial job losses in commercial farming.

The trends in the 1990s were associated with a shift toward greater capital intensity, so that increases in output and exports did not create employment on the necessary scale. Between 1998 and 2002, formal employment grew only about 1 per cent a year, or about half as fast as the population.

Labour absorption picked up from 2002, mostly because employment rose in construction, retail and security services. These sectors were highly cyclical, however, and growth could slow or even reverse if overall economic expansion declined.

Various indicators showed the trend toward a more capital-intensive economy through the early 2000s. The fastest growth in output occurred in the most capital-intensive sectors, led by telecommunications and basic non-ferrous metals. In contrast, light industry showed relatively little expansion.

As might be expected, the result of this growth pattern was a shift in the production structure toward heavy industry and away from light industry. The share of agriculture, gold mining, light manufacturing, public and most private services has declined. The winners were steel, platinum and aluminium refining; heavy chemicals; automobile; communications; and finance – all of which were relatively capital-intensive.

In short, growth since 1994 did little to diversify the economy. Instead, it was associated with continued dominance by mining and the heavy industries favoured under apartheid. This pattern resulted largely from the way South Africa integrated with the world economy. The expansion in retail, construction and security services after 2002 reflected the commodity-based boom rather than a long-term redirection of the economy.

The impact of trade on employment and poverty

Before 1989, when Nelson Mandela was released from prison, South Africa was relatively isolated from world trade, in part because of protectionist policies, in part because of resistance to apartheid and the disinvestment campaign. This situation changed rapidly from the early 1990s, as anti-apartheid sanctions disappeared, the political situation stabilized, and the country joined the General Agreement on Tariffs and Trade (GATT, now the WTO) at the cost of substantial tariff cuts.

The democratic government – or at least the Department of Trade and Industry (DTI) – embraced the philosophy of free trade with enthusiasm. According to its Integrated Manufacturing Strategy, "…the purpose of reforms [after 1994] was clearly aligned towards an opening up the economy, enhancing competitiveness, improved access to economic opportunities and greater geographic equity [within the country]" (DTI, 2002).

An initial belief that free trade in itself would stimulate growth gave way, by the 2000s, to a competitiveness strategy. In this approach, the State seeks to encourage a more efficient economy by improving infrastructure and skills, while maintaining a fairly narrow focus on promoting exports as the driver for growth (see DTI, 2002; PCAS, 2003). In 2004, the Government's medium-term Programme of Action emphasized improving infrastructure, cutting input costs, encouraging higher investment and bringing about "the earliest possible conclusion of trade agreements with Mercosur, EFTA, the US, India and China" (South African Government, 2004).

The opening of the economy saw rapid growth in South African trade. The spurt in imports in 2003 and 2004 reflected the strong appreciation of the rand. Between 1995 and the third quarter of 2004, in real terms, exports rose 37 per cent and imports by 43 per cent.

Despite the growth in volume, the structure of trade seemed unlikely to generate employment on the necessary scale. Specifically, South Africa's exports remained geared primarily toward relatively capital-intensive sectors – notably minerals, heavy chemicals and automobile manufacture. Expansion in these sectors did little to contribute to employment creation or more equitable ownership and control. Meanwhile, given relatively slow economic growth, increased imports of labour-intensive goods and services tended to displace domestic employment.

Very strong regional differences in the structure of trade also emerged. The Southern African Development Community (SADC) and the EU formed key markets for South African exports of labour-intensive products, while heavy industry dominated sales to China. Moreover, by 2004 China was fast becoming the dominant source of labour-intensive imports by South Africa.

South Africa's exports were considerably more capital intensive than its imports. Half of exports were relatively capital intensive, with R500,000 in capital for each employee. In contrast, just under half of imports were relatively labour intensive, with under R170,000 invested per job. This pattern suggests that increased exports did little to create employment directly, while rising imports displaced jobs on a larger scale.

The dominance of capital-intensive exports declined in the late 1990s, but regained some ground from 2002. The average capital intensity of South African exports was virtually the same in real terms in 2003 as it was in 1994.

In contrast, the bulk of South African imports were relatively labour intensive, although the share of highly labour-intensive imports declined from the late 1990s through the early 2000s. The average capital intensity of imports, excluding petroleum, rose by just over a quarter between 1994 and 2003.

Exports were capital intensive because they were dominated by minerals, automobile and heavy chemicals (largely derived from coal mining, as a result of heavy state investments in an oil-from-coal process before 1994). Between 1994 and 2003, as a percentage of total exports, automobile exports rose at the cost of mining and minerals, but little else changed. In contrast, almost half of all imports were machinery and equipment, autos and appliances of various kinds. Imports of transport equipment rose almost as fast as exports by the auto industry.

In short, the overall pattern of trade remained essentially characterized by exports of resource-based goods, with the exception of the automobile industry. Consumer and capital equipment still dominated imports, which were generally much more diverse. This pattern clearly limited the potential for job creation through trade. Moreover, it left South Africa vulnerable to shifts in world commodity markets, with little sign of the broader economic diversification needed for stable growth.

Underlying the overall trends in imports and exports were substantial differences in South African trade with different regions. The EU, United States and SADC were the main markets for relatively labour-intensive goods. In contrast, China, India and Brazil bought mostly minerals and heavy chemicals from South Africa, but exported mainly light industrial goods.

These patterns are largely reversed when it comes to imports by South Africa:[2]

- For the EU, minerals comprised 42 per cent of South Africa's exports, automobiles 9 per cent and agricultural goods 7 per cent. South Africa's imports from the EU were mostly transport equipment and automobile inputs (30 per cent of the total), machinery (20 per cent) and appliances (15 per cent).

- SADC imports from South Africa were much more diversified, and included a far higher share of manufactures – over three-quarters of the total. Chemicals comprised 15 per cent, machinery and equipment 12 per cent and food 10 per cent. SADC's exports to South Africa were dominated by mining and agricultural products, at around 25 per cent each.

- In contrast, some 60 per cent of Chinese imports from South Africa were mineral products, with heavy chemicals at 8 per cent. Meanwhile, China's exports to South Africa were predominantly light industrial goods: 25 per cent clothing, textiles and shoes, 20 per cent appliances and 22 per cent machinery and equipment.

The most notable trend was the extraordinary growth in imports from developing countries, especially China. While overall imports rose by just

---

[2] The following data are calculated from TIPS EasyData (downloaded in November 2004 from www.tips.org.za).

under 60 per cent in dollar terms between 1994 and 2003, imports from China, Brazil and India tripled. In contrast, South African exports to China doubled and to Brazil remained virtually unchanged. Only in the case of India did exports grow almost as fast as imports.

As a result of these trends, although China remained a relatively minor trading partner, its labour-intensive goods displaced competitors. In 1994, China accounted for 4 per cent of South African imports and 5 per cent of labour-intensive imports. In 2003, imports from China accounted for 7 per cent of the total and 13 per cent of labour-intensive goods. In clothing and footwear alone, China provided 40 per cent in 1994 and some 70 per cent in 2003. Meanwhile, China absorbed only 1 per cent of South African exports in both 1994 and 2003.

The trends with regard to the EU and the United States were almost the opposite, at least until the rand appreciated dramatically in 2002. While South Africa's total exports in dollar terms rose 37 per cent between 1994 and 2003, exports to the EU climbed 82 per cent and to the US, 66 per cent. Labour-intensive exports to the EU and United States increased relatively rapidly, especially between 1999 and 2003. But growth in labour-intensive exports slowed substantially with the strengthening of the rand in 2002.

Labour-intensive imports from the EU and the United States rose by only 14 per cent between 1994 and 2003, far slower than the average. Moreover, imports from the EU and the United States rose substantially less rapidly than total imports, growing by 42 per cent for the EU and by 30 per cent for the United States.

Finally, trade with SADC largely stagnated. Overall, exports rose 66 per cent between 1994 and 2003. But imports from SADC climbed only 25 per cent – half as fast as the world total.

In sum, analysis of South Africa's trade suggested that it probably contributed to the slow growth in employment after 1994. But the impact varied substantially by region. Increased trade with Europe and the United States supported relatively labour-intensive activities as long as the rand was at a reasonable rate. Trade with developing countries in general, and China in particular, was more likely to displace domestic light industry and employment. The benefits, however, appeared only in capital-intensive resource-based sectors, with limited gains for the majority of the population. Finally, although it was an important market for key manufacturing industries, trade with SADC remained neglected.

The effects of trade on the public treasury were more complex, since it is difficult to determine the extent to which growing trade in itself contributed to the (admittedly mostly slow) growth after 1994. Certainly the opening of the economy was the main factor behind the adoption of a conservative fiscal policy in 1996. The Government hoped that this stance, articulated in its Growth, Employment and Redistribution (GEAR) strategy (National Treasury, 1996), would prevent the rapid capital outflows experienced by some Asian countries and Mexico in that period.[3]

The GEAR strategy committed the Government to cutting its deficit relative to GDP from 5 per cent in 1997 to under 3 per cent in 2000. Given slow economic growth, the result was a 1 per cent fall each year in total government spending. Given the social and economic pressures arising from the political transition, the budget cuts caused considerable hardship. Moreover, it led to considerable pressure to downsize. Between 1994 and 1999, the State eliminated around 13 per cent of public-service positions, or over 100,000 jobs, mostly through attrition. Some big quasi-enterprises where the State has the majority of shares cut another 100,000 jobs.

From 2000, however, the State adopted a more expansionary stance. By no coincidence, delivery of basic services for the poor accelerated in this period – and so did economic growth. The Government also announced its intentions of increasing employment of health workers, teachers and police, although progress was very slow.

Finally, there is little evidence that cheaper imports translated into a lower cost of living for the poor. The available evidence indicated that the retail chains generally did not lower food or clothing prices when import costs fell (see Food Price Monitoring Committee, 2003). Electronic equipment and cars did decline in price, but constituted only a very small share of expenditure by the low-income group. In 2000, cars made up around 2 per cent and electronics about 0.5 per cent of spending by households earning under R2,500 a month (which included about half of all union members).

When analysing the expenditure by type of consumption by income quintile, the richest quintile accounted for over half of total consumption for all major consumer goods except for food. The rich dominated particularly in more sophisticated electrical and electronic equipment, which was more likely to be imported.

Overall, then, it appears that the opening of the South African economy had very mixed implications for unemployment and poverty. The focus on higher exports without adequate, targeted support for more labour-intensive sectors contributed to slower employment growth. Meanwhile, labour-intensive imports displaced employment. Moreover, the threat of capital outflows led to the adoption of a conservative fiscal policy through 2000, with devastating effects on government services.

---

[3] Conversations with GEAR authors in 1996.

Labour rights

Under apartheid, labour rights varied by race, gender and economic sector. White workers could organize, negotiate and strike, and were protected from forced and child labour. From the late 1970s, African workers in manufacturing also won some legal rights to organize and strike, although they faced considerable state harassment nonetheless. In mining and farming, however, workers enjoyed virtually no organizational rights. Child labour and prison labour were both found on white-owned farms.

After 1994, the democratic State moved swiftly to ensure normal labour rights for workers, with an end to unfair discrimination. The democratic order did not, however, much change the underlying conditions that generated high levels of un- and underemployment. In these circumstances, workers faced soaring unemployment and, despite improved organization in some sectors, falling real pay.

The following section outlines the changes in the formal legal framework for the labour market, and then explores the evolution of workers' conditions since 1994.

The legal framework

Progressively, from 1994, the Government worked to ensure equal rights for all workers. These efforts included stronger state support for workers whose conditions made unions hard to organize, especially farm, domestic and informal workers. More broadly, improved socio-economic rights enhanced workers' bargaining power as well as their living conditions. We here look at government efforts to protect workers' organizational rights and end discrimination, and to improve their overall socio-economic position.

Both the 1994 and the 1996 Constitutions included a separate section on labour relations. This section gave workers and employers the right to organize, and protected workers' right to form unions and strike. In addition, the Constitution banned forced and child labour, and provided that every South African might freely choose their occupation and place of residence. This provision effectively addressed apartheid practices around the migrant labour system, prison labour and job reservation.

The Labour Relations Act (LRA) of 1996 provided the basic framework for employer–employee relationships.

- It defined workers' rights to organize, negotiate and strike.

- In an effort to simplify and speed up dispute settlement, the LRA added a system of mediation and arbitration to the courts, through the state-funded Commission for Conciliation, Mediation and Arbitration (CCMA) and, for socio-economic disputes, through the National Economic Development and Labour Council (NEDLAC). The LRA also provided a legal framework for sectoral bargaining councils and workplace forums.

- The LRA laid out basic procedures for disciplinary and productivity procedures by employers, and workers' rights in this context.

The Basic Conditions of Employment Act (BCEA) of 1997 officially focused on issues of working time – especially leave and maximum daily working hours. It set a framework for sectoral minimum wages ("wage determinations") for workers whose circumstances made union organization difficult. It also banned paid or dangerous labour by children under 15 years old.

Perhaps the BCEA's biggest impact was in the definition of employee, which included all workers except the self-employed, irrespective of their contractual situation. This ruled out the previous distinction between casual/contract and permanent workers, ensuring much greater equity in legal protection across labour-market segments.

The Government made relatively little change in occupational health and safety legislation, beyond ensuring that the same standards applied in all sectors. The main innovation was the introduction of a legal framework for joint worker/employer committees on health and safety in large workplaces.

In light of the apartheid past, the Government prioritized efforts to end workplace discrimination. The 1996 Constitution banned unfair discrimination based amongst others on race, gender, disability, age or ethnicity, by either the State or private interests.

In effect, unfair discrimination only applies where there is no economic justification for differentiation. This approach seeks to ensure that anti-discrimination measures do not undermine productivity. But it means that, as long as black workers in particular have fewer formal qualifications and less experience than whites, employers can legally keep them in lower positions.

The Employment Equity Act (1998) both implemented the constitutional ban on unfair discrimination and went beyond it, by:

- Defining unfair discrimination explicitly to mean differentiation that does not follow from job requirements, and banning discrimination in hiring as well as existing employment.

- Establishing dedicated dispute-settlement procedures. If conciliation fails, the dispute goes, not as usual to binding arbitration, but to the Labour Court.

- Requiring designated employers to develop employment-equity plans with proactive, affirmative measures to promote black people, women and people with disabilities.

Finally, the Government moved rapidly to end racial discrimination in access to social insurance funds for unemployment and compensation for work-related injuries. Because these are formally insurance funds, however, with only small government subsidies, the Government felt it could not include many lower-income and more casual workers. The Unemployment Insurance Fund (UIF) only included domestic workers after 2000. The informal sector remained almost entirely outside the purview of social insurance.[4]

In addition to ensuring equitable rights in the labour market, the transition to democracy fundamentally changed the broader socio-political balance between workers and employers. Moreover, government efforts to improve conditions for the poor sought to open up alternative economic opportunities, improving workers' bargaining power.

Under apartheid, state action and employer power had been coordinated. The provision of equal rights to all citizens undermined this coherence. Above all, workers no longer needed to fear expulsion from urban areas or criminalization if they stood up to their employers. Special legislation protected farm workers' housing rights, so that losing their job should not automatically mean eviction.

These broader rights were particularly important for women workers, including those in unpaid labour. Government specifically sought to strengthen police action against family violence. Other measures worked to enhance women's economic independence. These included the extension of old age pensions and child-support grants to all poor families, as well as efforts to end discrimination against black women in home ownership and access to financial services.

Government also acted directly to increase the economic opportunities and resources available to workers, which should strengthen their position relative to employers. The strongest measures here included the establishment of a skills development strategy and the housing programme.

The skills strategy aimed to overcome the discriminatory policies of the past. It sought to ensure that every worker had access to skills and, on that basis, better jobs. It also tried to install mechanisms to provide certification for workers' informal skills. To support the strategy, the State imposed a 1 per cent payroll levy on all employers.

---

[4] For historical reasons, the UIF also did not include public-service workers, but since the public service provided almost permanent employment this did not prove a major disadvantage.

The housing and infrastructure policy effectively transferred over R50 billion in assets to poor households. Initially, this strategy was expected to expand opportunities for earning incomes through home-based production. In the event, however, service levels were generally low and costs high, limiting economic use.[5] Still, improved household appliances should ease the burden of unpaid home labour – caring and housework.

Support for small and micro-production, including through land reform and financial support for small enterprise, also aimed to provide alternatives to employment. Generally, however, these programmes had relatively little impact. Land reform affected only a small percentage of total arable land, despite the Government's long-standing commitment to transferring 30 per cent of the land to smallholders. Moreover, virtually all analyses showed that the Government failed to provide effective support for micro-enterprise.

Changes in workers' conditions, 1994–2003

Despite the improvements in workers' rights, their conditions on average deteriorated after 1994. The decline largely reflected the combined pressures of unemployment and rising international competition.

The available data indicate falling wages and salaries. The percentage of workers earning under R1000 a month in nominal terms rose from 36 per cent in 1995 to 39 per cent in 2001, and reached 41 per cent in March 2003 (calculated from Statistics South Africa, 1995, 2002 and 2003). In these eight years, inflation cut the purchasing power of R1000 by over half.

Rising unemployment was also linked to a falling share for labour in the national income. In 2002, remuneration accounted for around 51 per cent of national income, the lowest level in any year since records began in 1946 except for 1980 (which saw a soaring gold price). Labour's share fell particularly sharply in 1999–2002. In this period, profits rose from 29 per cent to 34 per cent of national income (calculated from SARB, 2003).

A particular problem lay in the growing informalization and casualization of labour. It appears that the informal sector expanded substantially in the late 1990s, but essentially stagnated in the early 2000s. The data on the informal sector fluctuate dramatically, however, because of a tendency to redefine informal work over time. Thus, the growth from 1995 to 1999 was exaggerated by the tendency increasingly to include unpaid labour, while the decline from 2000 probably reflected the shift from a general household survey to a more accurate labour force survey (Makgetla, 2004b).

---

[5] For instance, national government proposals in 2003 on free basic electricity would not provide enough to run a refrigerator, but anyone using more than the minimum might lose the free services altogether.

Only 30 per cent of workers in the informal sector were employed by someone else, compared with almost 95 per cent of those in the formal sector and domestic labour (calculated from Statistics South Africa, 2003). Most labour laws, however, do not apply to the self-employed. This in itself meant they did not much affect informal jobs.

The vast majority of informal workers did not earn enough to live on. In March 2003, three-quarters of informal sector workers earned under R1000 a month, compared with a quarter of formal-sector workers. Casualization also became a concern. In sum, in the absence of substantial growth in employment, the new labour laws did not ensure improved pay for workers as a whole. Union members generally did better than non-union members. But even they faced intense pressure as employers sought to adapt to increasing competition, sometimes through relocation, outsourcing and casualization as well as retrenchments.

Implications for engagement on trade

The South African experience indicates, first, that increased trade does not necessarily improve workers' conditions. Indeed, especially if it does not generate substantial gains in employment or leads to cuts in government spending, it may worsen the situation for labour. In these circumstances, even strong labour laws won't stop the race to the bottom, with employers forcing workers to compete with each other on the basis of declining pay and conditions.

In response to this situation, the Congress of South African Trade Unions (COSATU) called for a structural policy to replace the current emphasis on overall competitiveness. Such a policy would develop targeted measures to support sectors that can create employment on the necessary scale, whether they produce for international or domestic markets. Important sectors from this standpoint included agriculture, especially with accelerated land reform; light industry, both downstream from chemicals and minerals as well as to meet the needs of the poor; and services, including the public sector.

From the early 2000s, COSATU succeeded in gaining business and government support for tripartite work on sectoral approaches. By 2005, quite successful processes had been held in mining, clothing and textiles, information and communication technologies and the financial sector. More are under way for chemicals and metals. The financial sector process, in particular, led to substantial reforms in the sector to encourage diversification of investment as well as improved services for working class and poor households.

Still, it remained a problem that business in general and many government officials preferred to focus on competitiveness rather than job creation. Yet COSATU's experience over the past ten years demonstrates that measures to support competitiveness will not necessarily lead to substantially higher employment or equity. Indeed, some competitiveness measures may actually destroy employment.

The South African experience also demonstrates that an expansionary fiscal and monetary strategy, while inadequate in itself, is a critical necessity. The fiscal restrictions of the late 1990s certainly reduced the growth rate as well as cutting into services for the poor and employment. The relatively high interest rates of the early 2000s, while lower than the extraordinary rates seen in the late 1990s, contributed to the overvaluation of the rand. That, in turn, had a devastating effect on employment by blocking exports and accelerating imports.

Finally, trade negotiations must be consistently reviewed to ensure they support employment and poverty alleviation. Trade negotiators tend to substitute the end in view – ending obstacles to trade – for the real aim of accelerating development. In South Africa in the early 2000s, COSATU played an important role in ensuring that trade negotiations did not simply neglect the employment effects. In 2004, it concluded a policy framework with government and business that concludes that trade should support development and employment creation.

More fundamentally, it is important that trade negotiations leave governments in the South scope to support existing and new industries that can create jobs and raise living standards. That may mean targeted subsidies and protection in ways that the WTO disapproves.

In addition, South-South solidarity, while critically important in the realignment of forces at a multilateral level, cannot be equated to free-trade agreements. Rather, it should be developed in terms of mutually beneficial development programmes, possibly including fixed-preference agreements on trade. By themselves, pure free trade agreements may simply contribute to a race to the bottom.

The South African experience has implications for debates on trade policy in the international labour movement. In particular, it suggests that core labour standards are necessary, but not sufficient, to prevent a race to the bottom as a result of more open economies. Indeed, simply calling for core labour standards without finding a common position on protection for vulnerable or infant industries in both the South and the North has proven divisive.

From this standpoint, the international labour movement should work to develop stronger positions on how trade negotiations can:

- Ensure adequate scope for development policies in the South, including where necessary to protect infant industries and industries that serve basic needs; and

- Link to active labour market policies for workers in the North. Without support for these workers, they may end up bearing the cost of moves to increase the market access of Southern producers.

References

COSATU (Congress of South African Trade Unions). 2002. "Submission on industrial policy to the Trade and Industry Portfolio Committee and Select Committee on Economic Affairs", 30 Apr. Available at: www.cosatu.org.za [accessed Aug. 2003].

Department of Labour. 2003. *Improving the working conditions of all our people.* Available at: www.labour.gov.za [accessed Jan. 2004].

DTI (Department of Trade and Industry). 2002. "Accelerating growth and development: The contribution of an integrated manufacturing strategy". Available at: www.thedti.org.za [accessed Dec. 2004].

Food Price Monitoring Committee. 2003. *Final Report*, Pretoria, National Department of Agriculture.

Makgetla, N.S. 2004a. *Unpacking the unemployment data*, input to COSATU CEC (Johannesburg).

—. 2004b. "The post-apartheid economy", in *Review of African Political Economy*, Special edition on South Africa, Vol. 31, No. 100, pp. 263–281.

National Treasury. 1996. *Growth, employment and redistribution: A macro-economic strategy.* Available at: www.treasury.gov.za [accessed Dec. 2005].

PCAS (Policy Co-ordination and Advisory Services). 2003. *Towards a ten-year review: Synthesis report on implementation of government programmes* (Pretoria, Government Communication and Information System (GCIS)).

South African Government. 2004. *Government's Programme of Action – 2004.* Economics cluster. Available at: www.info.gov.za [accessed Aug. 2004].

SARB (South African Reserve Bank). 2003. Long-term data on national accounts. Available at: www.resbank.gov.za [accessed Sep. 2003].

—. 2004. *Quarterly Bulletin*, Dec. Available at: www.reservebank.co.za [accessed Jan. 2005].

Statistics South Africa. 1995. October Household Survey, Pretoria. [Database on CD-ROM.]

—. 2002. Labour Force Survey September 2001, Pretoria. Available at: www.statssa.gov.za [accessed Sep. 2002].

—. 2003. Labour Force Survey March 2003, Pretoria. [Database on CD-ROM.]

UNDP (United Nations Development Programme). 2003. *South Africa. Human Development Report – The challenge of sustainable development: Unlocking people's creativity.* Available at: www.undp.org.za [accessed Dec. 2004].

World Bank. 2004. *World Development Report 2005: A better investment climate for everyone* (World Bank and Oxford University Press). Available at www.worldbank.org [accessed Jan. 2005].

MIGRATION IN THE GLOBAL ECONOMY: CHALLENGES AND OPPORTUNITIES FOR CARIBBEAN TRADE UNIONS

9

Ann-Marie Lorde
Research Officer, National Union of Public Workers, Barbados

Introduction

The migration of people has existed from time immemorial and, with the dawn of the new millennium, migration has become a central issue of concern and debate among national and international policy-makers. It is accepted that migration can be productive for some economies, nevertheless it must be managed to serve as an engine of growth and development, and take place in a manner that fully respects the fundamental rights of all migrant workers.

The increased integration of culture, economies, societies and politics is supporting the present economic global order that is associated with the notion of flows. Whether it be the movement of "capital, data, ideas and people", the forces driving these migratory flows are many and not easily defined, and they present a series of multifaceted inter-relationships for policy-makers and governments (IOM, 2002). In essence, these increased flows are supporting a world that is rapidly becoming "a single place" (Marfleet, 1998).

By the end of 2000 three per cent of the world's population (175 million people) were living outside their country of birth or citizenship, with women accounting for an increasing proportion of international migrants, thus feminizing the face of migration (ILO, 2004). Substantial research reveals extensive migration for employment between developed countries where wage differentials are not very large (ILO, 2004).

In recent times there has been growing concern among trade unionists about the impact of international migration on the quality of social services, particularly the delivery of quality social services in developing countries, including the Caribbean.[1] This issue has been given high priority by organizations such as the ILO and Public Services International (PSI), especially in regard to the migration of health sector workers.

The Caribbean is presently witnessing with a measure of concern the migration of health-care workers, particularly caregivers. In Barbados, for example, its nurses are migrating to the United States and the United Kingdom. Of interest, however, is the fact that a large number of nurses contemplating migration are considering the United States because of the information being provided by American recruitment agencies visiting the islands. An area that is in need of further study is the migration of nurses to the United Kingdom who are then migrating to Saudi Arabia and Australia.

To add to the discourse this paper will examine the issue of migration in the health sector within the Caribbean at two levels: the notion of migratory flows from a Caribbean perspective; and the exploitation of migrant labour. In considering these issues this paper will also seek to identify some of the concerns that the Caribbean Public Sector Unions (CPSU) will need to address, specifically in light of Chapter 3 of the 2001 Revised Treaty of Chaguaramas Establishing the Caribbean Community including the CARICOM Single Market and Economy (CSME) which covers the "Establishment, Services, Capital and Movement of Community Nationals" (www.caricom.org).

One may argue that the CPSU are representative of the various faces of Caribbean public services, and thus must ensure that the rights of all workers, including migrant workers – regular or irregular – are safeguarded, and that decent work for all is promoted. The CPSU, therefore, have a pivotal role to play in the crystallization of the CSME which is being driven by the World Trade Organization (WTO) Agreement on Trade in Services (Mode 4) (www.wto.org). Concerns identified as affecting the issue of migrant workers are therefore central to developing a CPSU response to regional and international migrant flows, and must be considered in the light of globalization.

Migration flows

Migration is a systematic process that is influenced by a combination of macroeconomic and political forces as well as by "micro-level social networks, the formation of communities and interpersonal exchanges of information and remittances" (Simmons, 1998). One may argue that the high levels of remittances to the Caribbean, particularly Jamaica, have aided the development

---

[1] Interviews were conducted during 2003 with five female health sector workers in the Bahamas, 15 in Barbados, two in Guyana, one in Dominica and two in Dutch St Maarten. The leaders of the CPSU trade unions from Bermuda, Jamaica and Guyana were interviewed in 2004.

of Caribbean societies, however, there still remains the need to weigh the value of remittances against the loss of the "best brains" from Caribbean societies.

Within the Caribbean migration is nothing new. Historically, it has played a central role in the development and structure of the region, and has been shaped in the main by colonialism. The Caribbean has been more deeply influenced and affected by international migration than any other region in the world, responding to economic and political developments of the islands and the various shifts in migration policies in receiving countries including the United Kingdom, United States and Canada (IOM, 2001). This long history of labour migration from the Caribbean has varied significantly in numbers, characteristics, duration of stay abroad and frequency of return. It would therefore be noteworthy to consider migration in the context of the debate on trade unions and their role in the globalization process as it relates to shifting opportunities for low-skilled workers, skilled workers, professionals and civil servants, with civil servants being included in the category of professionals.

Extra-regional migration has been the dominant form of migration in the region; however, there exists an intra-regional network that has developed significantly in the last 50 years. Also to be considered is the element of circulatory migration which is increasingly changing the phenomenon of "brain drain" into that of "brain exchange" (IOM, 2001). Historically, Caribbean migrant workers have crossed borders intra-regionally and extra-regionally through one of three channels:

- permanent migration – primarily for family unification and for highly skilled workers to market their skills;

- temporary migration for all types of employment – primarily for guest workers who fill vacant jobs that persist, for example in the area of nursing; and

- temporary migration for time-bound employment – primarily for seasonal migrants in farm labour programmes and construction (ILO, 2004).

The key factors that are driving these facets of migration can be classified as pull factors, as in the case of the Bahamas, where tourism has stimulated the demand for foreign labour; and push factors, as in Jamaica, where high unemployment levels are increasing pressures to seek employment outside of Jamaica; and inter-country networks based on family, culture and history.

Over the years migration from the Caribbean to the United States and Canada consisted mainly of low-skilled workers who worked in farm labour programmes. In recent times skilled workers have been sought in the areas of construction, the hotel industry and nursing.

Skilled workers and professionals migrate for reasons such as better pay, better facilities and more opportunities for upward mobility. There is the argument that the resultant impact of the migration of these skilled and professional people is one of brain drain. As skilled workers and professionals migrate, especially in the health sector, a void is created leading to concerns of increased workloads, reduced contributions to social protection benefits, loss of mentorship to young workers and a reduction in the membership base of the trade union movement. However, within the region it is unclear whether this is now transforming from brain drain to brain exchange or brain gain in the Caribbean due to intra-regional mobility of labour and return migrants.

A situation of brain exchange is now developing in Jamaica through the successful Return of Qualified Nationals Programme. Increasing numbers of qualified professionals are returning home to reintegrate into Jamaican society and contribute to the development of their country. In contrast, Barbados and Dutch St Maarten witnessed a number of health-care workers leave their island homes as unskilled workers to return as trained professionals in nursing and other areas of medical care.

Members of this group exhibit two distinct characteristics of migration – returning nationals and that of circulatory migration. As returning nationals they state unequivocally that they have no intention of migrating again, thus exhibiting the concept of "brain gain" and "value-added brain". As circulatory migrants, they work sessionally at home and in their former adopted homes where many have established families and networks.

Migration of labour is, by its very nature, a trans-border phenomenon, tending to be more complex than trade or capital mobility (WTO, 2003). Today, Caribbean countries are points of origin, destination and transit for migrants. In recent years there has been growing concern about increased undocumented and irregular migration, with the flow of migrants being on the increase from the Caribbean to North America (IOM, 2001).

With the arrival of an integrated world economy there are profound implications for the socio-political structure of the Caribbean, where both labour and capital now circulate with increased freedom (Marfleet, 1998). However, with free movement of labour, migration appears to have been excluded from the process, with migrant workers being subject to the rules that promote the free movement of capital, goods, services and the integration of international business. Under the Revised Treaty of Chaguaramas, Chapter 3 speaks specifically to "Cross border employment of natural resources, human resources, capital technology and management capabilities for the production of goods and services on a sustained basis," (CSME Unit, 2004) where labour is limited to skilled workers (who must show verification of their skills), University of the West Indies graduates, journalists, musicians and cultural workers. These rules restrict the movement of labour and the exercising of labour rights, with migrant labour being viewed as a factor of production (ILO, 2002) – thus lending credence to the argument that population movements are a part of a notionally more fluid world of capital and information flows, and revealing starkly the ways in which new obstacles to free movement are being erected.

This is in sharp contrast to the movement of labour in colonial times, from the late seventeenth century until the 1960s. Colonial subjects emigrated to the "mother country" and inter-colonially as itinerant civil servants and as artisans with a view to bettering themselves. Colonial masters also immigrated to the Caribbean colonies as administrators, teachers and managers. This lends support to the view that Caribbean people were freer to move under colonial flags than they are now that a legal framework (Revised Treaty of Chaguaramas, 2001) governing the free movement of labour is being established.

Regarding the regulation of the temporary flow of migrants overseas there exists within the region a number of regulatory bilateral agreements with Canada and the United Kingdom. Within these agreements there are clauses that regulate the return of workers once their contract is completed. An example of such an agreement is the Canadian Farm Labour Programme between Barbados and Canada. In supporting the exchange programmes between Barbados and Canada there is a pre-departure preparation programme for temporary migrants, where nationals are prepared for their temporary integration into the Canadian labour market.

For the flow of migrant workers to Barbados there is a regulatory framework in place. Added to this Barbados is signatory to ILO Convention 97 (Migration for Employment Convention (Revised), 1949). Migrant workers are also protected under the Constitution of Barbados regarding protection of their fundamental rights and freedoms, including against forced labour and discrimination; they are to be treated no less favourably than citizens. Regarding the recruitment of migrant workers, there are short-term work permits not exceeding six months and long-term work permits which are also granted for specified periods. Immigrant visas for indefinite stays are also issued in special cases.

With respect to rights, benefits and social protection, regular migrant workers, though not family members accompanying them, receive the same benefits as nationals; irregular migrants on the other hand are only entitled to social benefits that include medical care, sickness benefit, old age benefit, maternity benefit, invalidity benefit and survivors benefit. Under national insurance legislation illegally employed migrants are insurable by the National Insurance Scheme (*The Barbados Advocate*, 12 October 2004). Nevertheless, these illegally employed migrants are disadvantaged, since deductions are made from their pay but not forwarded to the National Insurance Office (i.e. they are kept by the employer) and in the event of retirement, illness, death or unemployment these workers' families cannot claim any social security benefits.

By contrast, the Bahamas presently has no bilateral agreements in place concerning migrant workers, at least not in the traditional sense. However, the islands have for many years hosted migrant workers who entered the islands legally or illegally in search of work and a better standard of living for themselves and their families. The Bahamas, having ratified ILO Convention 97, passed legislation in 2001 to protect the rights of all workers within their borders regardless of their immigration status.

When the Bermudian situation is examined the island does not appear to have any major concerns regarding irregular migrant labour. Bermuda is an overseas territory of the United Kingdom and, until permission is given to become a full member of the Caribbean Community (CARICOM), it remains an associate member. As such the Public Service Union (PSU) is of the view that Bermuda's status as an overseas territory excludes it from issues surrounding illegal migrants. The PSU suggests that its migrant labour comes through the normal regulatory channels of immigration. An immigration policy is in place which ensures that all persons entering Bermuda to work are issued with a work permit. However, the PSU is of the opinion that once Bermuda becomes part of CARICOM then the question of open borders for CARICOM nationals may introduce the issue of irregular migrants.

The Caribbean context

There are four pillars that are key supports to any society's wealth and development – health, sanitation services, education and transportation/communication, with health being the most important.

Health-care workers are choosing to migrate; their reasons include remuneration, working conditions, lack of upward mobility and the opportunity that exists abroad for personal and professional development. Remuneration, although tabled as a motivating factor for some nurses choosing to migrate, can become a negative as working conditions in the receiving country may not be ideal. Some nurses indicate that promises made before they left their home country have not materialized in the receiving country, and that to compensate they need to work two jobs to sustain an adequate standard of living. Consideration must also be given to those health-care workers who choose to migrate for the experience of working in another country and return as a "value added" health-care worker.

For those health-care workers who do not migrate there is an increased workload. This is complicated by the fact that experienced personnel are leaving and the inexperienced workers who remain have very few qualified co-workers to help train and mentor them. This reality opens governments to malpractice lawsuits when serious mistakes occur. This begs the question, how ready is the region for the litigious habits of developed societies? Caribbean governments must take action to examine what is causing job dissatisfaction in this area, with a view to rectifying deficiencies, especially regarding the retention of nursing personnel in the 35 and older age group to allow for the mentoring and training process of the younger workers.

At present, Guyana is witnessing an exodus of labour, especially the highly skilled and professionals. It is questionable whether the rate at which Guyana can train and educate its workforce to deliver quality health can match the rate at which its most experienced and qualified are migrating. The Government is of the view that these workers can continue to leave and they will just train more. This view concerns the labour movement of Guyana not only because of the loss in membership, but also because it is the experienced and well-trained workers who are leaving. The reality is that Guyana is experiencing a brain drain.

In Dominica the situation is slightly different. In August 2004 the Government did not agree with the union that there was a shortage of nurses. The Government pointed out that of the 375 nurses working at the country's main hospital only 55 had migrated to the United Kingdom. In the Government's opinion this was an indication that they were training the best nurses in the region. However, the Government did point out that to alleviate the problems of nurses migrating they had increased the age of retirement for nurses from 55 years of age to 60 years of age. Also, included in the cost of the training programme initiated for registered nurse training is a fee to offset the cost of training in the event that trained personnel migrate (*Guyana Chronicle*, 28th August 2004).

For Barbados migration is viewed as being normal; reports indicate that among the Caribbean countries, Barbados has been the leading exporter of labour for the past 170 years (*The Daily Nation*, 7 July 2004). It is opined that too many assumptions are being made about the impact of migration on the delivery of health services, with the migration of nursing personnel in the 1960s and 1970s being more critical than it is now. Health care was at a critical turning point with the Queen Elizabeth Hospital (QEH) opening and coming on stream in 1964. Between 1959 and 1966 213 staff nurses left Barbados and there were only 100 graduates. Not enough trained personnel were available to replace the ones who had migrated.

During an interview with the Chief Nursing Officer of Barbados the following figures were made available on nurses migrating from Barbados between 1998 and 2003:[2] 1998 – 16, 1999 – 22, 2000 – 61, 2001 – 31 and 2002 – 45.

---

[2] Interview with the Chief Nursing Officer Barbados conducted on 10 November 2003.

In his opinion the figures have remained fairly constant, with the numbers being highest in 2000 when an entire graduating class migrated from Barbados because there were no available positions for them to fill. This occurred due to the fact that Barbados is a small island with one general hospital, which is an acute care institution and a teaching hospital, and one psychiatric hospital. These health-care institutions can only employ a certain number of nurses at any given time.

In examining the migration register for Barbados health-care personnel, it reveals that it is young workers who are leaving. One may argue that this is understandable since their upward mobility would be a challenge due to the limited number of available positions in the local hierarchy, compared with the perceived unlimited opportunities abroad to develop personally and professionally.

In Barbados tertiary level education and below is free and it has been suggested that nurses who benefit from free training should give it back in labour, i.e. that they should be "bonded". This suggestion has met with some disagreement. The argument being tabled is that there is only one general hospital and it is a teaching hospital, hence it can only accommodate a certain number of nurses. As well, the remittances (BDS$630 per month per student) paid to these students over the three years is not significant.

The Chief Nursing Officer also argued that it is not right to bond good workers who are receiving a salary, as in his view this is discriminatory since many skilled workers or university graduates leave Barbados as soon as they complete their studies, and they are not bonded. There is the recommendation, however, that it should be mandatory for the receiving countries to pay a recruitment fee or similar, towards the costs associated with educating and training these nurses.

In examining this recommendation, there are two elements that must be considered. Firstly, Barbados is also a receiving country, and as such the ability to compensate the sending country for its health-care workers comes into the equation. Secondly, when compensation is received, how can the Health Care Ministry guarantee this compensation will be channelled back into further training?

With respect to inward migration to Barbados, nursing personnel coming to work on the island are treated no less favourably than local nurses. What they do report is that the salary they receive is higher than they expected, but this is offset by the high cost of living on the island. This has resulted in them saving less than they had anticipated. There is also the observation that needs further examination that nurses coming to Barbados use the island as a stepping stone to migrate to the United States to continue their careers as nurses.

Added to this is the cultural barrier that appears to be given less attention. Nurses interviewed point out that migrant nurses are challenged by the dialect and cultural practices of the locals. There is also a language barrier when nurses are recruited who do not have English as their first language – this is cause for concern especially when crucial information is being taken from patients.

The concern has been raised by the Ministry responsible for nursing, the nursing fraternity, trade unions and the nursing school that when nurses choose to migrate, the Government should ensure that the conditions they go to should be no less favourable than those they currently work under. Recognizing that one cannot tell people not to migrate to what they deem to be better working conditions, the Government needs to ascertain what is causing the job dissatisfaction. One suggestion is to implement an exit survey, which should provide a consensus on the root causes and some suggested solutions. Furthermore, policies should not be implemented if there is no consensus on what the nurses want. Moreover, deciding which policies to implement should be carried out with the input of nursing personnel.

Migration occurs for many reasons and in varied ways but one of its least desirable aspects is trafficking for purposes of labour exploitation. Policy-makers in the Caribbean are becoming aware of the gravity of this activity but "information" is mainly in the form of anecdotes and information received from health-care personnel during union meetings. The data the CPSU have accumulated on this issue has been lacking; these organizations have not viewed it as of concern and or seen any urgency to collate such information. Therefore, at present there is very little systematic evidence and no documented case studies on the issue, and such paucity of information needs to be rectified.

Nevertheless, health-care providers in Barbados are gravely concerned with this issue, considering the fact that irregular migrants receive the same health care as citizens, the only difference being they are required to pay for medication. Since some of these people cannot afford to pay for medication the rules are bent to accommodate them and preserve the good health of the wider society. It is suggested that this has placed a strain on the available resources of the polyclinics and is leading to continuing increases in government finance to the health-care system. This lends support to the argument that the health-care system's need for funds appears to be insatiable, with the cost of delivery outstripping its ability to recoup the many injections of finance it receives.

Another concern tabled was the likely impact of migration not only on communicable diseases, but also on the instances of HIV/AIDS and the related delivery of health care in our societies.

The situation and consequences

The effects of labour migration in the Caribbean have been mixed. There are those who choose to migrate for the experience and to return home as value-added personnel. Then there are those who choose to migrate in search of greater opportunities at the expense of destroying familial relations.

The CPSU need to develop strategic partnerships not only across the region but internationally as well, with a view to protecting Caribbean workers as they move across borders. There is a need for cross-border cooperation to ensure that not only the human rights of migrant workers are protected but also that they work in decent and humane working conditions. Interviews often revealed instances where workers who choose to migrate were too embarrassed to return home, instead choosing to continue working abroad under substandard conditions of service and being treated like second-class citizens. One nurse stated that a co-worker whom she would consider to be a good friend had migrated with the understanding that she would be working as a nurse, but was in fact working as a nursing aid.

There is a need to provide a measure of empowerment to migrant workers, to give them a voice on the one hand and to eliminate any negative reactions of society on the other. This came into focus in Barbados in July 2004. Workers from Guyana and St Vincent were accused of coming and taking the jobs of local Barbadians. Members of the public had to be urged not to stir up or incite fear and xenophobia. Reassurance was also given to migrant workers that their rights would be protected while in Barbados (*The Daily Nation*, 7 July 2004). Such empowerment and the elimination of negative reactions can be successfully achieved through the CPSU by way of education programmes that are strategically planned and delivered.

In order to augment the positive and minimize the negative aspects of migration, the CPSU need to return to basics. These include working towards economic improvement for their members, social transformation for the labouring classes and promoting the democratic interests of its members. By focusing on the basics the CSPU will help transform the challenges of immigration into positive developments for both receiving and sending countries.

Recommendations

One important way the wealth of any society is gauged is principally by the delivery of and access to a quality health-care system. To retain nursing personnel they must be provided with adequate terms and conditions of service and reasonable remuneration – the provision of not only a decent wage but also an adequate living wage for all health workers. Other forms of compensation should also be considered, such as bilateral agreements that lead to cross-fertilization of ideas where those workers skilled in areas not available in the Caribbean would provide the training to local health-care workers and the workers who migrate would seek to enhance their skills. Also, noting that each ethnic group carries its own health-care problems these migrant health-care workers would also be able to transfer a measure of knowledge.

The concerns tabled here highlight the need to carry out greater research into the extent and impact that migration and Caribbean migration policies are having on the loss and retention of labour – unskilled, skilled and professional – and on matching the skills needed to the demands for labour. This reflects the growing concern about the loss of skilled personnel, particularly health sector workers, and the need for governments to fill the labour shortage gap (IOM, 2002). In addition, there is the need to study whether or not managed migration can counterbalance the expected impact of ageing on Caribbean societies.

Another area that needs consideration is how to attract those people who have raised a family, have a desire to enter nursing, are young enough to start a new career and are now willing to enter the workforce as caregivers. Moreover, the perception of nursing as one of changing bedpans and other menial tasks needs to be changed. Ways of attracting more men into the profession of nursing should also be considered.

There is also the need to examine the issue of increased remittances to the Caribbean. Such an examination must be considered in conjunction with the increased numbers of retirees who are now returning home and therefore increased remittances may actually be in the form of pensions or other social security benefits accruing to the Caribbean baby boomers, who would have migrated in the 1950s and 1960s to the United Kingdom, Canada and the United States and who now fall into the category of returning nationals.

Remittances are not appropriate compensation for taking the best brains, especially the health-care workers of the Caribbean. When there is large-scale exodus from a country, as in the case of Guyana, policies to tackle the brain drain in the sending country may not adequately deal with the root cause of the problems. Receiving countries and sending countries need to consider development policies that are purposeful; that place greater emphasis on temporary movement, with incentives to return home, and on remedying the institutional failures that cause both skilled and unskilled workers to leave their homes for greener pastures. Such integrated policy measures could provide for better development in the sending countries whilst at the same time help receiving countries with their labour shortages.

The CPSU need to initiate dialogue and develop research with a view to tabling policy on migration as it regards shifting opportunities for low-skilled, skilled and professional workers, on matching needed skills to the demand for labour and on the impact of ageing on Caribbean societies.

One final recommendation would be the examination of the concept of managed migration for the Caribbean. This has been defined by the Caribbean Community in 2005 as "a regional strategy for retaining adequate numbers of competent nursing personnel to deliver adequate health-care programmes and services to Caribbean nationals". This strategy should be examined in the context of, and from the perspective of, the CPSU who have a key role in ensuring that workers have a right to choose where they wish to work and live and that this right is respected. Consideration must also be given to what may be viewed as the expected counterbalance to be achieved through this strategy where improved terms and conditions of service, value and recognition for the work of health-care workers are recognized.

References

The Barbados Advocate. 2004. "NIS benefits for all", 12 Oct.

The Daily Nation. 2004. "Migrant workers in check", 7 Jul.

Guyana Chronicle. 2004. "Dominica nurses migrating", 28 Aug.

ILO (International Labour Organization). 2002. "Migrant workers", in *Labour Education*, No. 129, 2002/4 (Geneva).

—. 2004. *Towards a fair deal for migrant workers in the global economy*, Report VI submitted to the International Labour Conference, 92nd Session, Geneva, 2004 (Geneva).

IOM (International Organization for Migration). 2001. Background paper to the International migration policy seminar for the Caribbean, Kingston, Jamaica, 28 May–1 Jun.

—. 2002. *Report and Conclusions*, Follow-up Seminar to the International migration policy seminar for the Caribbean, Santo Domingo, Dominican Republic, 28–31 Oct.

Marfleet, P. 1998. "Migration and the refugee experience", in R. Kiely and P. Marfleet (eds): *Globalization and the Third World* (London and New York, Routledge).

OECD (Organisation for Economic Co-operation and Development). 2002. *Service providers on the move: A closer look at labour mobility and the GATS* [TD/FC/WP (2001) 26/Final] (Paris).

PSI (Public Services International). 2004. *Women and international migration in the health sector*, Final Report of Public Services International Participatory Action Research 2003.

Simmons, A.B. 1998. "NAFTA, international migration and labour rights", in *Labour, Capital and Society/Travail, Capital et Société*, Vol. 31, Nos. 1 & 2, Apr.–Nov.

WTO (World Trade Organization). 2003. *Labour mobility and the WTO: Liberalising temporary movement*, Global Economic Prospects 2004 (Geneva).

EUROPEAN UNION ENLARGEMENT, WORKERS AND MIGRATION: IMPLICATIONS FOR TRADE UNIONS IN THE UNITED KINGDOM AND POLAND

10

Jane Hardy
Business School, University of Hertfordshire, Hatfield, UK
and
Nick Clark
Policy Officer, Public and Commercial Services Union, London, UK

Introduction

On 1 May 2004 the EU was enlarged to include ten new Member States, eight of them from Central and Eastern Europe (known as the A8). In some quarters xenophobic fears have been raised through exaggeration, distortion and in some cases sheer invention. Although there will be some who enter the labour market in well-paid skilled work, the majority of migrant workers from the A8 States will be employed in the worst paid and most poorly organized sectors. Many workers from the A8 States had already been working in the United Kingdom before 1 May, but were unable to claim employment rights because of their lack of legal status. Legitimizing access to jobs should remove this potential advantage to unscrupulous employers. However, our concern is that the low level of labour regulation in Britain will leave migrant workers being exploited in low-paid jobs without security or access to trade union rights. The problem of migrant workers is made worse by the low level of protection that exists for some categories of workers, agency workers for example, and the difficulty in enforcing rights where they do exist. We explore this question through a case study of migrant workers from Poland in the United Kingdom.

This paper will review preliminary information available on migration patterns from Poland to the United Kingdom and then explore the issues raised for trade unions in both countries. The paper will be based on both primary and secondary information from the case study countries. Primary information has been gathered by one of the authors in his former role as International Policy Officer at the Trades Union Congress (TUC). In particular, it will report initial data gathered via contacts made by A8 workers with the TUC's Migrant

Workers Project, by TUC regions, and cases dealt with by affiliated unions and migrant organizations. The other author has extensive experience of researching on the restructuring of the Polish economy and its impact on Polish workers and trade unions. Interviews have been conducted with the representatives of the three major trade unions in Poland, as well as regional representatives of the Polish Solidarity (Solidarnosc) trade union from areas of high unemployment. In addition, a small number of interviews were conducted with migrant workers who had temporarily returned to Poland; these included students and bus drivers. Interviews were also conducted in the United Kingdom with the TUC National Organiser, a Solidarity worker seconded to the United Kingdom, and with full-time union officials from the Transport and General Workers' Union (T&G) who had been involved in disputes with Polish workers.

This case study is important on two counts. First, the treaties of accession to the EU included the option for existing members to restrict the right of new citizens to seek and take jobs in their labour market. The United Kingdom Government, unlike other EU nations, decided not to restrict the right of workers from A8 countries from seeking and taking up employment in the United Kingdom (*Financial Times*, 2004). Instead, workers from the A8 countries securing employment in the United Kingdom had to register their presence with the UK Home Office under the Workers Registration Scheme. Only those who completed 12 months' uninterrupted, registered employment would then be entitled to out-of-work benefits.

Second, Poland has been selected as the focus of the paper because with a population of 38 million it is the largest country in Central and Eastern Europe, therefore it can be taken as a case study and starting point from which to explore the implications for other accession countries. Home Office statistics for the first five months' registration, for example, showed workers from Poland as accounting for 56 per cent of registrations (Home Office and other departments, 2004).

Migration "push" and "pull" factors

This first section looks at the factors that are "pushing" workers from Poland to seek jobs in other EU countries, and the "pull" factors that are attracting them to the United Kingdom in particular.

Poland

In the early 1990s "shock therapy" introduced measures overnight, which liberalized the economy and introduced draconian cuts in spending. This was followed by a relentless drive to the market based on neo-liberal ideas which has increased insecurity and driven down living standards for large numbers of workers. Official Polish statistics show that in 2004 11.8 per cent of the population lived below the subsistence level compared with 6.4 per cent in 1994 (GUS, 2005). In 2005 unemployment averaged 20 per cent. This figure is higher for young people and those living in particular regions and towns. This is reflected in United Kingdom registration statistics where initial figures show 83 per cent of workers from A8 states as being aged between 18 and 34. Taken together these have been the push factors that have driven people to seek jobs beyond Poland.

United Kingdom

Many Polish migrants had already entered the United Kingdom lawfully under temporary entry schemes such as the Seasonal Agricultural Workers Scheme and the sector-based schemes for food processing and hospitality, as well as on self-employed visas under the EU association agreements. Others had entered and worked without authorization (Jordan and Düvell, 2002). Accession, however, has opened up the possibility of legally working in a wider spread of sectors, compared with illegal migrants often working under conditions of forced labour (Anderson and Rogaly, 2005). Polish newspapers are full of advertisements from agencies quick to profit from the new situation, offering jobs in a range of industries such as care (for the elderly and disabled), nursing, engineering and general factory work in the United Kingdom.

The lifting of restrictions in the United Kingdom has much more to do with labour shortages than with a liberal attitude to immigration. The overall unemployment rate in the United Kingdom in 2005 was 5.1 per cent, falling to as low as 3.8 per cent in the South East of the country. The economy has seen a polarization of income, with the wages and working conditions of public sector workers falling behind those in the private sector. Privatization of parts of welfare provision, notably care for the elderly, have driven down wages and made it harder to organize workers. Further, the deregulation of other areas of the economy such as transport services, particularly buses, means that there has been an intensification of competition through the use low-cost labour.

Emerging patterns of migrant Polish workers in the United Kingdom

The following section is based on the TUC's report *Propping up rural and small town Britain* (2004) and on Home Office statistics (Home Office and other departments, 2004).

Table 10.1 Requests by language

Language	Number of requests	Percentage of total
Polish	900	61
Slovak	189	13
Czech	135	9
Latvian	122	8
Hungarian	91	6
Lithuanian	25	2
Estonian	9	0.6

Source: TUC, 2004.

According to the Home Office, between May 2004 and May 2005, of the 231,545 migrant workers registered as working in the United Kingdom, 57 per cent were Polish. Thirty-two per cent of workers registered in the first five months had already been in the country before 1 May (and a further 13 per cent failed to state their arrival date). It is not clear that all workers who could register do so, for example those working for gangmasters.[1] Home Office figures show that 84 per cent of arrivals were between 18 and 34. In the first five months 47 per cent of applicants were female, and after 12 months this figure had fallen to 40 per cent.

One success of the TUC was an agreement with the Home Office that all workers registering received a TUC leaflet giving advice on employment rights (in English). By the end of October 2004 1,600 workers (or their friends and family) had contacted the TUC for translated versions (see table 10.1; now available in eight languages).

Regional patterns

Migrants can be found in every region of the United Kingdom, but there are significant regional variations. There are particular concentrations in the rural agricultural areas in the East of England (Lincolnshire, Cambridge, Peterborough, Norfolk, Luton, Kent and Sussex) as a result of the Seasonal Workers Scheme, as well as the outer boroughs to the east, north and west of London. Polish workers, too, were found in every region, but there were almost exclusively Polish concentrations in some towns, notably Luton and Southampton, and in Northern Ireland.

---

[1] Gangmaster is a historical term used for someone who provided temporary "gangs" of labour in agriculture and the food processing industry.

Sectoral patterns

Table 10.2 Number of requests by employer

Type of employer	Number of requests
Hotels	64
Pubs	7
Restaurants	3
Other leisure	7
Total hospitality	**81 (53 per cent)**
Farms	23
Other horticulture	5
Animal care, breeding and rearing	4
Agricultural wholesale	3
Food processing/manufacturing	8
Total agriculture and food	**43 (28 per cent)**
Care homes	4
Other services	5
Agencies	6
Total services	**15 (10 per cent)**
Other manufacturing	7
Other distribution	3
Transport	4
Others	**14 (9 per cent)**

Source: TUC, 2004.

These figures are generally confirmed by statistics from the Home Office who reported that the largest categories of registration were in hospitality and agriculture. However, business and administration featured significantly in the statistics which was not the case with the TUC figures (table 10.2). This is likely to reflect the high proportion of agency workers, whose direct employer may be classified into the service sector, but who are likely to identify their employer as being their actual workplace. According to the Home Office, 44 per cent were in temporary employment, but this rose to 82 per cent in "administration, business and management".

Hospitality, agriculture and food processing have all been covered by temporary labour schemes aimed at helping employers fill vacancies. However, anecdotal evidence suggests that once enlargement took place, workers who had previously been employed on temporary schemes registered and began looking for work where the pay and conditions were better. Provisional figures from the Home Office suggest that the temporary schemes, post enlargement, are drawing most workers from Bangladesh, Viet Nam, Ukraine and Bulgaria.

The recruitment of skilled and semi-skilled workers

One group of workers who are not prominent in the TUC survey are skilled and semi-skilled workers recruited directly by employers or their agents. For example, two groups of between 30 and 50 welders have been recruited directly to factories in the North East and the Midlands from the Gdansk region of Poland. As well as welders and electricians, specialized engineering skills are much sought after. One group of workers who have been the focus of recruitment have been drivers.

Problems of Polish migrant workers in the United Kingdom

This section summarizes the main problems faced by Polish migrant workers in the United Kingdom, and the issues these raise for trade unions.

Employer abuse

Gaining legal status in the labour market does not remove the threat of abuse by employers. However, it is clear that legislation does give some workers the confidence to find out about their rights, complain and seek to remedy problems.

Problems with recruitment and temporary labour agencies are substantial. Some agencies charge workers in their home countries for finding them jobs. There have been examples of hourly rates of pay being lower than promised, or lower than those paid to British workers, and of non-payment for some hours worked. In some cases wages have been reported as withheld for months.

Excessive working hours have been reported, in some cases with no rest day being provided or inadequate breaks between shifts. A frequent complaint is that no enhanced rates are paid for overtime. The differences in pay which have emerged are obviously of concern to unions, who want to avoid divide and rule strategies being used to depress wages.

Workers clearly do not understand the tax and social security contribution system, and sometimes suspect (perhaps with reason) that employers are defrauding both the worker and the State. It is a challenge to unions to explain to new arrivals the prevailing rates of pay, good employment practices and legal rights, and to organize these workers to defend themselves. Others problems include practical issues such as opening a bank account.

Housing

Many complaints centred on housing, which is frequently provided by the employers. The bad experience of accommodation for undocumented Polish workers was reported in a book published in 2002 (Jordan and Düvell, 2002). Many landlords are associated with the employer. In some cases early arrivals or already present family contacts will hire out rooms to new arrivals, often providing work as well.

Reports from TUC regions, unions and some employers suggest that the lack of affordable housing close to employers seeking workers for relatively low-paid jobs is a significant contributory factor to localized labour shortages. The experience of many migrant workers suggests that the solution to housing shortages cannot be left to the private sector.

There is widespread provision of overcrowded, overpriced and poor quality accommodation for single workers and this may resolve shortages in the short term. It may also help explain the preference of employers and agencies for young single people. However, it is not a long-run solution for practical and ethical reasons – it is hard to see how workers in such circumstances can exercise the right to family life promised to them by the European Convention of Human Rights (Council of Europe, 2007). The issue of housing needs to be addressed as a priority by regional development agencies and central government.

Women migrant workers

Traditionally Polish migrants have been men who worked, usually illegally, in the building industry. The main opportunity for the employment of women was as *au pairs*. However, through the sector-based schemes, significant numbers of women and young women in particular have entered to work in hotels and restaurants. This trend appears to be continuing since EU enlargement, with 44 per cent of those registering in United Kingdom being women. Although women migrants from Poland will face similar problems to migrant workers in general regarding pay and working conditions, interviews by the author found evidence of problems facing maternity leave and protection at work for pregnant women.

Xenophobia and racism

Despite the hostile tone in some English newspapers, there have been few examples of open xenophobia.

Trade union organization

A study of Labour Force Survey statistics for 2002 showed that workers not born in Britain were significantly less likely to be trade union members than the

British-born. Workers from Eastern Europe had the lowest level of membership at 11.7 per cent (TUC, 2003b). The TUC Congress in 2004 passed a resolution that, among other points, highlighted the importance of organizing and recruiting migrant workers. In order to address this issue with Polish workers, a programme is being developed.

A further survey of those contacting the TUC is planned, in conjunction with the Centre for Migration Policy and Society. This will build on questions already asked of Eastern European workers before enlargement regarding pay, hours and problems with employers (Anderson, 2004), and will also include questions which would give data comparable with those gathered by the German building workers union IG-Bau in researching the need for a migrant workers union (EIRO, 2004a).

Cooperation with the long-established Federation of Poles, the main organization representing Poles in the United Kingdom, is also being developed to include advice surgeries and help with the provision of translated information and advice. It is hoped that this initiative can be used to develop a cadre of Polish-speaking trade union activists.

A number of trade-union-based training initiatives which have been started with government funding are now being developed to include English-language training (ESOL) for migrant workers. This has already proved a valuable benefit for other migrant communities, such as the Portuguese.

Issues facing Polish unions

Impact of "drain" of members and potential members

For Solidarity and Ogolnopolskie Porozumnie Związków Zawodowych (OPZZ – the All-Poland Alliance of Trade Unions) migration poses the problem of a loss of members or the potential loss of members as young people seek employment outside Poland. The cyclical movement shown by many young Polish workers also means that workers will spend some time in Britain and some in Poland (or elsewhere). It is therefore likely that only organizations which can offer membership and protection in more than one country can hope to recruit and retain such mobile workers.

Improving the rights of Polish workers in the European Union

The key question here is the role that organized Polish workers can play in securing basic rights on pay and working conditions for Polish workers working in the EU. An additional challenge is that the nature of migrant workers is different, with young people dominating the movement of labour, and a significant proportion of young women.

On a more general political note, the major role being played by recruitment and temporary labour agencies is of particular significance. On 1 January 2004, new regulations governing temporary work agencies came into force in Poland. These are considerably more stringent than those operating in Britain (EIRO, 2003), but are still expected to lead to a rapid increase in the numbers of registered agencies and agency workers. Since enlargement Poland has been among the group of EU Member States (led by the United Kingdom) resisting the introduction of a Temporary Agency Work Directive which would grant agency staff parity with permanent workers with whom they work.

The abusive treatment handed out to Polish workers in the United Kingdom by some agencies (see for example *The Guardian*, 2005) highlights the consequence of the absence of such regulation. Potential clearly exists for joint union cooperation to address government inertia on this issue.

Improving the rights of migrant workers in Poland

At the same time as migrant workers from Poland seek better job opportunities and higher wages in the EU, workers from Ukraine and Belarus have migrated to Poland. This trend is likely to continue as the population of working age declines after 2020 (Iglicka, 2003). One anecdote tells of welders from Gdansk recruited to Telford (a town to the north of Birmingham), while Ukrainian welders filled their places in Gdansk.

The response of Polish unions

There are two main unions in Poland – Solidarity and OPZZ (the "official union" under the Communist regime). According to European Industrial Relations Observatory (EIRO, 2002) online, 6 per cent of the adult population are trade union members compared with 18 per cent in 1991 (EIRO, 2002). Solidarity and OPZZ have approximately 1.2 million members each and the remaining 1 million are members of a series of smaller trade unions.

A third new confederation, the Polish Trade Union Forum (Forum Związków Zawodowych or FZZ) was formed in the late 1990s. This includes unions representing workers significantly affected by migration such as nurses (OZZPiP – All Polish Union of Nurses and Midwives) and SFTU (Seamen's and Fishermen's Trade Union).

All three organizations are reported to have been hostile to the labour market restrictions being placed on Polish nationals in most EU Member States (EIRO, 2004b) and have advocated a free market in labour. However, there are contrasting views about how they should intervene in the issue of migrant workers.

Two different strategies of Polish unions

In the pre-accession period before May 2004 Solidarity ran a campaign to discourage their members from going abroad and taking "low wage" jobs. They are quite explicit that they do not aim to play the role of a "recruitment agency". However, as legal migration has become a reality in the post-accession period, their policy has changed to one where they try to reduce the exploitation of Polish migrant workers by making them as well informed as possible. Aside from concerns regarding the welfare of their individual members, they put forward the wider argument that migration should not be allowed to divide and rule workers and accelerate a "race to the bottom" in terms of low labour costs.

Solidarity's International Department is at the forefront of these new initiatives. Information points are planned in their largest 16 regional offices. Essentially these will provide information on countries that workers are considering migrating to, as well as specific information about particular sectors and jobs and any collective agreements that might exist. Importantly, there would be information about unions with which they are cooperating in order for workers to access further help and information on arrival. One aim is to discourage the migration of people who are "unfocused". Immediately after accession many hopeful workers arrived in London, in a sort of "gold rush" mentality, only to find that jobs were not readily available and accommodation was impossible.

The policy of opening information points is a double-edged sword. It uses scarce resources to assist members and potential members to leave the country, thereby reducing their membership. On the positive side, by providing this information service to a wider audience, they are able to raise the profile of the union and thus gain from the possibility of additional recruitment.

Although their approach may be considered the exception rather than the rule, the strategy of the SFTU has been very different. In the face of large-scale redundancies in their industry they have become active agents in the migration process. Between 1998 and 2002 there were 5,000 redundancies in the fishing industry due to the bankruptcies of the major state-owned enterprises. Approximately half of these workers were members of the union. The union took a policy decision that a major part of their activities would be focused on finding new employment opportunities for their members. This included putting resources into retraining workers or helping them update their skills. In particular, they have been active in seeking workplaces for their members abroad. To date they have found 400 jobs abroad for their members.

The new orientation of the SFTU was controversial and met with the disapproval of OPZZ, with which it was affiliated. This prompted the withdrawal of the union from OPZZ and their affiliation to the newly formed federation FZZ.

The argument of the SFTU is that they are actively and positively helping their members who would otherwise use "cowboy recruitment" agencies. According to the interviewee they can negotiate in advance the nature of the work, the payment, conditions of service and accommodation. Therefore, they are at least mitigating the exploitative conditions under which their members may otherwise be employed.

Issues for British trade unions

Problems with private sector trade unions

Polish workers tend to be employed in the private sector. In the United Kingdom, with only one in five workers in a trade union, organization is weak compared with the public sector. With the casualization of work this causes a double problem for trade union recruitment.

Temporary labour agencies

In the majority of cases workers are employed not directly but by agencies. It is at this level that trade unions need to recruit. There are hundreds of agencies with varying degrees of good practice. There have been successes with some unions negotiating and signing agreements with agencies. However, the challenge is first to get much more detailed knowledge on how Polish workers find work, through networks in Poland and the United Kingdom. The second area where research is needed is a mapping of and investigation into temporary labour agencies and their practices as well as the number of Polish workers they employ.

Integrating Polish activists into union structures

Rather than simply recruiting and acting on behalf of Polish workers it is important to try and build a base of activists who are trained and can act as a link between United Kingdom trade unions and the Polish workers.

The response of British trade unions

Grassroots projects and community cooperation

There are lots of examples of good practice and projects involving trade unions, communities, churches and sometimes employers in establishing rights for Polish workers in the workplace and the community.

Polish workers in unionized workplaces

Where Polish workers are employed in unionized workplaces workers have collectively taken up issues either with or on behalf of Polish workers. One notable success was in November 2005, when under the threat of balloting for a strike, a baggage handling firm at Luton airport was forced to give Polish workers the same wages and conditions as other airport workers. Ground staff at the airport were going to be polled on whether they would support a strike after the T&G exposed the exploitation of Polish workers. These workers, who had been supplied by an agency, were being paid substantially less than United Kingdom workers doing the same job. The union organizer said that it was vital that collective bargaining was maintained and not undermined. As a result of this success not only did the 15 workers join the union but it led to many enquiries from other Polish and migrant workers who were put in touch with union full-timers in other parts of the country.

Industrial action by bus drivers in the Midlands is another good example of how unity can be forged between British-born and Polish workers. In Autumn 2005 there was a series of one-day strikes over low pay and pensions with over 100 workers, British and Polish, joining the union.

Trades Union Congress special focus

Each year the TUC sets aside 10 per cent of its budget for innovative projects. One aspect of this work in 2005 was organizing migrant workers. After a visit to Solidarity's headquarters in Gdansk, one initiative was the decision to second a worker from Solidarity's Organization and Recruitment Department to the North West TUC. His role was firstly to raise the profile of trade unions with the Polish community. Second, he liaised with Polish workers and put them in touch with relevant unions. In the ten weeks of his secondment he recruited 150 new Polish workers to British trade unions from a variety of sectors such as construction, retail and food processing.

Cross-border collaboration

There are now some structures in place to try and provide information to prospective migrant workers, both in Poland and the United Kingdom. However, much more detailed information is needed about how migrant workers get jobs. In this respect more research on the role on employment agencies in the process is important.

The possibility of mutual recognition of union cards may enhance the attraction of union membership to a mobile workforce.

The TUC has already hosted some union organizers from Eastern Europe on training courses held in London (TUC, 2003a); examining the possibility of repeating this exercise should form part of the work in progress.

The identification of common campaigning aims – on the Temporary Agency Worker or Posting of Workers Directives, for example – will also be strengthened by joint work over migrant issues. There are also common labour market themes (over the minimum wage, labour market reforms and retention of skilled health workers, for example), where detailed consideration of the relationship between the two countries will prove valuable.

Although all interviewees emphasized that there was a huge task ahead, a good start has been made in trying to defend the rights of Polish migrant workers in the United Kingdom. Communities and trade unions in the United Kingdom and Solidarity in Poland have started to rise to this challenge.

References

Anderson, B. 2004. *Changing status, changing lives? The impact of EU accession on low wage migrants*, paper presented at Metropolis Conference on Migration, Geneva, 27 Sep.–1 Oct.

—; Rogaly, B. 2005. *Forced labour and migration to the UK*. Trades Union Congress, Feb. Available at: http://www.tuc.org.uk/international/tuc-9317-f0.cfm

Dorling, D.; Thomas, B. 2004. *People and places: A 2001 census atlas of the UK* (Bristol, Policy Press).

Council of Europe. 2007. *Convention for the Protection of Human Rights and Fundamental Freedoms as amended by Protocol No. 11*. Available at: http://conventions.coe.int/treaty/en/Treaties/html/005.htm [accessed 2 Aug. 2007].

EIRO (European Industrial Relations Observatory). 2002. "Declining trade union density examined". Available at: http://www.eurofound.europa.eu/eiro/2002/08/feature/pl0208105f.html

—. 2003. "Temporary agency work legislation approved". Available at: http://www.eurofound.europa.eu/eiro/2003/08/inbrief/pl0308103n.html

—. 2004a. "European Migrant Workers Union founded". Available at: http://www.eurofound.europa.eu/eiro/2004/09/feature/de0409206f.html

—. 2004b. "The Polish labour market and EU membership". Available at: http://www.eurofound.europa.eu/eiro/2004/01/feature/pl0401105f.html

Financial Times. 2004. "EU nationals harden their hearts against club's new members", 4 Feb.

—. 2004. "Restructuring the ideal of unity. But there are deep cultural fears of being overwhelmed by immigrants", 9 Feb.

The Guardian. 2005. "Polish workers lost in a strange land find work in UK does not pay", by Felicity Lawrence, 11 Jan.

GUS (Główny Urząd Statystyczny) [Central Statistical Office]. 2004. Available at: http://www.stat.gov.pl/english/dane_spolgosp/prac_ludnosc/bezrobocie_rejectrowane/2004

—. 2005. "The situation of households in 2004 in the light of the research into household budgets".

Hardy, J.; Rainnie, A. 1995. "Industrial relations in Poland: Solidarity and Polish industrial relations in the 1990s", in *Industrial Relations Journal*, Vol. 26, No. 4, pp. 267–279.

—; —. 1996. *Restructuring Krakow: Desperately seeking capitalism* (London, Mansell Publishing).

Home Office; Department for Work and Pensions; Inland Revenue; Office of the Deputy Prime Minister. 2004. *Accession Monitoring Report, May–Sep. 2004*. A joint online report, 10 Nov. Available at: http://www.ind.homeoffice.gov.uk/6353/aboutus/accession moniotoringreport6.pdf

Iglicka, K. 2003. *Priorities and developmental directions of Polish migration policy. Analizy i Opinie/Analyses & Opinions No. 13* (Warsaw, Instytut Spraw Publicznych).

Jordan, B.; Düvell, F. 2002. *Irregular migration: The dilemmas of transnational mobility* (Cheltenham, Edward Elgar).

TUC (Trades Union Congress). 2003a. *General Council Report*, Report to the 135th annual Trades Union Congress, 8–11 Sep., Brighton, UK.

—. 2003b. *Overworked, underpaid and over here – Migrant workers in Britain* (London).

—. 2004c. *Propping up rural and small town Britain: Migrant workers from the new Europe* (London).

MORE THAN BANANAS: SOCIAL RESPONSIBILITY NETWORKS AND LABOUR RELATIONS IN THE BANANA INDUSTRY IN THE URABÁ REGION OF COLOMBIA

Maria-Alejandra Gonzalez-Perez
and
Terrence McDonough
Centre for Innovation and Structural Change
National University of Ireland, Galway

Introduction

This paper seeks to apply a dynamic perspective to understanding the changing character of labour relations and associated social movements within the banana industry in Colombia and more specifically within the major banana-producing region of Urabá. It is based on of the results of a broader research on social responsibility networks (SRN)[1] and their role in improving working and living conditions for workers in banana-producing regions in the context of globalization.

Globalization has intensified many social problems and has exacerbated inequalities. It is widely believed that the same global movement of capital is also undermining the capacity of the State to effectively intervene to ameliorate these problems. The negative impact of globalization on communities and workers, along with the decline in the capacity of traditional political strategies to address these concerns, has led to challenges for labour and trade unions and other social actors (churches, NGOs, etc.). Unions and other organizations sympathetic to workers have adopted strategies of direct pressure on corporations, and collective bargaining is taking place around non-traditional issues. These new strategies and the corporate responses have contributed to new struggles and a discourse around issues of "social responsibility". It is to be expected that such a new strategy will be accompanied by both benefits and costs.

Traditionally, Colombia occupied third place in world banana exports after Ecuador and Costa Rica. In recent years, however, the Philippines have

---

[1] A social responsibility network (SRN) is a network of civil society actors and stakeholders as well as private corporations and state agencies that together provide a platform for social responsibility initiatives. Whether this concept is applicable outside the province of Urabá can only be determined by further research.

displaced Colombia to fourth place (FAO, 2006). The banana industry in Urabá employs 17,600 workers, of whom 15,000 are unionized, most of them with the National Trade Union of the Agriculture Sector, "Sintrainagro" (ENS, 2004; Torres and Guarnizo, 2004). The region of Urabá borders Panama and produces 83 per cent of the total number of bananas exported from Colombia. Ninety per cent of Urabá's economy is dependent on the banana industry (Torres and Guarnizo, 2004). The banana region includes four key towns: Chigorodó, Carepa, Turbó and Apartadó. Eight banana export companies operate in the region on a total of 344 farms. The banana industry in Urabá provides around 70,000 jobs – a means of employment and subsistence for more than 50,000 families (idem, 2004).

This paper is based on an ongoing study that is mainly a product of ethnographic research, using participatory methods. Multiple actors have been identified, though this study initially concentrates on three: trade unions, the employers' association and the Colombian State.

Particular emphasis is placed on:

- identifying relationships between the various groups of actors;

- exploring the capacity of different actors to undertake social responsibility initiatives and to demand such initiatives from others;

- describing the effects of different actors' strategies on the actions undertaken by the other actors, and

- analysing the developing nature of relationships within the context of an emerging SRN.

Banana business

Bananas are the world's most exported fruit in terms of volume. They rank first in export revenue for developing countries and second after citrus in terms of total value.

After more than a century, the banana business continues to be led by the "big four": three of them "dollar companies" (Chiquita Brands Int., formerly United Fruit Company; Dole Food Company Inc. and Fresh Del Monte Produce) and one Irish firm (Fyffes). These four, along with the Ecuadorian family enterprise Noboa, control distribution and retail sales in the global market. Even though there are many small and medium-size independent producers, most farms are owned by the big companies or supply fruit to them (Chambron, 1999; van de Kasteele, 1998; van de Kasteele and van der Stichele, 2005).

Since the beginning of the twentieth century, bananas have influenced South America, Central America and the Caribbean more than any other commodity. The transformation of the Americas into "banana republics" during the last hundred years has been the rubric under which the United States has been described as the colonizer of the rest of the hemisphere (Bucheli, 2005; Fonnegra, 1980; Litvin, 2003; Striffler and Moberg, 2003).

In Latin American countries, banana cultivation coincided with a wide succession of diplomatic, military and economic changes and movements. In the process of transforming the tropical rain forest into monoculture plantations, profound ecological, demographic, political and cultural changes took place. Banana companies developed towns, railways, roads, harbours, ports and electrification in the formerly impenetrable tropical forest. The integration of this frontier zone into the world marketplace, resulting from these structural changes, transformed the political and cultural identities of the indigenous people and immigrants as new forms of conflict, processes and actors emerged. The introduction of commercial banana cultivation presented new challenges for engineers, workers and entrepreneurs. From region to region in Latin America, the cultivation of bananas became connected to the process of capital formation, nation-building and labour migration both internally and internationally.

The early years of the banana trade generated demand for land, capital and labour. Banana companies needed to recruit a large number of workers both locally and abroad to establish the required infrastructure for large-scale banana production. Thousands of these workers sacrificed their lives in the malaria and yellow fever infested rainforest in order to make the banana trade possible.

Typically, technological progress has not been associated with good labour relations or democratic forms of governance. Labour unions, communist political parties and individual workers have resisted the attempts of foreign banana companies to impose poor working conditions and low wages. Often during these struggles, banana workers were divided by language, colour and national origin. While confrontational labour relations seem almost inherent in banana production, labour conflicts were resolved in distinct ways in different countries, and even within a single corporation, individual producers and managers designed diverse methods of labour control and recruitment.

Within the banana export sector, distinct roles have developed for MNEs, workers, contract farmers and the State. Vertically integrated enterprises are present in countries such as Colombia and Costa Rica where MNEs control all phases of production (Striffler and Moberg, 2003). This means the corporations own (or contract) plantations, sea transportation facilities and distribution networks in consuming countries. This is the best option to assure the coordinated flow of bananas, a highly perishable good, to the final destination. This perishability also demands a good relationship with most of the governments with which the corporation deals (Bucheli, 2005).

Colombia's main export product is oil, representing 26.2 per cent of total exports in 2006. In contrast, bananas represent 2.2 per cent of total Colombian exports (Mincomercio, 2006). In the year 2004, Colombia exported 67 per cent of its banana production to the EU and 33 per cent to the United States (FAO, 2006). Colombia supplies 11 per cent of the worldwide banana demand. Alongside banana production itself, there are associated industries such as logistics, cardboard production and box manufacturing, agrochemicals and marine operations.

In recent years the revaluation of the Colombian peso against the US dollar has reduced anticipated incomes for producers. The value of the US dollar decreased by 23 per cent from 2,962 Colombian pesos in March 2003 to 2,243 Colombian pesos in January 2006, lowering the peso value of sales denominated in US dollars (Portafolio, 2003 and 2006). Competition for entry into the European market and consequently for low-cost production is worsening labour conditions. In Latin America, there are variations in labour costs among banana producer countries due to wage differences, national labour markets, welfare regimes and labour efficiencies related to different types of landholding. Additionally, in order to compete, independent small producers are obligated to meet the same quality and environmental standards, food security regulations and efficiency levels imposed by the consumer markets as are large producers. These standards raise production costs, which in turn exert a downward pressure on labour wages and living conditions.

Due to the international character of the banana market, especially in the retail sector, and the extensive investment required in technology, logistics and marketing, more and more stakeholders are participating in the "banana global labour chain". Because of the importance of brands and private labels, competition makes banana companies increasingly sensitive to consumers' opinions and concerns as well as responsive to shareholders' demands. The companies must respond to claims concerning greater transparency, corporate governance, fair trade initiatives, human rights and sustainable environmental practices. Furthermore, the influence of secondary stakeholders (e.g. non-governmental organizations, the media, social movement activists), "best of" rankings, global standards, reporting initiatives focusing on multiple bottom lines rather than the traditional bottom line alone, and researchers and academics) impact on the practices and attitudes related to labour issues.

The EU imports 60 per cent of its banana consumption from Latin American countries and 20 per cent from the Africa, Caribbean and Pacific (ACP) countries. An additional 20 per cent of the bananas consumed in the EU are produced in the EU in such places as the Canary Islands (Spain), Madeira and the Azores (Portugal) and Crete (Greece), and also Martinique and Guadeloupe (France). After EU enlargement in May 2004, banana imports from the dollar zone (Latin America) increased by 70 per cent, and it is estimated that banana consumption will total 610,000 tonnes per year in the 25 EU Member States.

Labour relations and the socio-political background of Urabá

Colombia is a country with one of the lowest levels of union density in the world. However, in the banana industry, 95 per cent of the labour force is organized by trade unions. In the 1960s, trade union organizations were established in Urabá, including the Union of Agricultural Workers (Sintagro), the Trade Union of Banana Workers (Sintrabanano), the Union of the Workers of the Sevilla Fruit Company (Sinaltraifru), the Union of Agricultural Labourers (Sindejornaleros) and the Union of Banana Workers (Utraiban). At the end of the 1970s, the Revolutionary Armed Forces of Colombia and the Army of the People (FARC-EP) and the Popular Liberation Army (EPL) were actively involved in the two most important trade unions of the regions, FARC-EP in Sintrabanano and the EPL in Sintagro. The Army of National Freedom (ELN) also supported the trade union movement in Urabá (García, 1996).

The association of agricultural producers, Augura, is the trade organization which affiliates banana producers in Colombia. It exports 95 per cent of the banana production of Urabá (Augura, 2005). Furthermore, its trade organization functions as a national and international representative for the Colombian banana producers. Augura plays a critical role in collective bargaining and lobbying.

In Colombia, the 1970s and 1980s were a period of strong labour union development, notwithstanding the fact that this movement was mainly clandestine due to fear of being made redundant, potential imprisonment and death threats. Despite these obstacles, the labour unions attained organization and recognition. The early 1980s were a time of momentum for the labour movement in the Urabá region.

In 1984, collective bargaining was initiated on a farm-by-farm basis. Since there were more than 300 banana producers, negotiations were in progress for the whole year. For each production unit, bargaining was led by three worker representatives and one trade union official, a total of around 700 people. For security reasons, negotiations took place in the city of Medellin, 330 kilometres from Urabá, and the logistical costs were borne by the producers. At the same time, labour movement activists in the region of Urabá contacted banana workers in Costa Rica in order to learn about their experiences and to develop an international perspective concerning labour issues in the banana industry.

In 1985, the first banana workers' strike in Urabá took place. The aim of the strike was union recognition and freedom of association. As a result, a labour relations commission was established, representing the national and state governments and the employers' federation, to attempt to mediate future labour conflicts. From 1989 until 1995, labour relations in the banana industry in Colombia were characterized by collective industry-wide industrial contracts. Social order in the region was added to labour conditions as an objective of collective bargaining.

In the 1990s, the labour union movement underwent a process of political and institutional development. In the official constitutional referendum in 1991, Colombian society agreed to a new social contract in which different social actors could take part in the resolution of conflicts. This new social contract had three main elements: civil rights; participative democracy in social, political, administrative and cultural issues; and local autonomy. Despite this, the often deadly conflict in Colombia has obviously continued. At the same time, in 1991, the largest illegal armed movement in the region of Urabá, the Popular Liberation Army (EPL)[2] demobilized after a three-year process. Sintraingro decided to support the social reintegration process for the demobilized members of the EPL politically. The banana trade association, Augura, also supported the process of demobilization. This decision was pivotal for the region because it led to the creation of a network of social commitments within the labour movement and the banana trade organization, aimed at the integration of armed elements on the basis of social dialogue and social cooperation. Former members of the EPL were trained as banana workers and were offered employment contracts in the region. This initiative was crucial because, through this network, social security linked to employment had implications for the regional and national political and economic situation. The politics of employment in the region as a method of ending armed conflict in Urabá was led mainly by networking the banana producers' association Augura, the trade union Sintraingro and the Catholic Church. Armed groups in Colombia played a significant role in creating and sustaining employment for the working-age population, and it was through the process of social incorporation of those who voluntarily decided to lay down their arms and participate in the banana labour market that the pacification and social "integration" of the Urabá region was achieved.

Nevertheless, the politics of employment in the banana production enclave of the region were complex, and conflicts of interest between various social groups and armed groups were involved. In the following years, banana

---

[2] In Colombia as a whole, FARC was much larger than the EPL. A minority of EPL militants refused to demobilize, leading to serious conflict between the different factions.

workers were unwillingly caught up in conflict between armed factions of both the left and the right in the region. Many were killed, disappeared, or were forced to migrate.[3] These deadly attacks on banana workers were confronted and denounced to the world by trade unions and other NGOs such as the Catholic Church, with the support of the IUF and COLSIBA (the Latin American Coordinating Committee of Banana Workers' Unions, grouping 40 banana workers' unions in eight countries of Latin America). Sintrainagro and its membership were supported by the IUF and COLSIBA and gained international recognition for their struggle, which greatly raised the morale of the labour movement in Urabá. The trade union movement in the region of Urabá together with the Catholic Church developed a social commitment to political education. The active incorporation of former leaders of the EPL influenced a project of political emancipation, facilitating the establishment of a new political party as an alternative to the traditional parties in the region. The former illegal armed guerrilla group the Popular Liberation Army (EPL – Ejercito Popular de Liberación) was transformed into a legal political party, keeping the same initials. As a political party EPL was renamed Colombia Hope, Peace and Liberty (Esperanza, Paz y Libertad) in 1991, and today EPL maintains active democratic participation in the regional government.

Trade unionism and labour relations in general in Colombia have changed structurally in the last decade. In 1996, a Verification and Monitoring Commission replaced the earlier labour relations commission and added representatives from the trade unions and the Church. Secondly, the inclusion of an element in each contract referred to as a "Preambulo" was mandated. Each contract must include a statement of principles, values and goals which will set the framework for ongoing labour relations. Such principles include the harmonization of conflicting interests, training and information for worker committees, and continuing improvements in work and living conditions, as well as the adoption of social indicators and the observation of legal norms.

Between 27 May and 11 June 2004, 319 farms in the Urabá region went on strike for 16 days, with the participation of 14,900 workers unionized by Sintrainagro. Banana producer companies lost US$25.5 million, and workers' lost earnings amounted to US$5.44 million. The strike had three aims: a) a wage increase of 8 per cent, b) a contribution of 105,000 Colombian pesos per cultivated hectare towards a common housing fund and c) the introduction of a model to prevent outsourcing of secondary labour tasks (*El Tiempo*, 2004).

---

[3] Urabá was portrayed as the most violent corner of the world in the 1990s. The IUF reported that in 1995 more than 700 people were killed in Urabá. Of these 111 were active in the trade union movement, most of them being members of Sintrainagro (Iglesias and Pedraza, 2006). Trade union and political leaders of the region – such as the mayors of Apartadó and Chigorodó and the Vice-President and the General Secretary of Sintrainagro – were killed (Torres and Guarnizo, 2004).

The banana companies announced a plan to contract labour, through temporary manpower cooperatives and associated enterprises, to perform non-regular tasks on the plantations. Workers and Sintrainagro believed the introduction of this model would replace the current system of direct contracts and would damage the trade union movement in the region. Producers pioneered this model of contract in 2001 with Generación de Empleo y Soluciones Técnicas Ambientales (GESTA),[4] a cooperative with a membership of 230 women, aged between 19 and 65, who were heads of households and were widowed during the period of violence. These women collected nylon and plastic and recycled these materials to sell to other industrial sectors in different regions of Colombia. Their labour facilitated banana producers' compliance with environmental regulations on "clean production". The affiliated workers were compensated at an agreed rate according to individual performance (the amount of nylon and plastic collected in a working day measured in kilos). Trade unions criticize this model because cooperatives provide neither social security benefits nor regular wages. Also, these workers are not represented by a labour union.[5]

Both the Sintrainagro and the Sinaltrafru trade unions have proposed a type of contract called the *contrato sindical* (trade union contract), created and implemented by a trade union in a plastic producing company in Medellin, in which the trade union acts a contractor and employer but at the same time continues its role as a labour union. This model has its critics. Social movement activists, such as other trade unions and some left-wing political parties, have raised objections to the dual role of the trade union organization as the workers' representation body and as the employer, especially in the region of Urabá where a significant number of trade union organizers have run for local elections. This potentially would make the trade union organization a force for political, social, labour and capital control in the region.

As result of the 2004 strike, workers secured a wage increase of 7.63 per cent and a contribution to the common housing fund of 80,000 Colombian pesos per cultivated hectare. The 2004 collective agreement had as one of its objectives to respond to productivity and other demands imposed by commercial globalization and to protect labour rights. For this negotiation, the Verification and Monitoring Commission was constituted, with six members: two members from the trade union organization (Sintrainagro),

---

[4] The name of this cooperative translates to English as Employment Creation and Technical Environmental Solutions.
[5] As Rosa Luxemburg (1900) stated, "Workers forming a co-operative in the field of production are thus faced with the contradictory necessity of governing themselves with utmost absolutism. They are obliged to take towards themselves the role of capitalist entrepreneur – a contradiction that accounts for the usual failure of production co-operatives which either become pure capitalist enterprises or, if the workers' interests continue to predominate, end by dissolving."

two banana producer representatives, one representative from the Ministry of Social Welfare and one representative of the Catholic Church.

In 2004, banana producers presented to the Verification and Monitoring Commission proposals to modify contract conditions through the introduction of flexible work contracts. The implementation of this measure for the Urabá region would imply salary reductions and would impact on the quality of the life in the region. This measure would change income distribution in favour of the employers. The Escuela Nacional Sindical (ENS) found this measure would increase net profit to 44.69 per cent, and labour costs would be reduced to 10.7 per cent (ENS, 2004).

At present, the well-being of the Urabá region is under threat. As well as ongoing local security issues, the region faces intensifying international competition. On November 2004, the local social responsibility network, Fuerzas Vivas de Urabá (Urabá's Vital Strengths) was formed, led by Sintrainagro, Augura and the Catholic Church and with the participation of local government leaders, political parties, non-governmental associations, the Colombian army, the regional police department, local media and other trade unions. The objective of that regional assembly was the establishment of an agenda of active social and economic goals to compel the state to meet its responsibilities[6]. It focused on three main areas: the future of the banana industry; regional welfare concerns such as health, education, housing, employment and infrastructure; and security and public order for the region.

On 11 May 2006, 86.6 per cent of Urabá banana workers who were members of Sintrainagro voted either in favour of a strike or to go to an arbitration court, after failing to secure from the banana producer companies a new collective agreement and a wage increase of 10 per cent (Sintrainagro, 2006). Banana producers argued they were unable to meet workers' demands for an improvement in their living conditions due to the restrictions on access to the European market imposed by the EU, in addition to the revaluation of the Colombian peso, which created a loss estimated at 100 million US dollars. This revaluation has been partially compensated by government aid. The strike was averted when a three-year agreement was reached on 25 May 2006. It secured a wage increase of 6.5 per cent for the first year, full cost of living adjustments in the second and third years and an additional 1.5 per cent in the third year. Banana-producing companies will also arrange substantial financial contributions to the social, educational, cultural, recreational and sports funds (*El Tiempo*, 2006; IUF, 2006).

---

[6] As is clear from the previous list, many of the participants are themselves part of that very state.

Observations

- The threat of a collapse of the Colombian banana industry on international markets generated a network of social actors whose main participants are producers, trade unions, workers, the Church, political parties and the Colombian State.

- As a consequence of this network, trade organizations (both trade unions and the producers' union) and their members allocated resources to regional social infrastructure development and compelled the State to address its responsibilities.

- The demobilization of armed forces in the region provided space for the creation of the SRN in the Urabá region which in turn provided a space for social dialogue with the various armed forces, achieving a process of pacification in the region. Just as trade unions sometimes serve as a recruiting ground in armed conflicts, they can also play an active role in the resolution of such conflicts. The presence of unions at the heart of the local economy and employment opportunities greatly facilitates this role. The Urabá experience indicates that conflict resolution will involve engagement with a wide range of social actors and members of civil society.

Globalization and changing labour relations in Urabá

The Colombian banana industry is itself an outcome of an earlier era of internationalization. Specifically, the industry in Urabá dates from the 1960s, the height of the post-war Pax Americana. The challenges facing the region today stem from multiple aspects of the current establishment of global neo-liberalism. Paradoxically, these factors are pushing the region in two opposite directions. These opposing forces are at the centre of the decisions confronting the region today.

On the one hand, the current hyper-globalization of the banana market has led to a situation of oversupply on the international markets. In this way, the situation in bananas mirrors that in many other industries in the current period. Because bananas are a primary product produced in many developing countries, this has rapidly resulted in downward pressure on prices. This situation is exacerbated by demands from an increasingly centralized global retail industry for more competitive pricing.

The pressure of the international market for lower prices is becoming particularly acute because of expected changes in the EU banana regime. Currently, the EU is the only large importer which does not allow completely open un-tariffed access to its banana market for the "dollar" banana producers, which include Colombia. A regime of quotas and tariffs on imports above the quotas is imposed on the dollar producers, as a way of protecting banana producers in the former European colonies from competition. This system has resulted in dollar producers diversifying into the protected European zone and may have been a factor in Chiquita's and Dole's decisions to sell production operations in Urabá to local production companies.

This protectionist regime was challenged in the WTO by the United States. The WTO's GATT dispute mechanisms found that the EU regime contravened GATT rules. In 1997, the WTO dispute panel found the EU's tariff quota regime acted in a discriminatory way. A WTO ruling two years later allowed the United States to impose US$191.4 million in trade sanctions against EU goods and this led to the "banana war". In 2001, the EU agreed to change its import system and negotiated a unified tariff for all exporters. On October 2004, the EU announced its intention of imposing a duty of €230 per tonne of bananas when the new regime entered into force in January 2006. This tariff level, when combined with tariff preferences granted to the ACP countries, disadvantages Latin American producers. Latin American banana-producing countries have argued that an increase in the tariff "would bring about disastrous economic and social consequences for Latin American countries, eroding national incomes and destroying jobs throughout the region, where the banana industry is a substantial source of income and employment" (Bianchi, 2004).

At the same time, the elimination of quotas means that within Latin America, low-cost producers like Ecuador will be favoured over higher-cost areas like Urabá. All of these factors have conspired to produce a downward pressure on prices. Low wages and extremely poor working conditions have been imposed in Ecuador. This low-road strategy threatens a race to the bottom in conditions within the industry.

In contrast to the Ecuadorian industry, the Urabá region is currently pursuing an alternative strategy analogous to the high-road strategies pursued by some developed countries' industrial producers (albeit at the end of a protracted and bloody conflict). The viability of this high-road strategy in the banana industry is also conditioned by pressures emanating from the global market. The emergence of global marketing has created competition around the quality of the product. Unfortunately, this has more to do with the size, appearance and price of the banana than either taste or nutrition. Of perhaps more importance is the emergence of marketing concern for the ethical "quality" of the product. Historically, bananas have been marketed as a sunny, fun and sexy product. Widespread knowledge of impoverished workers, terrible working conditions and environmental damage threatens this happy image. It has consequently become possible to pursue a higher-priced strategy in conjunction with selling social responsibility and a consequently guilt-free product.

Moves in this direction in the Urabá region were conditioned by, on the one hand, the demobilization process of a significant faction of the armed struggle in the region and the temporary bankruptcy of Chiquita in 2001, associated with the restrictions on access to the EU market for Latin American bananas. Chiquita adopted a policy of "good citizenship" as a way of rowing back into the market's good graces. It concluded agreements with the Rainforest Alliance to certify the environmental performance of its suppliers, Social Accountability 8000 labour and human rights standards, and EurepGAP food safety in all its operations in Latin America. It also signed an important labour agreement with the IUF/COLSIBA federation of unions in 2001. These agreements have been associated with a recovery of its stock price.

Nonetheless, this "exemplary citizen" face of Chiquita was challenged in the international media after its public admission in April 2003 of protection payments made to a right-wing paramilitary group in order to ensure the safety of its employees in Colombia (Chiquita, 2004a). Not long after this news, Chiquita sold its banana operations in Colombia to a Colombian-based producer, C.I. Banacol S.A, for US$37 million (Chiquita, 2004b)[7] as part of a cost-cutting strategy and a move to higher-value products. Unions in Urabá were consulted regarding the sale agreement, in which the new company undertook to respect the union contract and to maintain the environmental, social and safety standards previously introduced for eight years. Furthermore, Chiquita committed itself to buy Banacol production for a period of eight years.

During the ILO's 95th International Labour Conference in Geneva (31 May to 16 June 2006), a tripartite agreement was reached between the Colombian Government, employers and workers, providing for a permanent ILO presence in the country. The agreement includes technical assistance to the Decent Work Country Programme and the promotion and defence of fundamental workers' rights, in particular as regards the right to life and freedom of association and expression, as well as collective bargaining and freedom of enterprise for employers (ILO, 2006).

Despite these efforts, exponentially multiplying pressures to reduce costs and lower prices and the unpredictability of market access politics put this strategy in jeopardy. The pursuit of this strategy has risks for employers, workers, and their communities, and also the participating multinationals. The

---

[7] After a federal court case initiated in March 2007, Chiquita Brands International received a sentencing memorandum from the United States Department of Justice on 10 September 2007, imposing a fine of US$25 million (Chiquita, 2007). The sentence was handed down after the company was charged with making payments of US$1.7 million to paramilitary groups during the period 1997–2004. The court decision sparked outrage by the Colombian Government and others who accused the company of buying impunity. Colombia's Government requested the US$25 million be transferred to the region of Urabá to be allocated to social programmes in aid of victims of paramilitary violence (*El Tiempo*, 2007). According to testimony given at the court case by the paramilitary group, all banana companies operating during that period in the region made payments to paramilitary groups (*El Tiempo*, 2007).

strikes in May of 2004 and the negotiation process in May 2006 indicate that the long-term conflict of interest between worker and employer has not disappeared. In the global capitalist market, any strategy intended to avoid participating in the threatening race to the bottom in terms of standards of living and working conditions walks a fine line, with precipices of deteriorating social conditions on one side and the loss of international markets to cheap competition on the other. So far, developments in Urabá have been somewhat encouraging. The future, however, remains deeply uncertain.

References

Augura. 2005. "Asociación de Bananeros de Colombia: Quién es y que hace?". Available at: http://www.augura.com.co/augura_es.htm

Bianchi, S. 2004. "Developing countries prepare for 'banana battle'". Available at: http://www.globalpolicy.org/socecon/trade/2004/1028bananas.htm

Bucheli, M. 2005. *Bananas and business: The United Fruit Company in Colombia, 1899–2000* (New York, NY, New York University Press).

Chambron, A.-C. 1999. *Bananas: The "green gold" of the TNCs* (London, UK Food Group). Available at: http://www.bananalink.org.uk/images//greengold_anneclaire.pdf

Chiquita Brands International. 2004a. "Department of Justice investigation", 10 May. Available at: http://www.chiquita.com/

—. 2004b. "Chiquita agrees to sell operations in Colombia", 11 Jun. Available at: http://www.chiquita.com/

—. 2007. Chiquita Brands International statement on U.S. Department of Justice sentencing memorandum, 11 Sep. Available at http://www.chiquita.com/

El Tiempo. 2004. "Los 16 mil trabajadores bananeros de Urabá levantan huelga tras 16 días de cese de actividades", 11 Jul.

—. 2006. "En la negociación, que terminó el jueves en la madrugada, se acordó un aumento salarial del 6,5 por ciento para el primer año de vigencia", 25 May.

—. 2007. "¡Indignados con Chiquita!" 24 Sep.

ENS (Escuela Nacional Sindical). 2004. *Sector bananero colombiano: Evolución y perspectivas* (Medellin, Sintrainagro).

FAO (Food and Agriculture Organization). 2006. *Banana Statistics 2005*, Commodities and Trade Division. Available at: http://www.fao.org/es/ESC/common/ecg/109399_en_BAN_STAT_06.pdf

Fonnegra, G. 1980. *Bananeras testimonio vivo de una epopeya* (Bogotá, Ediciones Tercer Mundo).

García, C.I. 1996. *Urabá: región, actores y conflicto, 1960–1990* (Medellin, Universidad de Antioquia, Instituto de Estudios Regionales).

Giraldo Ramírez, J. 2005. *Mejoramiento de las relaciones laborales en Colombia: Dinámica laboral 1994–2003* (Lima, ILO). Available at: http://www.oit.org.pe/osra/documentos/colombia_dinamica_laboral_1994_a_2003.pdf

Iglesias, G.; Pedraza, L.A. 2006. *Sintrainagro (I). Mucho más que una negociación colectiva: Entre dignidad y el fatalismo neoliberal*. Available at: http://www.rel-uita.org/sindicatos/ [accessed 15 May 2006].

ILO (International Labour Organization). 2006. "ILO's 95th annual Conference concludes". Available at: http://www.ilo.org/public/english/bureau/inf/pr/ 2006/35.htm

IUF (International Union of Food, Agricultural, Hotel, Restaurant, Catering, Tobacco and Allied Workers' Associations). 2006. *Strike averted with new collective agreement for Colombian banana workers*. Available at: http://www.iufdocuments.org/cgi-bin/dbman/db.cgi?db=default&uid=default&ID=3517&view_records=1&ww=1&en=1.

van de Kasteele, A. 1998. *The Banana Chain: The macro economics of the banana trade*, paper prepared on behalf of IUF for the 1998 International Banana Conference. Available at: http://www.ibc2.org/text/PAPER1E.pdf

—; van der Stichele, M. 2005. *Update on the Banana Chain*, paper read at International Banana Conference II: "Reversing the race to the bottom", 28–30 Apr., Brussels, Belgium.

Litvin, D. 2003. *Empires of profit: Commerce, conquest and corporate responsibility* (New York, NY, Texere).

Luxemburg, R. 1900. *Social reform or revolution* (London, Militant Publications). Available at: http://www.marxists.org/archive/luxemburg/1900/reform-revolution/index.htm

Mincomercio (Ministerio de Comercio y Turismo de la República de Colombia). 2006. *Exportaciones totales por séctor*. Available at: http://www.mincomercio.gov.co/VBeContent/Documentos/estadisticas/expo/periodo/sector/sector.xls

Pedraza, L.A. 2006. *Representación permanente de la OIT: Un triunfo del sindicalismo nacional e internacional*. Available at http://www.rel-uita.org/sindicatos/

Portafolio. 2003. "Histórico de dólar en 2003", Dec. Available at: http://www.portafolio.com.co/porta_dono_online/DOCS_DOLAR_PORTA/dolar2003/index.html

—. 2006. "Histórico de dólar en 2006", Jun. Available at: http://www.portafolio.com.co/porta_dono_online/DOCS_DOLAR_PORTA/dolar2003/index.html

Sintrainagro. 2006. *Comunicado de Sintrainagro: Cese de actividades en el Urabá Antioqueño*. Available at: http://www.rel-uita.org/sindicatos/ [accessed 15 May 2006].

Striffler, S.; Moberg, M. 2003. "Banana wars: Power, production, and history in the Americas", in G.M. Joseph and E.S. Rosenberg (eds): *American encounters/global interactions* (Durham, NC, and London, Duke University Press).

Torres, J.F.; Guarnizo, C.J. 2004. *Experiencia del sector bananero* (ILO, Bogotá). Available at: http://www.oit.org.pe/osra/documentos/en_la_busqueda_del_mejoramiento_de_las_relaciones_laborales.pdf

12

THE LABOUR PLATFORM: AN ALLIANCE OF TRADE UNIONS IN TURKEY

Seyhan Erdoğdu
Department of Labour Economics and Industrial Relations
Faculty of Political Sciences, Ankara University, Turkey

The issue – the policies of the international financial institutions

Neo-liberalism has dominated the policies pursued by various governments in Turkey since the 1980s. Within two decades, Turkey has become a country whose economic policies were almost totally shaped by the International Financial Institutions (IFIs),[1] and the chances of democratic government have been weakened.

Turkey has passed through successive International Monetary Fund (IMF) agreements, the most recent being signed on 11 May 2005. The results of the implementation of IMF policies, characterized by liberalization of goods, services and capital markets; privatization of state economic enterprises, utilities and social services; cuts in public investment, expenditure and employment; deregulation of labour markets; and elimination of agricultural subsidies, have had adverse consequences for workers and trade unions. The unions were partly successful in preventing a reduction in the wage levels and working conditions of their members, as compared with non-union and informal workers; but due to the loss of their members in the public sector, and faced with difficulties in organizing the private sector, they have become smaller organizations with less influence. The civil service union movement that developed after 1990 also faces the threat of deregulation measures introduced in 2004–2005 under the regulatory reform

---

[1] In this paper the term globalization is used to define the stage after 1980, in the internationalization and restructuring of capitalism, facilitated by changes in generic technologies. Neo-liberalism is both the social philosophy and the political strategy of this capital-driven globalization. In economic terms neo-liberal policies are imposed globally by the market forces of both multinationals and financial capital. Furthermore, these policies are imposed upon the developing countries additionally by the IFIs.

of central and local administration which entails retrenchment in public employment, privatizations, flexible work patterns and contract work.

Background on trade union representation in Turkey

In Turkey the total number of wage and salary earners is 11,948,000 (54.1 per cent of total employment) (TURKSTAT, 2005). Of these, 42 per cent are public and private sector "workers", employed under the Labour Act of Turkey (No. 4857) and covered by the social security system (ÇSGB, 2005a). Twenty per cent are "civil servants" and "contracted personnel" employed in the public sector and covered by their special social security system (Emekli Sandığı, 2005). The rest, approximately 38 per cent, are undeclared labour (i.e. not declared to the authorities and hence not covered by social insurance schemes. Undeclared labour exist both in the informal and formal economy. An ever-increasing part of undeclared labour is in the formal sector).

The official statistics of the Ministry of Labour and Social Security on the total number of workers organized in trade unions (2,945,929 in July 2005) are inflated due to trade union competition and percentage rules on representation.[2] An unofficial but more realistic estimate would be only half of this figure.[3] Thirty-six per cent of organized workers are employed in the public sector. The workers' unions are organized under the umbrella of three different confederations: TÜRK-İŞ, DİSK and HAK-İŞ. TÜRK-İŞ is the largest confederation, with 70 per cent of the unionized workers, DİSK is the second with 13.4 per cent and HAK-İŞ is the third with 12.5 per cent (ÇSGB, 2005b).[4]

The total number of civil servants organized in trade unions is 747,617 in 2005 (47 per cent). The civil servants' unions are also organized under the umbrella of three major confederations: KESK (35 per cent of total membership), Türkiye KAMU-SEN (42 per cent) and MEMUR-SEN (21 per cent) (ÇSGB, 2005c).[5]

---

[2] Under the Trade Unions Act No. 2821, to have the right to represent the workers at a given work place, unions must prove that they organized at least 10 per cent of all workers within the industry.

[3] For example, the total membership of YOL-İŞ, the construction workers' union in Turkey, is given as 130,000 in the official statistics for 2005 whereas the real figure is only 44.8 per cent of this (YOL-İŞ, 2005).

[4] The main union organization, the Confederation of Turkish Trade Unions (Türkiye İşçi Sendikaları Konfederasyonu – TÜRK-İŞ) was founded in 1952 and is the oldest. The Confederation of Progressive Workers' Trade Unions of Turkey (Türkiye Devrimci İşçi Sendikaları Konfederasyonu – DISK) originated from a faction of TÜRK-İŞ and was founded in 1967. Confederation of Turkish Just Workers' Unions (Türkiye Hak İşçi Sendikaları Konfederasyonu – HAK-İŞ) was founded in 1976. A small number of unions remain independent.

[5] Confederation of Public Labourers' Trade Unions (Kamu Emekçileri Sendikaları Konfederasyonu – KESK) was founded in 1995. Its affiliates have been the forerunners of the public employees' trade union revival after 1989. Confederation of Public Employees' Trade Unions of Turkey (Türkiye Kamu Çalışanları Sendikaları Konfederasyonu – Türkiye KAMU-SEN) was founded in 1992. The Confederation of Civil Servants Trade Unions (Memur Sendikaları Konfederasyonu – MEMUR-SEN) was founded in 1995. The differences between the three confederations are mainly political. A small number of unions belong to other confederations.

The central challenge for labour: How to influence policies

One alternative for the trade unions in Turkey would be to accept the core economic policies imposed by the IFIs, while trying to reform them through conditions of good governance and a social plan for restructuring. However, in spite of the fact that trade unions have become smaller organizations with less influence, they have not accepted these policies. While rejecting the policies of the IFIs, they have been able to develop their own alternative economic programme and to defend it at various levels.

The Labour Platform and its alternative economic programme

Since 1999, Turkish trade unions have taken the novel step of forming the Labour Platform. In 1999, the confederations of the labour and civil service unions, professional organizations and various associations in Turkey came together to form an informal alliance called the Labour Platform. The motivating force behind this alliance was opposition to neo-liberal economic policies.

In 2001, the Labour Platform adopted its own economic programme (revised in 2002) which contained provisions for national planned development, publicly provided services, public investments in various sectors, control of capital movements, rescheduling of public debt and an immediate halt to privatizations not only of social services but also of utilities and state economic enterprises, including state banks.

The aim of the present study is the examination of the development and main contents of the policies and the alternative economic programme of the Labour Platform, and its impact, if any, on the stand-by agreements[6] with the IMF.

The research gaps on labour resistance to globalization

This study is the first of its kind on the Labour Platform and aims to fill some of the gaps in research on labour resistance in Turkey to corporate-driven globalization. Until the middle of 1990s, the crises of the trade unions went hand in hand with the decline of industrial action and labour militancy all over the world. There were strong reasons for arguing that labour movements had ceased to be the actors of social transformation (Castells, 1996 and 1997;

---

[6] Since 1998, Turkey experienced one close monitoring agreement (1998) and three successive stand-by agreements (1999, 2002 and 2005) with the IMF.

Gorz, 1982; Laclau and Mouffe, 1985; Touraine, 1986). However, starting from the mid-1990s and the search for alternative economic policies to corporate-driven globalization, labour unrest grew in many countries and was reflected in various types of militant labour action, often in coalition with the other social movements (Silver, 2003). In many developing countries, such unrest was closely related to the policies imposed by the IFIs. But these acts of labour resistance to capital-driven globalization, especially those in developing countries, are not well recorded and in many cases have not been empirically studied. There are various reasons for the weakness of research in this area, the insufficiency of data being one of them (Silver, 2003). There is a strong need to fill the gap in social research on labour resistance to neo-liberal globalization and on alternative economic policies. National-level research on trade union resistance can be carried to the global level by comparative research. Such comparative research will also help the trade unions to overcome national bias and country/region-centred approaches to alternative trade union policies in the era of globalization.

The Labour Platform is not a formal, legally established organization. The organization acting as the mouthpiece for the alliance changes periodically. This practice, which is an advantage for the democratic working of the Platform, is a disadvantage when it comes to collecting and preserving Platform documents. Collecting information on the activities of the Platform's local branches is also difficult and can only be done by scanning press coverage. Our wider research is based on the examination of the complete set of primary documents (Declarations of the Presidential Committee, press releases and correspondence with the member organizations) collected from the archives of the member organizations of the Platform (Labour Platform, 2004). Periodicals, general congress documents and other reports of the member organizations are used as secondary resources. Personal participation at Platform demonstrations held in Ankara has also been an asset for the evaluation of the primary documents.

Formation and structure of the Labour Platform

The formation of the Labour Platform is connected with the effects of the 1997 Asian and 1998 Russian crises on the Turkish economy and with the signing of the Close Monitoring Agreement with the IMF in June, 1998 (IMF, 1998). The agreement, which was to last for 18 months, contained conditions that had direct effects on the trade unions and workers, such as wage restraint in the public sector, the elimination of indexation from collective agreements, privatizations, cuts in public investment and social expenditure, social security reform and the acceptance of international arbitration for concession contracts,[7] paving the way for costly build, operate and transfer (BOT) energy projects.

In December 1998, the workers' confederations (TÜRK-İŞ, DİSK, HAK-İŞ) made a joint declaration stating both their urgent short-term demands and their long-term macroeconomic demands. Regarding the latter, the unions called for the abandonment of IMF policies and privatizations (TÜRK-İŞ et al., 1998). In January 1999, the three civil servants' confederations KESK, Türkiye KAMU-SEN and MEMUR-SEN joined in. This was the first time in Turkish labour history that all the trade unions had formed an alliance to defend workers' rights and to develop an alternative to the current economic policies (TÜRK-İŞ et al., 1999).

In mid-1999, the draft law on social security, which was one of the conditions of the IMF Close Monitoring Agreement, began to be discussed in parliament. The national social dialogue channels on social security reform being closed as a result of the IMF agreement, the unions resorted to the creation of a wider, permanent alliance for resistance. In July 1999, the six workers' and civil servants' union confederations, the three pensioners' associations, the professional associations of doctors, veterinarians, pharmacists, dentists, engineers and architects and financial consultants formed the Labour Platform.

The Platform is an informal organization. Each member organization has equal representation rights and decisions are consensus-based. The proposals for mass action coming from the bigger union confederations naturally carry more weight. Relations between the constituents of the Labour Platform are not without internal conflict, due both to trade union competition and to political differences (TÜRK-İŞ, 1999). The loose and informal character of the Platform also does not help its proper functioning. Each member organization tries to activate the Platform when they need it most for their own issues and problems.

The member organizations of the Labour Platform represent workers and civil servants with different political views and party political attachments. Even though it is not possible to assess the real political tendencies of the membership, looking at the election results in Turkey we can safely say that the majority of organized workers and civil servants are far from being "leftist", let alone being radical anti-capitalists. The adoption of a strong anti-IMF/

---

[7] When a private company enters into an agreement with the government to have the right to invest and operate a public utility for a given number of years, this contract is called a "concession contract". According to the Turkish Constitution, concession contracts were considered to be under public law, making them subject to the review of the Council of State in the name of public interest. In 1999, under pressure from the IMF, the Constitution was amended to allow the application of private law and international arbitration to concession contracts. This facilitated privatization in the electricity sector in the form of build, operate and transfer schemes which included price and purchase guarantees for investors. Such BOT projects resulted in "the purchase of expensive electricity by the state" (OECD, 2002, p.85).

anti-globalization programme from the start by the Platform had no political or ideological choices attached to it and was basically a response to the real-life experiences of its members.

Activities of the Labour Platform: 1999–2004

The activities of the Labour Platform during the years 1999–2004 developed in conjunction with the stand-by agreements signed with the IMF.

In the formative months, the constituents of the Platform agreed to an action plan against neo-liberal economic policies (e.g. wage restraint for the public sector, cuts in public investment and social expenditure, social security reform, privatizations in telecommunication and energy sectors and elimination of backward indexation in labour contracts, pension adjustments and agricultural price subsidies) prescribed by the Close Monitoring Agreement with the IMF. The action plan included local and national demonstrations, partial work stoppages and sit-ins. The Platform also initiated the informal, de facto organization of local Labour Platforms (Labour Platform, 2004).

In December 1999, Turkey signed a stand-by agreement with the IMF for the period 2000–2002. This agreement had all the characteristics of a typical IMF structural adjustment programme. A pre-announced exchange rate path set the depreciation rate at 20 per cent for 2000 (Turkish Treasury, 1999).

During 2000, the Labour Platform and its local branches engaged in protest actions and demonstrations in all major cities in Turkey. Hundreds of thousands of people took part, denouncing the IMF policies (Labour Platform, 2004).

In February 2001, the IMF programme collapsed after a financial crisis. The Turkish lira was devalued. Many workers including salaried employees in manufacturing, banking and telecommunications lost their jobs. There was a new IMF programme, this time with a floating exchange rate regime to replace the 1999 pegged regime and with further structural changes entailing the liberalization of markets, elimination of agricultural subsidies and privatization of state economic enterprises and public utilities (Turkish Treasury, 2001).

The Labour Platform denounced the bankruptcy of the IMF policies and asked for a strong national social dialogue to overcome the economic problems. The Platform constituents agreed to initiate an alternative economic programme to the IMF policies. In March 2001, a labour policies symposium was organized with the participation of representatives from the Platform organizations and academics and the programme of the Labour Platform was adopted (Labour Platform, 2004). In 2001, Labour Platform workplace meetings and demonstrations in major cities against the new IMF programme were repeated and the alternative programme of the Labour Platform was widely publicized (Labour Platform, 2004).

In February 2002, the 2000–2002 stand-by agreement with the IMF was replaced by a new stand-by agreement for 2002–2004, with an increased target of 6.5 per cent primary surplus (Turkish Treasury, 2002). Among other things, retrenchment of 45,800 workers from the public sector was specified as a performance criterion for the agreement.

The Labour Platform was relentless in its opposition to the IMF agreements and reacted with an increased surge of demonstrations (TÜRK-İŞ, 2003). The main item on the Platform's agenda in 2004 was the draft laws for public administration reform supported by the IMF and the World Bank, which meant the downsizing of the central administration, privatization of public utilities and public services, and downsizing and deregulation of public employment (Labour Platform, 2004).

On the political level, campaigns on two issues marked the Platform's activities: the national elections and the occupation of Iraq. The political stand of the Labour Platform regarding the early elections of 2000 reflected the political differences among the member organizations. The Platform asked its members not to vote for parties which did not support the demands listed in its alternative Labour programme. However, this call did not meet with a corresponding political response, and the grassroots voted independently in accordance with their personal political leanings.

The Labour Platform was politically very active against the war in Iraq and nationwide demonstrations and meetings were organized (Labour Platform, 2004). It campaigned for non-interference by Turkey in the war and contributed to the parliamentary rejection of Turkey's involvement in the occupation of Iraq.

The programme of the Labour Platform

The structure of the alternative programme of the Labour Platform has some eclectic characteristics due to the structure of the Labour Platform itself, which brings together groups of workers and civil servants with different occupations, status, wage levels and so on. But overall, it is a national, democratic, social programme placing strong emphasis on the public sector as the channel for planned national development. Nowhere in the programme is this stated explicitly, but some of the policies suggested are national–Keynesian. The distinguishing feature of the programme is that it combines an alternative national macroeconomic programme with the demand for trade union rights and other labour standards (which goes further than the demand for a social clause). Its corollary on the global level would be a programme similar to the New International Economic Order as advocated by the Independent Commission (1977–1983) headed by the former German Chancellor Willy Brandt and supported then by the ICFTU (Gumbrell-McCormick, 2000).

In the programme, the economic policies implemented by governments under the direction of the IMF and the World Bank are cited as the main cause of the crisis and of the economic/social problems in Turkey. Privatizations and downsizing of the state are rejected and the importance of the public sector is emphasized. A national and social development plan is seen as the way out of the country's economic instability, stagnation and poverty. The programme calls for rescheduling of the internal and external debt, control of short-term capital movements, reform of the state banks instead of their privatization, tax reform, public investments, an increase in the public expenditures for education, health and social security, and the cancellation of all IMF-imposed legislation (concerning sugar, tobacco, electricity, natural gas, public contracts, international arbitration, Central Bank, foreign investments and so on).

The effects of the activities of the Labour Platform and its alternative programme

The activities of the Labour Platform and its alternative programme did not have a direct effect on the macroeconomic policy framework imposed by the IFIs. This may be attributed to the unaccountability of these institutions to the people of Turkey and to the people represented by the Labour Platform.

It had limited effects on the implementation of these policies, through national social dialogue and political pressures on the government. The public sector unions were able to keep the indexation clauses in their collective agreements and protect the real wages of their members, so also pulling up the average wage levels by constituting a growth point.

The activities and alternative programme of the Labour Platform brought some results in an indirect way by creating a climate of public opinion that favoured the labour demands. Several laws adopted by parliament were sent back by the President to the parliament with a request for reconsideration. Also worth mentioning are the postponement and/or annulment by the constitutional court and the administrative courts of some of the arrangements relating to the implementation of the IMF economic programme, among which there were major privatization deals.[8]

Social dialogue with the International Monetary Fund

Right from the start, the Labour Platform had sought social dialogue with the Government and employers on the adoption of short-term measures to

---

[8] Many unions lodged cases with the administrative courts against the privatization deals. The total or partial cancellation of several critical privatization deals were effected through court decisions.

improve the working and living conditions of its members, the implementation of ratified ILO Conventions and a macroeconomic policy framework which would be an alternative to the IMF programmes. Apart from the formal social dialogue bodies, the informal dialogue channels with Government have always been kept open.

The IMF also supports national social dialogue but for different purposes. In the IMF stand-by agreements and the periodic reviews, national social dialogue was promoted as a tool for securing the consent of the trade unions on certain issues such as the elimination of wage indexation from collective agreements, the downsizing of public employment, privatizations and social security reform. In IMF parlance, "social dialogue" has been a euphemism for securing trade union concessions on neo-liberal restructuring.

In the period between 1999 and 2004, Turkey signed two stand-by agreements with the IMF (1999, 2002) which were periodically reviewed, but neither the IMF nor the World Bank in any way incorporated the criticisms made by the trade unions into the formulation of their policies and strategies towards Turkey. The dialogue between the IMF and the trade unions, which was to have been the local counterpart of the global social corporatism to be realized by the GUFs, did not develop at all.

In the primary documents of the Labour Platform (1999–2004) there is no mention of any contact with the IMF/World Bank representatives or local offices. In the documents of the most representative workers' confederation, TÜRK-İŞ, only one contact with the IMF has been recorded. In June 2004, the Head of the Turkish Desk of the IMF visited TÜRK-İŞ and asked for support for IMF structural adjustment policies, while the President of TÜRK-İŞ heavily criticized the conditionalities in the stand-by agreement and the periodic reviews (TÜRK-İŞ, 2004, pp. 15–17). As explained above, all trade unions in Turkey, whatever their political leanings, strongly oppose the IMF policies. In addition to producing extensive publications criticizing those policies, they were involved in almost continuous street protests, demonstrations, sit-ins and so on, at both national and local levels. To that extent, the IMF's representatives did not need to visit the trade unions in order to know their thoughts on IMF policies. Therefore, the IMF visit to the TURK-İŞ confederation can be seen simply as a public relations exercise, and not social dialogue.

Conclusions

Economic reality is both the environment and the result of social interaction by human beings. It has been common practice to treat the labour movement as passive recipients of capital-driven globalization. They may be scattered and weak, but there are national and local examples of trade unions' trying to create a counterforce to the dominant global alliance of TNCs, some governments and the IFIs. The Labour Platform of Turkish trade unions is a national-level example of such practices.

The Labour Platform lives on, despite some internal difficulties, and its economic programme has been widened to include the joint labour demands against "the regulatory reform of the State" and "the reform of the social security systems" as imposed by the IMF and the World Bank. The Labour Platform and its constituents were able to delay, if not prevent, the implementation of IFI policies through grassroots action and other activities. What is more, they were able to challenge the supremacy of the neo-liberal project and upheld the belief in the possibility of "another world" through their alternative economic programme which had a national, social and developmental character based on a strong public sector.

This paper does not aim to discuss the feasibility and/or the sustainability of the policies and alternative programme of the Labour Platform. It attempts to show, through the examination of the policies and alternative programme of the Labour Platform, that the implementation of neo-liberal policies causes responsive changes in the organizational forms and policies of the trade unions and that the trade union movement tries to resist and change the socio-economic environment created by liberal policies, through its social practice. In Turkey, the responsive policy of the Labour Platform has been the rejection of the basic tenets of globalization and, however rudimentary, the creation of their own development programme.

Such responses, if expanded spatially and politically, have the potential to change the policies of capital-driven globalization and the anti-democratic rules of global governance. However, it is equally true that if spatial and political expansion do not occur, such responses may eventually prove ineffective. The Labour Platform itself may not escape the same fate.

Trade unions do have structural limitations in their quest for change in liberal economic policies, and social researchers cannot foretell the outcome of their social action. However, neglect of labour resistance to the core policies of neo-liberal globalization, and an overemphasis on strategies of reforming the IFIs' policies through local and global social dialogue and a social plan for restructuring, not only may mislead people in their search for truth but may also constitute an ideological barrier to change.

References

Castells, M. 1996. *The information age: Economy, society and culture. Vol. I: The rise of the network society* (Oxford, Blackwell).

—. 1997. *The information age: Economy, society and culture. Vol. II: The power of identity* (Oxford, Blackwell).

ÇSGB (Ministry of Labour and Social Security). 2005a. *İstatistikler*. Available at: http://www.calisma.gov.tr/istatistik/cgm/sendikalasma_oranlari.htm [accessed 10 Aug. 2005].

—. 2005b. *İstatistikler*. Available at: http://www.calisma.gov.tr/CGM/4688_istatistik_2005.htm [accessed 10 Aug. 2005].

—. 2005c. *İstatistikler*. Available at: http://www.calisma.gov.tr/CGM/4688_istatistik_2005.htm [accessed 10 Aug. 2005].

Emekli Sandığı (Pension Fund for Civil Servants). 2005. *İstatistikler, İstirakçi Sayısı*. Available at: http://www.emekli.gov.tr/ISTATISTIK/istirakci.html#im11 [accessed 10 Aug. 2005].

Gorz, A. 1982. *Farewell to the working class: An essay on post-industrial socialism* (London, Pluto Press).

Gumbrell-McCormick, R. 2000. "Facing new challenges: The International Confederation of Free Trade Unions (1972–1990s)", in M. van der Linden (ed.), *The International Confederation of Free Trade Unions* (Berne, Peter Lang), pp. 341–518.

IMF (International Monetary Fund). 1998. *Turkey memorandum of economic policies*, 26 Jun. Available at: http://www.imf.org/external/country/TUR/index.htm?pn=0 [accessed 20 Dec. 2004].

Labour Platform. 2004. Declarations of the Presidential Committee, press releases and correspondence with Labour Platform member organizations, 1999–2004 (collected from the archives of the Labour Platform Constituents) (Ankara, Labour Platform).

Laclau, E.; Mouffe, C. 1985. *Hegemony and socialist strategy: Towards a radical democratic politics* (London, Verso).

OECD (Organisation for Economic Co-operation and Development). 2002. *Regulatory reform in Turkey: Critical support for economic recovery*, SG/RR (2002)3 (Paris).

Silver, B.J. 2003. *Forces of labour. Workers movements' and globalization since 1870* (Cambridge, Cambridge University Press).

Touraine, A. 1986. "Unionism as a social movement", in S.M. Lipset (ed.), *Unions in transition: Entering the second century* (San Francisco, CA, ICS Press.), pp. 151–173.

TÜRK-İŞ (Confederation of Turkish Trade Unions). 1999. Declaration of the TÜRK-İŞ Committee of Union Presidents, 5 Aug., Ankara.

—. 2003. *Çalışma Raporu (General Congress Report) 1999–2003* (Ankara).

—. 2004. *TÜRK-İŞ Dergisi* (*TÜRK-İŞ Periodical*), No. 361 (Ankara).

—; HAK-İŞ; DİSK. 1998. Joint Declaration, 29 Dec., Ankara.

—; —; —; KESK; Türkiye KAMU-SEN; MEMUR-SEN. 1999. Joint Declaration, 27 Jan., Ankara.

Turkish Treasury. 1999. Stand-by arrangement, Letter of intent, Turkey. Available at: http://www.hazine.gov.tr/imf_standby.htm [accessed 12 Nov. 2004].

—. 2001. Stand-by arrangement, Letter of intent, Turkey, 3 May. Available at: http://www.hazine.gov.tr/imf_standby.htm [accessed 12 Nov. 2004].

—. 2002. Stand-by arrangement, Letter of intent, Turkey. Available at: http://www.hazine.gov.tr/imf_standby.htm [accessed 12 Nov. 2004].

TURKSTAT (Turkish Statistical Institute). 2005. Employment, Unemployment, Wages; Labour Force Statistics; Statistical Tables; Periodic Results of Household Labour Force Survey (Turkey, Urban, Labour), Table 7. Available at: http://www.turkstat.gov.tr/VeriBilgi.do [accessed 18 Feb. 2006].

YOL-İŞ (Union of Road, Building and Construction Workers). 2005. Membership figures, unpublished union data.

TRANSNATIONAL UNION NETWORKS, FEMINISM AND LABOUR ADVOCACY

13

Mary Margaret Fonow
Arizona State University
and
Suzanne Franzway
University of South Australia

Union feminists are playing an important role in mobilizing women's participation in transnational campaigns for labour rights and economic justice. Our research suggests that union feminists, with their structural ties to both organized labour and the women's movement, are in a unique position within both movements to mobilize in response to the issues and concerns that rapid economic globalization raises for all workers. Because union renewal depends on developing new ideas and resources for organizing new types of workers and new types of workplaces, it is important for unions to create a central place for the participation of union feminists in their organizations, campaigns and struggles.

We view union feminism as goal-oriented collective action taken on behalf of the rights of women as a group. Union feminism emerges out of the day-to-day struggles by women for equality, respect and dignity at home, in the workplace, in their unions and in society as a whole. Union feminists use discursive tools (conference resolutions, policy statements, educational programmes, websites, newsletters, etc.) as well as institutionally sanctioned spaces (conventions, workshops, labour schools, committee structures, etc.).

They use these tools to fashion a network of resources that can be called into action to mobilize union members and their potential supporters at strategically important moments. This network helps to establish and sustain more permanent structures of organizational participation, as well as a collective identity based on the belief that social and political action taken by a group can make a difference (Fonow, 2003).

We examine several sites where union feminists are using transnational labour networks to build international solidarity, to create new discourses of advocacy, and to build alliances with activists from grassroots organizations,

NGOs and other social movements. Our examples and illustrations are drawn from research we have conducted on the work of union feminists within the ICFTU[1] and the International Metalworkers' Federation (IMF).

Union feminists and transnational networks

As a political environment, globalization has reconfigured the opportunities for politics and the repertoire for collective actions available to social movements (Moghadam, 2001). For example, emerging new political opportunity structures such as transnational labour advocacy networks provide union women with the opportunity to participate in the ongoing construction of transnational labour solidarity. Networks can serve both as actors in politics and as a way to mobilize and structure the actions of participants. However, the existence of networks in and of themselves does not produce collective action; networks have to be framed by movements as useful avenues for mobilization.

Unions have always been involved in international labour networks, but more recently their networks have become stronger and more diverse. There has been a proliferation of political spaces where the interests of labour overlap with other movements and with advocacy organizations concerned with labour rights and development. Increasingly, campaigns for labour rights are organized and funded with non-union support from churches, foundations, NGOs and universities. Labour conferences and periodicals focus more on non-contract issues such as worker empowerment, organizing, union democracy and feminism. Contract issues are being defined in new ways, and many unions are actively engaged in equity bargaining (Kidder, 2002). New players from the non-profit sector and activists from other social movements are joining with unions as strategic partners in the growing transnational advocacy network for labour rights.

Some unions have taken the step of creating their own transnational non-governmental agencies that link unions to grassroots organizations and to NGOs. For example, Canadian steelworkers have created the Steelworkers Humanity Fund. Established in 1985, the fund supports 31 international aid and development projects in 13 countries, including seven women's NGOs in Bangladesh, Bolivia, Guatemala, Mexico, Nicaragua, Peru and South Africa. Because of the active participation of union feminists, the projects sponsored by the fund are required to reflect principles of gender equity, democratic participation and environmental sustainability. Applicants must demonstrate how the design, implementation, and evaluation of their project incorporates

---

[1] In November 2006, ICFTU, WCL and a number of previously unaffiliated unions created the ITUC. As the research was carried out before the creation of the ITUC, the term "ICFTU" will be used.

the involvement of women and how the project will affect gender and the division of labour, property relations and access to education and training. The guidelines go even further by acknowledging that the power differentials between women and men affect economic development, "Development activities have historically affected women differently than men. This reflects the greater poverty and dependence women experience in most parts of the world and the inequality of women relative to men in their political, economic and social power" (Fonow, 2003, p. 179).

Women are encouraged to discover their own unique approaches to empowerment and to develop leadership and communication skills through their participation in community-based organizations serving women. One example of this principle in action is the Women's Integral Training Institute (IFFI) in Bolivia which received union funding for an educational programme that brought together about 750 women from more than 40 women's organizations working in poor neighbourhoods. The curriculum was designed to increase the capacity of women to exercise and influence power in both the public and private spheres. According to Carmen Zabalga, IFFI's Director, "We're involved in teaching women about their rights, and have been successful in our campaign to enact legislation prohibiting domestic violence. Unless we get involved politically, our work won't be self-sustaining. We have to institutionalize change if we want to endure" (Fonow, 2003, p. 181).

These collaborations help to expand traditional ideas about the roles unions can play in the movement for global justice. Transnational labour advocacy networks have become mobilizing structures for feminists and labour activists. They have opened the way for union feminists to play an active role in shaping the discourses and mobilizing strategies of organized labour. Within these networks union feminists challenge conventional notions: first, of the class-based solidarity of the labour movement, by acknowledging the differences of gender, race, sexuality and ethnicity within class; and second, of the gender-based solidarity of the women's movement by recognizing the class differences among women. The creation of gender-specific, class-based political demands defines who is or is not included in the process of developing social movements, thus creating new types of political claims and new solidarities, which Curtin (1999) labels contingent solidarities.[2] In the case of union feminists, these contingent solidarities are mediated through activists' and advocacy networks.

---

[2] As a tool of analysis, the concept of contingent solidarities provides a framework for identifying how and why women have defined their political interests the way they have within particular political fields. This concept "allows for a cross-national analysis of the ways in which class, welfare state, labour markets and cultural discourse have included or excluded women and how women trade unionists themselves have influenced the construction and formulation of claims, strategies and solidarities" (Curtin, 1999, p. 60).

In the context of intensified globalization, new interconnections of networks and communities produce new alliances and reveal common needs and concerns. In our research, we identify a number of spheres where union feminists have mobilized resources to address the impact of globalization on women's labour rights and to forge collective identities as transnational activists. These alliances can be sites of labour renewal, including formal organizations, networks, and forums such as the ILO, ICFTU, the GUFs and the WSF and less formal alliances such as international campaigns for pay equity and against sweatshops and unfair trade agreements. We have even identified some surprising platforms, such as gay pride festivals. Below we analyse two agencies of transnational labour advocacy, the IMF and the ICFTU, where union feminists are playing an important role in advocating for labour rights and economic justice.

Feminist networks within the global union federations

As alliances of advocacy, unions bring workers together within and across workplaces, firms and communities, and within and across national borders. This can occur at the international level through a union's formal membership in international trade union secretariats and confederated labour bodies. And, less formally, through strategic partnerships and alliances with intergovernmental agencies, transnational social movements and NGOs.

One site of increasing importance to union feminists is the network of women's committees and equity offices within the ICFTU and GUFs.[3] The women's committees of each federation are networked through the coordinating activities of the ICFTU, which in 2005 renewed its major campaign to significantly increase women's membership in unions worldwide, and to increase their representation and participation in union programmes, activities and decision-making structures. The organizing campaign, "Unions for Women and Women for Unions", targets specific groups of women workers including women working in the informal economy, young women, migrant women, women from ethnic minorities and women employed in EPZs.

In February 2003 the ICFTU brought women union leaders from 225 unions and 148 counties to Melbourne, Australia, for the 8th World Women's Conference. The event was hosted by the Australian Council of Trade Unions (ACTU). Delegates participated in workshops and panels on a wide range of topics, ranging from those closely associated with trade unions, such as collective bargaining, to more pressing political issues such as the war in Iraq.

---

[3] For an in-depth discussion of the role of union feminists in the ICFTU see Moghadam, 2005.

Delegates passed a strong feminist anti-war measure that spelled out the specific ways war impacts women and girls. The ICFTU conference organizers made an effort to include in the conference programme prominent feminist leaders from the non-profit development sector. Elmira Nazombe of the Women's International Coalition for Economic Justice (WICEJ) addressed the delegates about building alliances between labour and transnational NGOs. The WICEJ, founded in 2000, is a transnational network of 45 women's economic and human rights organizations from every region of the world. It focuses on the link between gender, race and macroeconomic policy within international inter-governmental policy circles. The coalition works with labour bodies such as the ICFTU, American Federation of Labor–Congress of Industrial Organization (AFL-CIO) and PSI to get governments to pay greater attention to ILO core labour standards. The coalition is actively involved in the WSF, UN Commission on the Status of Women (CSW) and UN Financing for Development process. The coalition has developed a methodology that allows activists, unions and NGOs to conduct an analysis of the way gender and race intersect with globalization.[4] Nazombe told the delegates that improving relations between unions and NGOs is a challenge but necessary if the economic lives of women are to improve. She believes that spontaneous organization of women workers outside union structures has increased the awareness of unions for the need to cooperate with women's rights organizations. "The unions themselves are increasingly aware of the need to meet the demands of women workers. But that will require informing women about the unions and their work, which will in turn mean increasing exchanges between the unions and organizations working with women" (Fonow, 2005, p. 221).

Our second example of feminist union networking involves one of the oldest global union federations, the IMF, founded in 1883. Today the IMF represents 24.8 million metal industry workers in steel, auto, shipbuilding, electronics and precision instruments in 101 countries, and nearly one-third of its membership is female.

A women's conference was held on the day prior to the opening of the 31st World Congress of the IMF held in Vienna in May of 2005, in which 126 of the women delegates came together to strategize how to increase their visibility and effectiveness at the congress. The women introduced two resolutions at the congress. The first resolution, "Women's work under globalisation"

---

[4] The elements of this methodology involve collecting and reporting data that are disaggregated by race, gender, ethnicity, descent, citizenship status and other categories of difference; contextualizing the disaggregated data by focusing on social and historical factors such as slavery, colonialism and religious differences that exacerbate the inequities of globalization, and; reviewing policy initiatives and systems of implementation through the lens of the disaggregated data and their context.

(IMF, 2005a), called for the IMF affiliates to take a stand against inferior forms of employment for women; to gather information on gender segmentation and equal pay and use the information to ensure that women are not restricted to the lowest-paid, lowest-skilled work; and to work with women's organizations to organize women workers in EPZs and the other ghettos of globalization to improve the lives of working women. The second resolution, "Statement on gender equality" (IMF, 2005b), focused on steps that the IMF and the affiliates should take to ensure that women are given the opportunity to participate in IMF events and to develop as leaders at every level of the federation. The resolution cited the need to support the work of women's committees, to continue to organize new women members, and to take up the unique needs of women through collective bargaining. The discourse framing the resolutions reflected a feminist understanding of how globalization is gendered. The resolution states, "Women's employment under globalization is precarious. Millions of young women throughout the world are hired at minimal wages, only to be laid off when they get married or start a family. Women's jobs are the first to be lost, often forcing them into even more marginal and potentially dangerous means to earn a living, or to migrate in search of work" (IMF, 2005b).

The IMF Congress included several keynote addresses and roundtable discussions that dealt specifically with global justice and how organized labour can build alliances with other social movements, with NGOs and with civil society to protect and advance workers' rights. Sharan Burrow, President of the ACTU and the first woman elected to the presidency of the ICFTU (elected in 2004), addressed the IMF Congress on the theme of workers' rights and referred to herself as a "feisty feminist and woman warrior". She told the congress that it is essential for labour to enhance its capacity to hold governments and corporations responsible for respecting the hard-won rights of workers throughout the supply chain. One way to do this, she argued, is for unions to build stronger alliances with NGOs and the rest of civil society. According to Burrow, this will require multiple strategies including organizing new workers in the EPZs, fighting for the rights of migrant workers, enhancing human rights in China, joining the fight against poverty, and linking workers' rights with shareholder activism and consumer power (IMF, 2005c). In our interview with Burrow, she told us that union feminists play an important role in helping unions understand how to close the gap between the organization of women and the low labour standards underpinning women's work.

The most dramatic and moving appeal for building new social alliances came from Janet Barzola, President of the Central Nacional de la Mujer Minera, a national organization in Peru that seeks to support the labour rights of subcontracted workers in the mining industry against the practices of multinationals. Barzola works with the wives of these mostly unorganized miners to improve living conditions in mining communities. Her organization is working with an IMF affiliate in the region to organize these miners. She vividly described the conditions of poverty in the mining camps and communities and the hardship those conditions impose on women and children. Alcohol consumption is encouraged among the men who work in the mines, which makes women more vulnerable to domestic violence. The children are undernourished and have no opportunity to go to school. In a speech on advancing workers' rights delivered in Vienna in 2005, she said, "the children have very little to smile about and no teeth to smile with because they must drink polluted water" (IMF, 2005c).

The increased visibility of women and feminists at the 2005 IMF World Congress reflects decades of struggle on the part of women against discrimination in the metal trades and for greater representation within the IMF and its affiliates. However, the movement has picked up steam since the last World Congress in Sydney in 2001 where women delegates confronted the IMF about its poor record of representing women's interests. In fact, the IMF was the last GUF to add women to its highest decision-making body.

Jenny Holdcroft, director of equal rights, EPZs, at the IMF, convened an advisory group to begin rejuvenation of the work of women's committees. The group also addressed the question of organizing women and increasing their

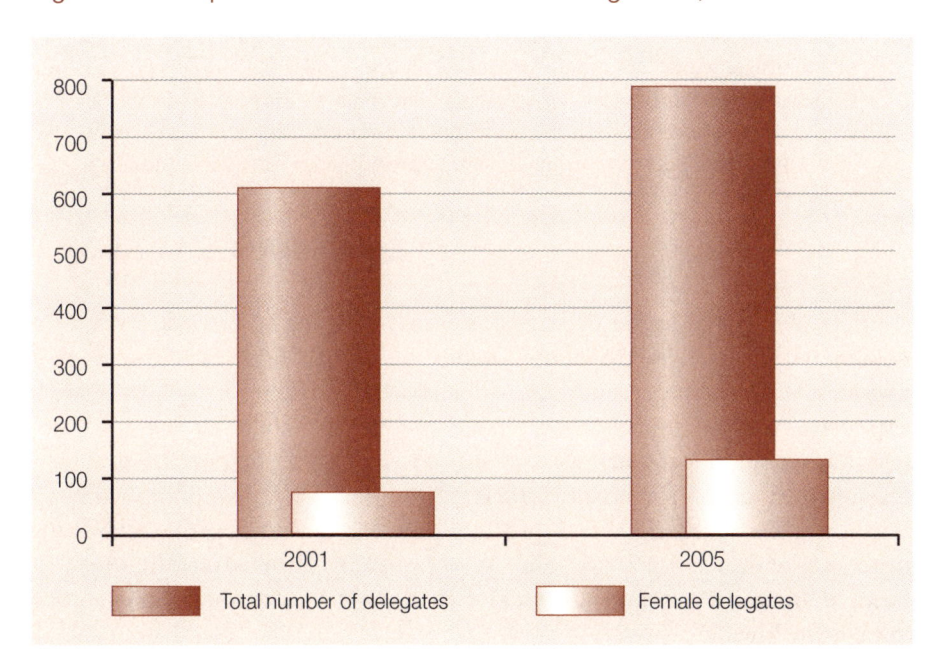

Figure 13.1 Representation of women at IMF congresses, 2001 and 2005

representation in the deliberative bodies of the IMF and its affiliated unions. A small group of women representing metal industry unions from: Brazil, Canada, Colombia, the Czech Republic, Germany, Ghana, Mexico, Sweden, Switzerland, South Africa, Uganda, the United Kingdom and Zimbabwe met in Geneva in October 2002 to map out a strategy to increase the power of women within the IMF. They proposed adding at least six seats specifically for women to the IMF executive. They also proposed establishing women's structures at global, regional and subregional levels, setting a 20-per-cent target for women's participation at meetings of the central committee and congress, and holding women's conferences.

As the result of the women's demands for greater representation within the IMF and its affiliated unions, the IMF recently selected eight women to serve on its highest executive body. In addition each affiliate was required to ensure that 20 per cent of their delegation was women, and to include a section in their activity report that detailed their efforts to increase the membership and participation of women within their unions. These projects range from gender equality training for shop stewards to dialogues or forums on strong families, legal rights of women, and so on.

All of the proposals were eventually accepted, and it seems unlikely that women would have achieved such success without the quotas. Marcello Malentacchi, General Secretary of the IMF, admitted as much when he said in April 2001:

> During our long history, we have always rejected the idea of quotas for groups of members which are not represented in the governing bodies of our Federation in the most appropriate way. However, if we are unable to achieve improvements in terms of the level of women's representation, it will become increasingly difficult to continue rejecting proposals to introduce quotas in order to attain this goal.
>
> (Fonow, 2005, p. 230.)

The discursive frame of inclusion is used to justify reserving seats for women within the policymaking bodies of the IMF. It is assumed that women's increased representation will make the IMF and its affiliates more responsive to the concerns of female members. While quotas may not guarantee such an outcome for women, it is one of the important strategies developed by union feminists to increase the likelihood that some women's voices will be heard. This is a precondition for developing the mobilizing structures within unions that can be co-opted by feminists to build transnational solidarity, contingent on acknowledging the power differences among women worldwide.

Because global federations such as the IMF are organized by region and by sector, activists can develop agendas and approaches that address women's rights in the workplace and their representation in unions. Such an agenda must take into account cultural specificities and the differential effects of globalization in different types of workplaces and sectors. This structure becomes an obvious advantage when negotiating with MNEs. The IMF has already negotiated 15 international framework agreements (IFAs) with companies such as DaimlerChrysler, Renault and Volkswagen that require a common set of core labour standards across all locations of a particular company. The core labour standards were established by the ILO and include freedom of association and protection of the right to organize, the right to collective bargaining, the abolition of forced labour, equality and non-discrimination, and the elimination of child labour. Discrimination on the basis of race, colour, sex, religion, political opinion, nationality, sexual orientation or social origin is outlawed in the model framework agreement.

The IMF has abandoned corporate codes of conduct in favour of IFAs because workers and their unions have more of a say in crafting their terms and conditions. Corporate codes of conduct tended to be unilateral, less comprehensive in terms of the types of rights protected and who is covered, and tended to provide workers with little input into the monitoring of codes. By contrast, because they are negotiated, the IFAs require dialogue between management and unions and involve the unions more in the implementation of labour standards. In the hands of activists, these global instruments can and are being used as leverage with other stakeholders such as consumers and stockholders. They can be useful to feminists because they contain strong equity clauses, including protection for the rights of gays and lesbian workers.[5]

Conclusion

Those concerned with the renewal of the labour movement must come to terms with the fundamental way that gender structures neo-liberal globalization, labour markets and free trade agreements. We argue for gender analysis because sexual politics is integral to trade unions, globalization and efforts to challenge the neo-liberal agenda. The labour movement already has within its ranks a group that can significantly aid the necessary renewal – union feminists. Union feminists already active within the network of GUFs understand the tensions and contradictions between productive and social

---

[5] For a review of the literature on gay and lesbian labour activism see Fortescue, 2000; Hunt, 1999; Irwin, 1999 and Krupat and McCreery, 2001.

reproductive spheres,[6] the sexual politics of trade unions and the importance of building transnational solidarities contingent on an understanding of cultural and social differences among workers (Franzway, 2001).

Union feminists weave together strengths and strategies that emerge from the labour movement and the women's movements. By building and mobilizing transnational networks and alliances between these various movements, union feminists create political spaces for new workers. They also create a new understanding of workers' issues and concerns that arise out of the rapidly changing impact of globalization on both workplaces as well as personal lives.[7] However, for labour to benefit from the work of union feminists unions must increase and enhance the participation of women within their ranks. This requires a rethinking of structures and practices that perpetuate male dominance in the labour movement.

References

Bakker, I; Gill, S. 2003. "Ontology, method, and hypotheses", in I. Bakker and S. Gill (eds): *Power, production and social reproduction* (London, Palgrave), pp. 17–41.

Curtin, J. 1999. *Women and trade unions: A comparative perspective* (Brookfield, VT, Ashgate).

Fantasia, R; Voss, K. 2004. *Hard work: Remaking the American labor movement* (Berkeley, CA, University of California Press).

Fonow, M.M. 2003. *Union women: Forging feminism in the United Steelworkers of America* (Minneapolis, MN, University of Minnesota Press).

—. 2005. "Human rights, feminism, and transnational labor solidarity", in W. Kozol and W. Hesford (eds): *Just advocacy? Women's human rights, transnational feminism, and the politics of representation* (New Brunswick, NJ, Rutgers University Press), pp. 221–242.

Fortescue, R. 2000. "Mardi Gras: The biggest labour festival of the year", in *Hecate*, Vol. 26, No. 2, pp. 62–65.

Franzway, S. 2001. *Sexual politics and greedy institutions: Union women, commitments and conflicts in public and private* (Sydney, Pluto Press).

---

[6] Social reproduction as defined by Bakker and Gill (2003, p. 18) "involves the institutions, processes and social relations associated with the creation and maintenance of communities – and upon which ultimately, all production and exchange rests." These activities include biological reproduction, socialization of children, care of elders and other dependent family members, the organization of sexuality, and how food, clothing, and shelter are made available. Most social reproduction occurs within the family unit.

[7] Fantasia and Voss (2004, pp. 107–108) argue for a new "labor metaphysic" that addresses organizationally and symbolically the spaces between unions. They believe union renewal lies in the active cultivation of the spaces between existing unions and between unions and other institutions (communities, churches and religious organizations, civic associations, social movements, etc.) and between the labour movement and those stigmatized groups previously ignored by the labour movement. This is the way for labour to regain some of its former significance in the symbolic vocabulary of society.

Hunt, G. 1999. *Laboring for rights: Unions and sexual diversity across nations* (Philadelphia, PA, Temple University Press).

International Metalworkers' Federation (IMF). 2005a. "Resolution 4: Women's work under globalisation", IMF World Congress, Vienna. Available at: http://www.imfmetal.org/main/congress2005/index.cfm?n=494&l=2&c=11695 [accessed 31 Jan. 2007].

—. 2005b. "Resolution 5: Statement on gender equality", IMF World Congress, Vienna. Available at: http://www.imfmetal.org/main/congress2005/index.cfm?n=494&l=2&c=11698 [accessed 31 Jan. 2007].

—. 2005c. Speech by Sharan Burrow, IMF World Congress, Vienna. Available at: http://motor.aic.at/metaller2005/index.php?show=stream&id=1&open=http://motor.aic.at/metaller2005/videos/burrow_3_2.rm [accessed 31 Jan. 2007].

—. 2005d. Speech by Janet Barola, IMF World Congress, Vienna. Available at: http://motor.aic.at/metaller2005/index.php?show=stream&id=1&open=http://motor.aic.at/metaller2005/videos/barzola_4_2.rm [accessed 31 Jan. 2007].

Irwin, J. 1999. *"The pink ceiling is too low": Workplace experiences of lesbians, gay men and transgender people* (University of Sydney, Australian Centre for Lesbian and Gay Research).

Kidder, T. 2002. "Networks in transnational labor organizing", in S. Khagram, J.V. Riker and K. Sikkink (eds): *Restructuring world politics: Transnational social movements, networks, and norms* (Minneapolis, MN, University of Minnesota Press).

Krupat, K.; McCreery, P. (eds). 2001. *Out at work: Building a gay-labor alliance* (Minneapolis, MN, University of Minnesota Press).

Moghadam, V.M. 2001. "Transnational feminist networks: Collective action in an era of globalization", in P. Hamel, H. Lustinger-Thaler, J.N. Pieterse and S. Roseneil (eds): *Globalization and social movements* (New York, NY, Palgrave).

—. 2005. *Globalizing women: Transnational feminist networks* (Baltimore, MD, Johns Hopkins University Press).

Workers online. http://www.workers.labor.net.au/139/ [accessed 31 Jan. 2007].

ACTION RESEARCH IN THE GARMENT SECTOR IN SOUTHERN AND EASTERN AFRICA

14

Esther de Haan
Centre for Research on Multinational Corporations, Amsterdam, the Netherlands
and
Michael Koen
Civil Society Research and Support Collective, Durban, South Africa

Context

Chapter 8 has shown the ambiguous effects of increased trade on labour in South Africa. This chapter looks at the impact of preferential trade dispensations, such as the United States African Growth and Opportunity Act (AGOA) on the countries of Southern and Eastern Africa between 2000 and 2005, which has been mixed. Research in the garment sector over this period reveals that the impacts cannot be viewed in isolation from the broader trade environment and the rules emerging from the WTO on the one hand and the consequences of neo-liberal economic policy on the garment sector in these countries.

Labour in this environment has been faced with a number of central challenges. In many countries, the opening of markets and the rise of the trade in used clothing as well as the import of cheaper garments marked the destruction of the domestic garment and textile markets. Unions had little impact in stemming the tide of closures.

Through preferential trade access – as is arranged through AGOA – export-based production in Southern and Eastern Africa has risen. In several cases, it more than replaces the jobs lost during the demise of the domestic sector. These jobs, however, turn out to be of a very temporary nature. And early research revealed the conditions of workers in these export-focused factories to be highly exploitative. Unions' traditional organizing methods seemed to have little impact. Unions were, initially, ineffective against the mostly Asian TNCs that started producing in their countries, paying low wages and employing workers in bad working conditions.

This created an environment where workers and unions were forced to learn new ways of struggling for better working conditions – this time, in an environment that demanded a much broader policy response across the subregion and not one purely focused on domestic practice. International solidarity, as a method of fighting workplace issues, has become increasingly important. This paper traces the use of action research (see below) to support these attempts in a rapidly shifting economic and policy environment.

Between 2000 and 2004, labour conditions in garment supply chains in Southern and Eastern Africa were researched for trade unions and campaigning organizations. Efforts towards improving labour conditions have been intensified by connecting research with concrete actions and follow-up. The Centre for Research on Multinational Corporations (SOMO) and the Civil Society Research and Support Collective (CSRSC), together with the regional office of the GUF in the sector – the ITGLWF Africa – and the national garment unions in the different countries, have developed and conducted this research.

Introduction to action research

The establishment of an African regional office of the ITGLWF at the same time as SOMO launched a research project in the Southern African region proved to be a unique window of opportunity to develop activities to map factory locations, buyers, investment policies and integration of the research findings in union activities and strategies at regional and national level. At the same time, in the year 2000, the AGOA was introduced, granting quota- and duty-free entry for certain African exports to the United States, with a specific focus on garments. The AGOA served to bolster garment production in several African countries (at present, 37 sub-Saharan African countries qualify to export to the United States under AGOA), directed for export towards large American clients such as GAP, Sears, Target and Wal-Mart.

The research project started with mapping factory locations and researching the working conditions in factories in five countries in the Southern Africa region – Botswana, Mauritius, Madagascar, Lesotho and Swaziland – and with establishing who were the most important buyers in the different countries and factories. At the same time, the project served to discuss the possibilities of using these buyers' voluntary codes of conduct to help unions to improve labour conditions in the different countries, to give input to the regional and national discussions on campaigning and to develop material for workers and unions in the region. The research project linked campaigns on improving labour conditions, through urging brand-name producers and retailers to take responsibility, to the unions in the Southern African region. The access to new campaigning opportunities to support organizing efforts gave new impulses to the activities of national unions and regional solidarity initiatives.

Action research methodology

The research that has been conducted has used an action research methodology and spans a number of different projects over four years. By following a consistent methodology and integrating research into strategic planning and education processes, it has played a meaningful support and enabling role.

During the research, workers were interviewed in focus groups outside the factories, facilitated by the union. The factories were visited and the management interviewed as were government officials in labour departments and investment agencies, who provided information on company movements within the region, reasons for investment, management attitude and perception of the unions. The research gave an overview of the most urgent labour issues that needed to be addressed, and the specific problems the unions were facing in the different countries as well as specific problems at every factory researched. Other desktop data, such as trade statistics, were integrated to develop a full picture of the industry and its prospects, employer practices and union capacities. Various information sources were exploited as often there was conflicting information from management and worker interviews.

Action research takes into consideration the concerns, needs and knowledge of those participating in the research and allows needs on the ground to control the research agenda to a large degree. By providing feedback on the research findings, at different stages of the research, to national and regional unions, and international (campaigning) organizations, action research is linked directly with taking action and making changes. Throughout the project, the needs of the different unions were taken into account in the specific research undertaken in each country and the workshops organized. In this way, the constituencies should be enabled to make a final decision on the use of the research and the actions to be taken. Should there be a call for pressure to be put on a supplier, it is up to the union and the workers to take the decision.

Growth of the garment sector in Africa

Foreign investment in the garment industry in Southern Africa started in the 1990s – with the notable exception of Mauritius – and came mainly from Asia, drawn by a favourable investment climate. Most importantly, export possibilities were presented by favourable and quota-free entry to the United States and European markets. In recent years the advantages of quota- and duty-free export to the United States under the AGOA have increased the share of exports to the United States.

The United States has expressed a great deal of optimism that the implementation of the AGOA will, in addition to causing economic reform, lead to economic growth and development in the SADC region. The 2001 AGOA report to the US Congress claims that after only one year of implementation, the AGOA "generated a strong trade and investment response" (Office of the United States Trade Representative, 2002). The AGOA is mentioned by the US Government as a factor "expected to help countries diversify their exports and to assist them in building a manufacturing base to support long-term economic growth" (Office of the United States Trade Representative, 2001). This seems questionable. The countries fuelling the growth in trade are quite limited, as well as the number of sectors involved. American exports to Africa are dominated by aircraft and oilfield equipment with, in 2003, 62.9 per cent of American exports to sub-Saharan Africa going to three countries: South Africa, Nigeria and Angola. Meanwhile, South Africa, Nigeria, Angola and Gabon accounted for 82.9 per cent of sub-Saharan exports to the United States in 2003, which were mainly limited to crude oil exports and, in the case of South Africa, also platinum, diamonds and motor vehicles. Garments exported to the United States are the second largest export article, accounting for only 5.9 per cent of sub-Saharan exports under the AGOA, after the oil exports, which represent 69.6 per cent (Robinson-Morgan, 2004).

But unquestionably, the only sector that has created a significant number of jobs under AGOA has been the apparel sector due to the labour-intensive nature of garment-producing factories. Of the US$2.2 billion non-energy exports under the AGOA in 2002, apparel accounted for 40 per cent. Some of these jobs in the sector in fact pre-existed the AGOA or were associated with trade with other countries. Malawi, for example, used to export to South Africa predominantly. Since the AGOA came into existence, producers in Malawi have shifted focus to the United States market, although employment in the sector has remained much the same. Mr K.K. Desai, the Chairman of the Malawi Garment and Textile Manufacturers' Association, reported in an interview in August 2003 that there has been no new investment in Malawi since the introduction of the AGOA (De Haan, Koen and Mthembu, 2003).

Where the sector has expanded due to American trade, it has not spread across sub-Saharan Africa but tends to be associated with pockets of investment. The major exporters of apparel under the AGOA are Lesotho, Kenya, Madagascar, Mauritius, South Africa and Swaziland. Lesotho is the top exporter with exports having grown from US$111 million in 1999 to around US$454 million in 2004 (United States International Trade Commission, 2002 and 2005).

Apparel products are subject to the AGOA "Apparel Rules", under which only 25 of the 37 AGOA countries are eligible for exceptions (AGOA, 2006). Under these rules, raw material used in the production of apparel for export under the AGOA must come from local sources, other AGOA-eligible producers or the United States. There was a notable exception, until October 2007, to this rule in that it is not applied to countries that are considered least developed countries (LDCs) under a "special rule" also known as the "third country fabric provision". It is the benefits of this rule that have attracted most of the investment in the sector as it means that producers located in LDCs are able to use fabric imported from other countries in the manufactured garments for export. There has been very limited investment in the textile sector – an exception being the setting up of a large textile mill by the Taiwanese company Nien Hsing in Lesotho. Where there has been limited or no investment in the textile sector, countries are very vulnerable to the loss of investment after October 2007.

The rapid growth of the sector, the precarious nature of the thus established industry, dependent on short-lived trade "favours" and global trade developments, such as the phasing out of the Multifibre Agreement (MFA) at the end of 2004,[1] has posed a challenge for the unions in terms of organizing in such an unstable sector.

Challenges for the unions

Despite similarities in terms of membership, the unions operating in the sector across the countries have had mixed successes and failures. They have been in existence for a number of years and as such date back to a period when the garment industries in these countries were more focused on supplying domestic and regional demand, often as a result of import substitution strategies that predated the neo-liberal onslaught on labour standards. Whilst all the unions have ultimately come to draw on the social capital of international solidarity efforts, through both research and campaigning efforts, in order to alleviate some of the most severe resource restrictions, it became clear that the extent to which international solidarity has been used to directly pressure employers for change has rather depended on the union model adopted in the different countries. For example, in the more militant model of engagement adopted in Lesotho and Swaziland by the Lesotho Clothing and Allied Workers Union (LECAWU) and the Swaziland Manufacturing and Allied Workers Union (SMAWU)[2] respectively, substantial international support and solidarity efforts have been sought in direct action campaigns concerning employer and government conduct.

Growth in the sector, mainly as a result of the AGOA, gave obvious organizational opportunities for unions in terms of increased membership, revenue, greater worker solidarity and increased organizational stability. At the

---

[1] A GATT agreement that placed quotas on volumes of garments and textiles from the main textile and garment producing countries (mostly Asian countries) to mostly North America and European countries.
[2] The exposure of unionists to more radical forms of union engagement in South Africa during the apartheid regime seems to play a role in the organizational forms and tactics adopted by the unions in neighbouring States.

same time this rapid growth, associated as it is with highly mobile capital and competitive international labour market conditions, brings its own problems, as is evident in the relative successes and failures of various unions operating in the sector. Prior to sector growth, most unions suffered a chronic lack of resources, poor to non-existent administrative processes and leadership crises, in addition to which the application of labour laws and the exercise of trade union rights were problematic in most countries.

It was therefore important for the region to develop regional strategies, facilitated by the ITGLWF African regional office, and drawing on information that came out of the research.

Liberalized trade and the African garment industry

The AGOA, which was initially only intended to last for a period of eight years, has been extended, including the period during which lesser-developed countries can use textiles sourced outside of AGOA-eligible countries and the United States for garment export under the AGOA (United States Congress, 2004). This extension might potentially be a stay of execution for thousands of jobs in those very lesser-developed countries, as Africa has limited quality textile production capacity and US textiles are too expensive. This suggests the view that when producers in Africa can no longer get textiles from internal sources, they will rapidly withdraw from a country, rendering the devastation of the garment industry in that country complete. The whole process has been accelerated by the phasing out of the MFA at the end of 2004. Through the MFA it was possible for some countries to build up a garment industry as most of the larger economies, for example China, India and Taiwan (China) were restrained by quotas. This strategic issue was publicly ignored by policy-makers from both the United States and Africa when AGOA started in 2000, and even in 2005 when the consequences of the phase-out become clear.

The growth of the sector in recent years has not necessarily led to improvements in development and labour conditions for the countries concerned. Investment policies are exacerbating the garment industries' problems. Among countries that benefit from agreements such as AGOA, competition has increased for investment. Governments have responded by offering incentives such as duty-free imports, tax breaks, and relaxed labour laws. Government incentives have been described as not a main factor in drawing the industries, but they do make a difference for companies in choosing which African country to produce in. When these benefits end, companies are prone to leave. The Sri Lankan company Tri Star for example has been producing in Kenya for many years. When tax and other incentives ended, as per the time allotted in the Kenyan EPZ Act, the company increased its already existing capacity in Uganda and opened a new factory in the neighbouring United Republic of Tanzania, which had just created EPZ legislation.

However, for the countries offering the incentives, the consequences of such concessions might make the difference between profiting from FDI or failing to gain any real benefits for the country. Incentives for investors, such as caps on wages, tax holidays or restrictions on union activity can mean that workers lose out not only in economic terms but also in social terms. With the phasing out of the MFA, the governments in Africa will be even more desperate to keep the industries, particularly in light of the fact that the destruction of a domestically based industry has made workers and their families wholly dependent on the foreign capital.

Sourcing policies and labour practices of Asian companies in Africa

Drawn by trade agreements and other incentive programmes to countries desperate for foreign investment and jobs, investors, including Asian investors, have been able to circumvent local labour laws (for example, minimum wage and social security requirements) as well as the standards for good labour practices set out by the ILO. In Swaziland, for example, where violations documented at Asian-owned factories include forced overtime, verbal abuse, sexual intimidation, unhealthy and unsafe conditions (including locked doors), unreasonable production targets, and anti-union repression, the Department of Labour admits that in an attempt to keep investors happy it does not pursue labour law violations to its fullest ability. They say they "can't push investors too hard", but instead are "very gentle and persuasive" (De Haan and Phillips, 2002). While investors see profitable returns on their investments, critics wonder if workers and their communities really benefit when wages and conditions are substandard and tax abatements and subsidized infrastructure mean little money goes back into the community.

Asian investors in the garment and textile industries have proven to be as mobile as Western buyers, "cutting and running" from one location to another as suits their interests. Mauritius developed a significant clothing export industry directed to the EU, among others fuelled by investment from Hong Kong companies. Now that wages are lower and preferential trade incentives are better in nearby countries, this location is less attractive to investors.

Information on the Asian companies and accounts of their movements were essential for the unions to deal with organizing in these companies, as well as drawing on solidarity from organizations and trade unions in Asian countries. This moved beyond the classic North-South campaigning issues into "triangular solidarity"; workers in Asian production factories in African countries drawing into their struggle organizations and trade unions in the country where the production company has its head office, as well as organizations and trade unions in the export destination countries.

Using action research in organizing and campaigning

Organizing in most African countries is extremely difficult, especially considering the levels of poverty that beset working class communities in many countries there. Whilst domestic struggle is a prerequisite for any solidarity action, regional and international exposure and support adds a strong strategic advantage to these efforts. Therefore one can argue for the strategic necessity of expanding struggle and awareness of issues beyond the borders of the country. For this reason, research can be linked to both internal organizing and external campaigning and awareness efforts.

The trade unions, which in many cases had seen a radical decline during the shift in industrial policy, were poorly resourced and ill-prepared to deal with the wave of sweatshops that mushroomed in response to the AGOA. Whilst ITGLWF Africa set about a drive to address some of the organizational crises that beset the labour movement, research played a major and integrated role in the strategy developed by the ITGLWF and the affiliates to reverse the downward trend in conditions in the region.

The research in all countries since 2000 (among others in Botswana, Kenya, Lesotho, Madagascar, Malawi, Mauritius, Swaziland, Tanzania U. R. and Uganda,) has been conducted in close partnership with the local union and the ITGLWF. The research has been useful in capacitating local trade unionists in the process of collecting information, as well as educating unionists on the issues around codes of conduct, monitoring labour conditions and the process of global campaigning. These processes have effectively begun to link consumer markets in the North and campaigning organizations in the South with workers in the South.

For example, as the contacts amongst the unions increased after the establishment of an African office, research was used selectively to target major abuses by suppliers. This strategy forced the Government of Lesotho to begin to enter into dialogue around some of the excesses being perpetrated by investing multinational manufacturers. One consequence of this was to force companies to grant some organizational rights to the union. This initial research was followed by more detailed sectoral research in Lesotho and other countries. ITGLWF Africa has been using the research findings to work with the union on building membership. Despite militant action, there was little progress in securing recognition for the union organizing the garment workers in Lesotho, LECAWU, particularly in Asian-owned companies.

By 1999, LECAWU had organized only about 4,000 of the 18,000 workers in the sector. However, this membership increased tremendously in the following years. The ITGLWF has been instrumental in the strategy and played a major role in brokering a deal that eventually saw LECAWU officials entering the employer's premises and actively recruiting members.

The research also played a role in identifying patterns of ownership in the region and linking ownership across borders. This was key in developing international campaigning and illustrating this with evidence of particular factory abuses where ownership links had been established.

International support and research, however, are not a substitute for effective grassroots unionism. Lesotho is a case in point which saw rivalries over union leadership in the sector eventually leading to a collapse in LECAWU's membership despite Lesotho enjoying more international investment and campaigning attention in the garment sector than most other countries.

Pressuring Asian manufacturing multinationals to take responsibility for their role in respecting workers' rights can present special challenges. Labour rights advocates will get less leverage from the threat of tarnishing brand image with these "unseen" companies. However, a more integrated response, pressuring the retailers that these manufacturing multinationals produce for as well, can yield results. Campaigns, as in the Nien Hsing case (see box 14.1), that have utilized an approach mobilizing stakeholders at various levels of the garment industry supply chain have demonstrated a potential to open up space for workers to successfully voice their demands.

Increasingly, more research is being done to understand and assess the role of Asian manufacturing multinationals in global supply chains and in the regions where they operate. The growing importance of manufacturing multinationals from regions and countries such as Hong Kong, the Republic of Korea and Taiwan (China) has led to a need for more information, including tracing production chains. Also needed are campaigns on such manufacturing multinationals, based on links between regions. Asian research partners have also now been drawn into the process to assess ownership structures in the producer's home countries.

As has been mentioned, the other key area where research is used by unionists on the ground is to identify brands and retailers that are purchasing from producers in their country. The real downward pressure on wages and conditions as well as the volatility of investment (as a result of changing sourcing decisions) lies very squarely at the door of these groups. Initial campaigning efforts have led these groups to formulate codes of conduct in order to alleviate some of the damage caused to their public image. Where a factory is supplying a retailer or brand which has a code of conduct, the

> **Box 14.1 Case study: C&Y Garments and Nien Hsing Textile Company in Lesotho persuaded to recognize LECAWU**
>
> Nien Hsing opened its first factory in Lesotho, C&Y Garments, in 1991. By 2002, it employed about 4,000 workers. In January 2001, the company opened a second jeans factory, Nien Hsing, which employed about 3,500 people in 2002, 95 per cent of whom were women. Nien Hsing Textile Company wholly owns both factories. The two factories can be found opposite each other in the Thetsane Industrial Area, east of Maseru. Both companies produce jeans for the United States. Known buyers include Bugle Boy, Kmart, Sears, Casual Mail, Gap and Cherokee jeans for Canada. Nien Hsing is building a US$8.6 million textile mill a short distance from the Nien Hsing factory.
>
> C&Y Garments and Nien Hsing were identified as two very large and exploitative employers early on in the interaction between LECAWU and ITGLWF Africa. As such, they were researched and information was generated about practices in these factories.
>
> A variety of problems were reported at the Nien Hsing facilities: taking advantage of Lesotho's high unemployment rate, workers were employed on a "casual" basis, at a lower minimum wage. This is legal for casuals employed for less than six months. However, at C&Y some workers had been employed as casuals for ten years. Workers also reported verbal harassment, physical abuse, unsafe conditions (including locked emergency exits) and non-payment of benefits. ITGLWF Africa and the Clean Clothes Campaign took up the case, as did unions and NGOs in the United States, Canada, Taiwan (China) and Nicaragua, where another of Nien Hsing's factories was producing. In July 2002, ITGLWF Africa and LECAWU started an organizing campaign at the two Nien Hsing factories. With increasing pressure on all these fronts, LECAWU and Nien Hsing signed a memorandum of understanding committing the company to recognize the union and enter into collective bargaining negotiations on the condition that the international action was stopped.

opportunity exists to demand of the retailer or brand to make good on its word and make sure the situation improves at the producer. The problem is that codes are often cosmetic and constant monitoring by unions is necessary to make them work. The other difficulty is that it is the very sourcing practices and the nature of the demands for low prices and fast delivery that cause many of the practices in the producing factories. It therefore also makes sense to have specific campaigns on these issues internationally.

Action research and strategy

The research conducted detailed the players in the supply chain and played a central role in the process of strategic planning with the ITGLWF and local unions in the region. This was assisted by the research not just detailing employers but also looking at the unions and identifying strategic areas for intervention.

At a more macro level, research has helped the ITGLWF and its affiliates to formulate policy responses to issues of trade and industrial development as well as uncovering potential solidarity partners in actions against Asian manufacturing multinationals. The detailed knowledge developed around the supply chain mostly involving Asian manufacturing multinationals led to the targeting of Nien Hsing for international campaigning actions by multiple organizations. Initial efforts of the research partner organizations established a methodology and exposed unions to research practice and its links to organizing and global campaigning. The interventions of ITGLWF Africa worked on capacity, and research organizations participated actively in both education and strategic forums to assist in this process. The approach has at all times attempted to broaden access to information and options open to unions. At the final stage, unions are beginning to collect and assimilate information themselves, coordinated through ITGLWF Africa.

The future of the garment export industry in Africa

The introduction of trade agreements or phasing out of quotas also influences decisions to relocate. Both government officials and factory managers interviewed in the research projects mentioned the MFA quotas as one of the main reasons that Southern Africa was attractive to the garment industry. Garment export from Southern Africa was not hampered by quotas, as faced by many garment-producing countries in Asia. Many doubted the sustainability of Southern and Eastern Africa's garment industry following the phase-out of these quotas and the increased competition from Asian countries. By May 2005, the closure of a substantial number of factories confirmed pessimistic thoughts about the sustainability of the sector in Southern and Eastern Africa, even for the extended period of the AGOA. Duty- and quota-free access to the American market as a result of the AGOA helps to enhance the countries' competitiveness, but, as said before, the limited duration of its provisions is seen by all involved in Southern Africa's garment industry as a major pitfall.

One of the early indications of shifting investment as a result of changes in the trade regimes at the conclusion of the MFA was when several factories in Lesotho, employing thousands of workers, failed to reopen in January of

2005. In May 2005, Southern and Eastern African unions at a meeting in Swaziland calculated their losses and came up with the staggering figure of 52,669 workers losing their jobs as a consequence of factories closing in Namibia, Malawi, Lesotho, South Africa, Tanzania U. R., Kenya and Mauritius.

Conclusions

In conclusion, some of the broad lessons of the research and the union organizations involved in the garment sector in South East Africa are drawn out below, followed by a brief commentary around labour agenda research gaps in the region.

The research has been most effective when linked to organizing and participatory strategic planning. A flexible approach with researchers who are knowledgeable about labour issues is key in developing broader derivative research efforts addressing organizational development and organizing strategy development.

An action orientation allows needs on the ground to control the research agenda to a greater degree, making the research relevant to beneficiary and not organizational or funding needs. Through linking to different partner organizations, connecting to a wide variety of both campaigning organizations and trade unions, the impact of action-oriented research is multiplied.

Genuine regional solidarity is a precursor to improvement in standards for all in sub-Saharan Africa. Paying lip service to solidarity whilst practising protectionism when it comes to jobs will only serve to further undermine labour conditions. Recognizing differences between countries and industries is imperative. The level of investment in Lesotho, for example, permits more robust forms of engagement than would be possible in Malawi, given the precarious nature of the industry there.

Within this broad array of issues, a number of labour research agendas emerge. There is a need to quantify the cost of investment incentives and investment policies more broadly for the countries in the region, given the investment agenda of the predominantly Asian companies and the short-sighted approach of the governments who draw in the investment with costly incentives. Ongoing research about closures and possible responses to these closures is becoming increasingly important post-MFA, as well as developing adequate responses.

References

AGOA (African Growth and Opportunity Act). 2006. "General country eligibility provisions". Available at: http://www.agoa.gov/eligibility/country_eligibility.html [accessed 10 Dec. 2006].

Bahadur, A.; Koen, M.; Mthembu, N. 2004. *Impact of second hand clothing on the textile and garment sector in Southern and East Africa* (SOMO and Workers' College, Durban), pp. 3–4.

De Haan, E.; Phillips, G. 2002. "Taking the devil's rope: Swaziland", in *Made in Southern Africa* (Amsterdam, Clean Clothes Campaign), pp. 15–21. Available at: http://www.cleanclothes.org/publications/02-12-southern-africa.htm

—; Koen, M. Mthembu, N. 2003. *Garment production in Malawi* (Amsterdam, Centre for Research on Multinational Corporations). Available at: http://www.somo.nl/html/paginas/pdf/Garment_production_in_malawi.pdf

Office of the United States Trade Representative. 2001. *Comprehensive report on US trade and investment policy toward sub-Saharan Africa and implementation of the African Growth and Opportunity Act*, first of eight annual reports, pp. 4–6. Available at: http://www.agoa.gov/resources/annual_1.pdf

—. 2002. *Comprehensive report on US trade and investment policy toward sub-Saharan Africa and implementation of the African Growth and Opportunity Act*, second of eight annual reports, pp. 23, 27–28. Available at: www.agoa.gov/resources/annual_2.pdf

—. 2004. *Comprehensive report on US trade and investment policy toward sub-Saharan Africa and implementation of the African Growth and Opportunity Act*, fourth of eight annual reports, pp. 31–33. Available at: http://www.agoa.gov/resources/2004-05-agoa.pdf

Robinson-Morgan, A. 2004. *US–African trade profile* (Washington, DC, US Department of Commerce), Apr., p. 4. Available at: http://www.satradehub.org/CXA_html/docs/reports/US-African%20Trade%20Profile%202004.pdf [accessed 10 Dec. 2006].

United States Congress. 2000. *The African Growth and Opportunity Act* (Washington, DC). Available at: http://www.agoa.gov/agoa_legislation/agoatext.pdf [accessed 10 Jan. 2005].

—. 2004. *Summary of AGOA acceleration act of 2004–AGOA III* (Washington, DC). Available at: http://www.agoa.gov/agoa_legislation/AGOAIII_text.pdf [accessed 30 Aug. 2005].

—. 2005. "General country eligibility provisions". Available at: http://www.agoa.gov/eligibility/country_eligibility.html [accessed 5 Jan. 2005].

United States International Trade Commission. 2002. "Lesotho: US exports, imports, GSP imports, and AGOA imports, by major commodity sectors, annual and year to date Jan.–Dec". Available at: http://reportweb.usitc.gov/africa/by_country.jsp [accessed 10 Sep. 2002].

—. 2005. "Lesotho: US exports, imports, GSP imports, and AGOA imports, by major commodity sectors, annual and year to date Jan.–Dec". Available at: http://reportweb.usitc.gov/africa/by_country.jsp [accessed 16 Feb. 2005].

CONCLUSION

Verena Schmidt
Bureau for Workers' Activities, ILO, Geneva

The issues discussed in this publication show that the labour movement is developing creative responses to react to the complex impact of globalization. Trade unions have increasingly enlarged their agenda to include issues such as engaging with international organizations to influence their policies. Due to the growing power of multinational companies, trade unions are also involved in international social dialogue through IFAs, organizing global campaigns as well as extending and deepening their cooperation at the transnational level. There are three common themes which emanate from the present book as important trade union responses to globalization, firstly the need for enlarging the trade union agenda, secondly the role of network and alliance building and thirdly the role of the ILO and labour standards in achieving a fair globalization.

Enlarging the trade union agenda

The international trade union movement has recently focused on a number of emerging themes to respond to the challenges of globalization. Besides the institutional involvement of the ITUC within the ILO and TUAC in the OECD, the global unions (consisting of the ITUC, GUFs and TUAC) are engaging with the large international organizations such as IMF, the World Bank Group, the United Nations and their programmes and funds, WHO and WTO to influence their rules and regulations with view to achieving a fair globalization.

The ITUC is actively involved in influencing the ongoing WTO negotiations beyond labour provisions in trade agreements, demanding that developing countries are not to be pressured into making disproportionate tariff reductions which would seriously affect their industrial development and employment, or take up other commitments that would undermine or hamper their development. TUAC and its affiliates are negotiating to influence the OECD and the G8 to change the corporate governance system with a view to ensuring good corporate governance and accountability, wider market integrity and global markets balanced by an effective social dimension.

The global unions have worked hard on procurement standards as one important way to implement core labour standards. They have done this by firstly influencing the World Bank's procurement policy and secondly by engaging in campaigns on World Bank financed activities, including procurement standards.

Since the late 1990s, global union leaders have lobbied for inclusion of the ILO core labour standards in World Bank lending and procurement practices. Since May 2006 the International Finance Corporation (IFC) has required that all enterprises borrowing from the IFC abide by the core labour standards. In December 2006 the World Bank announced that it would extend the core labour standards requirement to public works projects financed by the International Bank for Reconstruction and Development and the International Development Association. The bank started including the core labour standards requirement in its procurement contracts in May 2007. In a second stage, the World Bank will promote the incorporation of the new core labour standards requirements into the harmonized basic Standard Bidding Document for Procurement of Works used by all regional development banks. The inclusion of rights in World Bank lending and procurement has engendered a lot of international attention and is linked to the more general question of how government and policies can limit the externalities of private sector practices and ensure that they promote general public goods. It is therefore crucial to build up a coherent framework between the ILO and the World Bank group (starting from the ILO supervisory system), since it is clear that any judgement on implementation of core labour standards can only be decided by the ILO.

Regarding the procurement for the Olympics 2008, the ITUC, ITGLWF and the Clean Clothes Campaign have embarked on the PlayFair 2008 campaign which calls on the International Olympic Committee (IOC) to enter concrete discussions on the IOC's responsibilities to ensure respect for workers' rights in the production of all Olympics merchandise. BWI, in partnership with European and global trade unions and NGOs, launched a campaign in 2007 on "Decent Work in Football". The campaign mobilizes for decent working conditions from the construction phase onwards for the companies contracted to build and/or renovate football stadiums for the football world championship 2010 in South Africa.

International framework agreements between companies and unions are another important tool for the protection of workers' rights and the effective implementation of labour standards. IFAs provide a practical example of international solidarity and can be seen as a platform for better social dialogue and organizing. They are also a tool in building alliances among unions in the North and South.

Building networks and alliances

Building networks between trade unions along global production systems is an example of transnational cooperation. The production of goods and services is not only ever more dispersed but also more coordinated by international producers, buyers and retailers. Unions have to deal with sophisticated and often anti-union human resource management strategies at a local level within global production systems. They also face the question of how to respond to more difficult representational situations as a result of sourcing decisions. However, the concept of value chains also presents some opportunities for labour. To benefit from these opportunities, unions try to develop strategies with a view to organizing and to bargaining collectively along the value chains. Organizing along supply chains could be a way to focus efforts and move beyond existing North–South cooperation arrangements.

However, one potential conflict of interest exists between workers of the global North and the global South when it comes to offshoring and outsourcing. Indeed, there is a need for active labour market strategies in the global North to avoid workers in the North bearing the cost for outsourcing. It is also important to stop a race to the bottom especially between countries of the global South. Here, the ILO has an important role to play.

The enlarged agenda of trade unions requires a closer alliance with other civil society groups. This was already acknowledged in 2000 by the ICFTU at their World Congress in Durban (ICFTU, 2000). By proactively organizing women and increasing the proportion of women in trade unions the organizational culture of many trade unions has changed. Union feminists, with their strong ties in trade unions and the women's movement, have played an important role in mediating between the different organizational cultures of trade unions and NGOs. Changes in the organizational culture are beneficial for including other underrepresented groups within trade unions, such as migrant and ethnic minority workers and those with different sexual orientations, which will encourage diversity and push changes in organizational culture still further.

Cooperation between trade unions and other civil society groups is, of course, not always harmonious and does not always result in positive outcomes. As the above-mentioned ICFTU decision emphasizes, one important prerequisite for constructive cooperation between NGOs and trade unions is that

NGOs understand the unique role of trade unions as mass organizations which represent workers (ICFTU, 2000).

The role of the ILO and of international labour standards

International labour standards are an important campaign tool to improve working conditions. However, it is not enough to refer to international labour standards in relation to trade. The assumption that trade supports development needs to be continually questioned. The opportunity costs of international trade need to be carefully checked against the advantages it may bring.

While core labour standards must be respected in all member States of the ILO[1] regardless of whether they have been ratified by the countries, the ILO's *Application of International Labour Standards* (ILO, 2007) and the ICFTU's *Annual Survey of Violations of Trade Union Rights* (ICFTU, 2006) show that the reality is very different. The international labour movement is mobilizing the international community to put pressure on those countries which do not respect the core Conventions to make the necessary changes. At the same time, as the core labour standards refer only to fundamental rights at work, the international labour movement continues to struggle for the promotion, ratification and implementation of international labour standards beyond the core Conventions.

The ILO is working towards codifying the Decent Work Agenda – hence emphasizing the importance of standards in areas such as occupational safety and health, social security, wages, work and family and labour inspection. This is encouraged and supported by the international labour movement. Also, the Decent Work Agenda is being further realized through the Decent Work Country Programmes which need to be built around core labour standards as well as the areas mentioned above.

The international trade union movement has recently addressed other important new areas. One such topic is the negative impact of private equity and hedge funds. The global unions are calling for governments and international agencies to ensure proper regulation, taxation and transparency concerning the activities of private equity and hedge funds.

This book has shown various examples of how trade unionists have improved the situation of workers by enlarging the agenda and cooperation at international, transnational and national levels, as well as through their alliance building with other civil society groups. All changes and new ideas were

---

[1] On 31 August 2007 the ILO had 181 member States.

met with scepticism and resistance by some as would be the case for the implementation of changes in any organization. However, the challenges of globalization can only be met if the trade union movement continues to address new issues and change its organizational structures accordingly.

The promotion and implementation of international labour standards is one important tool to achieve a fair globalization. A strong and unified trade union movement, with a vision of social justice for all, coherent concepts for social and economic policy, effective collective bargaining and a modern and inclusive form of trade union structures, is a key factor in achieving this objective.

References

ICFTU (International Confederation of Free Trade Unions). 2000. Congress Statement on Trade Unions, NGOs and Tripartism. 17th ICFTU World Congress, 3–7 Apr., Durban, South Africa. 17GA/ 8.13 (final).

—. 2006. *Annual Survey of Violations of Trade Union Rights* (Geneva).

ILO. 2007. *Application of International Labour Standards 2007 (I). Report of the Committee of Experts of the Application of Conventions and Recommendations.* International Labour Conference, 96th Session.